131 3206

Single-Level Home Plans

Publisher James D. McNair III

Cover Photography by John Ehrenclou
Cover Design by Judy-Ann Konopka
Interior Layouts by Paula Mennone

Library of Congress No.: 95-81707/ISBN: 0-938708-66-X

TABLE OF CONTENTS

D1027765

Submit all Canadian plan orders to:
The Garlinghouse Company
20 Cedar Street North
Kitchener, Ontario N2H 2WB

Canadians Order only: 1-800-561-4169
Fax#: 1-519-743-1282
Customer Service#: 1-519-743-4169

REFER TO PRICE CODE A

Design 34150

PHOTOGRAPHY BY JOHN EHRENCLOU

CLASSIC RANCH DESIGN

INTERESTING ANGLES

C onsider this plan if you work at home and would enjoy a homey, well-lit office or den. The huge, arched window floods the front room with light. This house offers a lot of other practical details for the two-career family. Compact and efficient use of space means less to clean and organize. Yet the open plan keeps the home from feeling too small and cramped. Other features like plenty of closet space, step-saving laundry facilities, easily-cleaned kitchen, and a window wall in the living room make this a delightful plan.

• Main floor	1,492 sq. ft.
• Garage	462 sq. ft.
• Bedrooms	Two, possible Third
• Bathrooms	2(Full)
• Foundation	Basement, Slab, Crawl space
▼ Total living area	1,492 sq. ft.

An **EXCLUSIVE DESIGN**
By *Karl Kreeger*

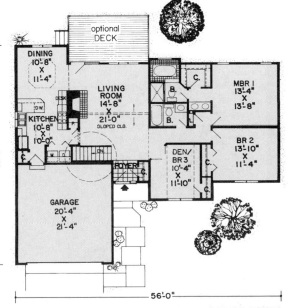

FOUNDATION OPTION

optional DECK

DINING
10'-8" X 11'-4"

LIVING ROOM
14'-8" X 21'-0"
SLOPED CLG.

KITCHEN
10'-8" X 10'-0"

MBR 1
13'-4" X 13'-8"

BR 2
13'-10" X 11'-4"

DEN/ BR 3
10'-4" X 11'-10"

FOYER

GARAGE
20'-4" X 21'-4"

48'-0"

56'-0"

MAIN AREA

TRADITIONAL BRICK DESIGN

Stacked windows fill the wall in the front bedroom of this one-level home, creating an attractive facade and a sunny atmosphere inside. Around the corner, two more bedrooms and two full baths complete the bedroom wing, set apart for bedtime quiet. Notice the elegant vaulted-ceiling in the master bedroom, the master tub and shower illuminated by a skylight, and the double vanities in both baths. Active areas enjoy a spacious feeling. Look at the high, sloping ceilings in the fireplaced living room, the sliders that unite the breakfast room and kitchen with an adjoining deck, and the vaulted-ceilings in the formal dining room off the foyer. The photographed home has been modified to suit individual tastes.

Design 20100

Design 20100

An
EXCLUSIVE DESIGN
By Karl Kreeger

PHOTOGRAPHY BY JOHN EHRENCLOU

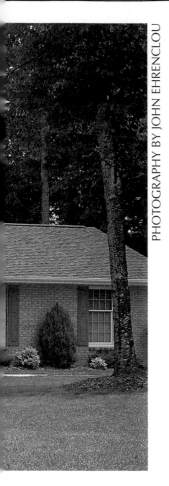

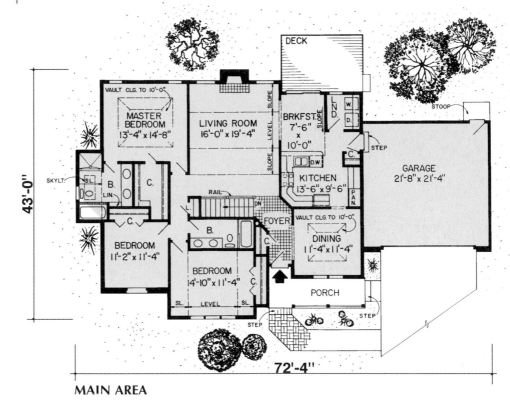

MAIN AREA

43'-0"

72'-4"

DECK

VAULT CLG. TO 10'-0"
MASTER BEDROOM
13'-4" x 14'-8"

LIVING ROOM
16'-0" x 19'-4"

BRKFST.
7'-6"
x
10'-0"

GARAGE
21'-8" x 21'-4"

KITCHEN
13'-6" x 9'-6"

STOOP

STEP

SKYLT.

B.

C.

LIN.

RAIL

DN

PAN.

D.W.

BEDROOM
11'-2" x 11'-4"

B.

FOYER

VAULT CLG. TO 10'-0"
DINING
11'-4" x 11'-4"

BEDROOM
14'-10" x 11'-4"

C.

PORCH

LEVEL

SL.

SL.

STEP

STEP

C.

PLAN INFO:

• Main floor	1,737 sq. ft.
• Basement	1,727 sq. ft.
• Garage	484 sq. ft.
• Bedrooms	Three
• Bathrooms	2(Full)
• Foundation	Basement, Slab, Crawl space
▼ **Total living area**	**1,737 sq. ft.**

REFER TO PRICE CODE B

STUCCO DESIGN FOR A HILLSIDE

A tiled threshold provides a distinctive entrance into this spacious home. There's room for gracious living everywhere, from the comfortable living room with a wood-burning fireplace and tiled hearth, to the elegant dining room with a vaulted-ceiling, to the outside deck. Plan your meals in a kitchen that has all the right ingredients: a central work island, pantry, planning desk, and breakfast area. A decorative ceiling will delight your eye in the master suite, which includes a full bath and bow window. The photographed home has been modified to suit individual tastes.

Design 20066

Design 20066

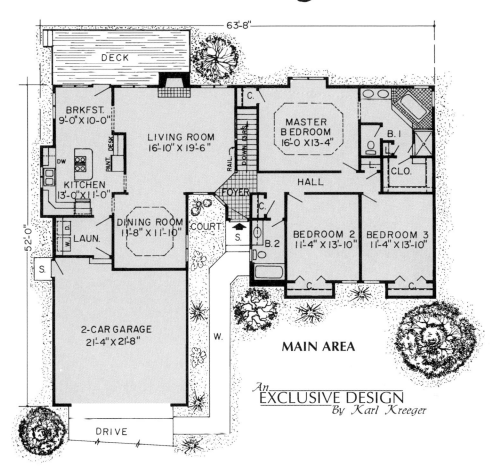

63'-8"

52'-0"

DECK

BRKFST.
9'-0" X 10'-0"

LIVING ROOM
16'-10" X 19'-6"

C.

MASTER
BEDROOM
16'-0 X 13'-4"

B. 1

DW

PANT. DESK

RAIL.

DOWN

CLO.

KITCHEN
13'-0" X 11'-0"

HALL

W. D.

LAUN.

DINING ROOM
11'-8" X 11'-10"

FOYER

C.

S.

COURT

S.

B. 2

BEDROOM 2
11'-4" X 13'-10"

BEDROOM 3
11'-4" X 13'-10"

C.

C.

2-CAR GARAGE
21'-4" X 21'-8"

W.

MAIN AREA

An
EXCLUSIVE DESIGN
By Karl Kreeger

DRIVE

REFER TO PRICE CODE C

PLAN INFO:

• Main floor	1,850 sq. ft.
• Basement	1,850 sq. ft.
• Garage	503 sq. ft.
• Bedrooms	Three
• Bathrooms	2(Full)
• Foundation	Basement
▼ **Total living area**	**1,850 sq. ft.**

RANCH DESIGN WITH UNIQUE FEATURES

This Ranch home features a large sunken Great room, centralized with a cozy fireplace. The master bedroom has an unforgettable bathroom with a super skylight. The huge three-car plus garage can include a work area for the family carpenter. In the center of this home, a kitchen includes an eating nook for family gatherings. The porch at the rear of the house has easy access from the dining room. One other bedroom and a den, which can easily be converted to a bedroom, are on the opposite side of the house from the master bedroom. The photographed home has been modified to suit individual tastes.

Design 10839

Design 10839

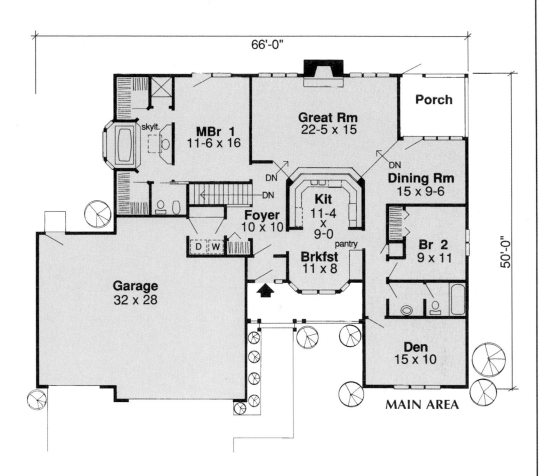

66'-0"

50'-0"

Porch

Great Rm
22-5 x 15

skylt.

MBr 1
11-6 x 16

DN

DN

Dining Rm
15 x 9-6

Kit
11-4
x
9-0

pantry

Br 2
9 x 11

Foyer
10 x 10

DN

D   W

Brkfst
11 x 8

Garage
32 x 28

Den
15 x 10

MAIN AREA

REFER TO PRICE CODE B

PLAN INFO:

• Main floor	1,738 sq. ft.
• Basement	1,083 sq. ft.
• Garage	796 sq. ft.
• Bedrooms	Two
• Bathrooms	2(Full)
• Foundation	Basement, Slab, Crawl space
▼ **Total living area**	**1,738 sq. ft.**

SINGLE LEVEL OPEN FLOOR PLAN

You'll find an appealing quality of open space in every room of this unique one-level home. Angular windows and recessed ceilings separate the two dining rooms from the adjoining island kitchen without compromising the airy feeling. A window-wall flanks the fireplace in the soaring, skylit living room uniting the interior spaces with the outdoor deck. The sunny atmosphere continues in the master suite, with its bump-out window and double vanity bath. The photographed home has been modified to suit individual tastes.

Design 20099

An
EXCLUSIVE DESIGN
By Karl Kreeger

Design 20099

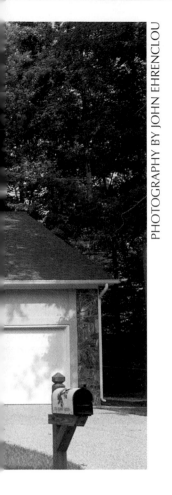

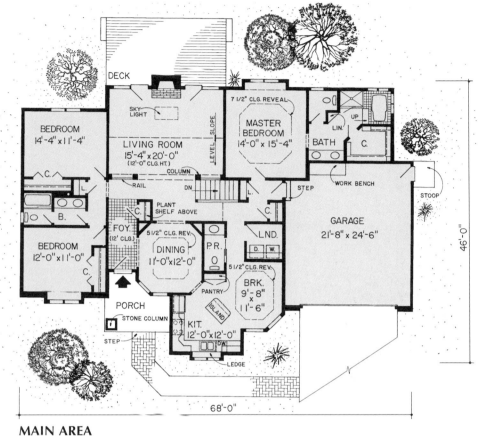

DECK

SKY-LIGHT

BEDROOM
14'-4" x 11'-4"

LIVING ROOM
15'-4" x 20'-0"
(12'-0" CLG. HT.)

LEVEL SLOPE

7 1/2" CLG. REVEAL

MASTER BEDROOM
14'-0" x 15'-4"

UP

LIN.

BATH

C.

C.

RAIL

COLUMN

DN

L.

STEP

WORK BENCH

STOOP

B.

L.

FOY.
(12' CLG.)

PLANT SHELF ABOVE

C.

5 1/2" CLG. REV.

C.

LND.

GARAGE
21'-8" x 24'-6"

BEDROOM
12'-0" x 11'-0"

C.

DINING
11'-0" x 12'-0"

P.R.

D. W.

5 1/2" CLG. REV.

BRK.
9'-8"
x
11'-6"

PANTRY

PORCH

STONE COLUMN

ISLAND

KIT.
12'-0" x 12'-0"

STEP

DW.

LEDGE

46'-0"

68'-0"

MAIN AREA

PLAN INFO:

• Main floor	2,020 sq. ft.
• Basement	2,020 sq. ft.
• Garage	534 sq. ft.
• Bedrooms	Three
• Bathrooms	2(Full), 1(Half)
• Foundation	Basement
▼ **Total living area**	**2,020 sq. ft.**

RUSTIC CONTEMPORARY DESIGN

This one level contemporary is a one-of-a-kind design just made for the sun lover. With a huge front deck featuring pass-through convenience from the kitchen, a rear patio and an abundance of windows, you're guaranteed a cheerful atmosphere, even on the coldest day. The central focus of this contemporary charmer is the sunken living room, with its three window walls and massive fireplace. Open to the kitchen, foyer and handy bar area, this elegant room seems even larger because of its soaring ceiling. Just behind the fireplace, an indoor hot tub turns the skylit sunspace into a private spa. The foyer separates active areas from the front bedroom and vaulted master suite.

Another bedroom shares a quiet spot behind the garage with a full bath and utility area. The photographed home has been modified to suit individual tastes.

Design 10619

Design 10619

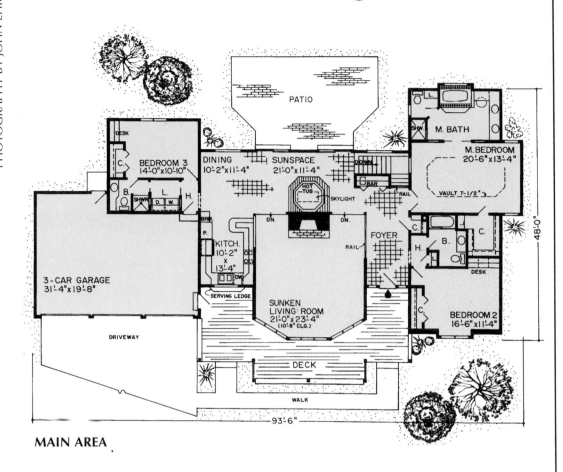

MAIN AREA

R E F E R   T O   P R I C E   C O D E   D

PLAN INFO:

• Main floor	2,352 sq. ft.
• Basement	2,352 sq. ft.
• Garage	696 sq. ft.
• Bedrooms	Three
• Bathrooms	3(Full)
• Foundation	Basement
▼ **Total living area**	**2,352 sq. ft.**

COMPACT RANCH DESIGN

*T*his wonderful Victorian-featured Ranch design incorporates many luxury conveniences usually offered in larger designs. The master bedroom is expansive with an oversized full bath, complete with a walk-in closet, an individual shower, a full tub, and a two-sink wash basin. A large kitchen area is offered with a built-in island for convenience. The kitchen also has its own breakfast area. Located next to the kitchen is a half-bath. The living area is separated from the dining room by a half-wall partition. Two large bedrooms complete the interior of the house. They have large closets and share a full bath. A two-car garage and a wood deck complete the options listed in this design. The photographed home has been modified to suit individual tastes.

Design 20058

Design 20058

MAIN AREA

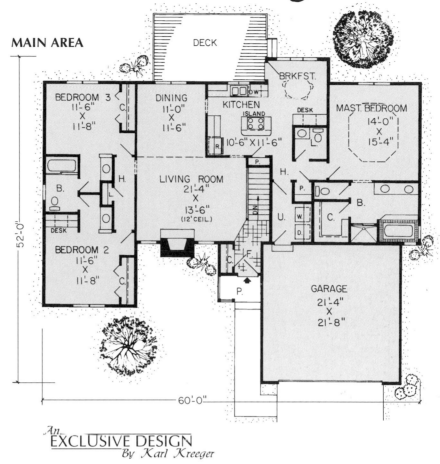

DECK

BRKFST.

BEDROOM 3
11'-6"
X
11'-8"

DINING
11'-0"
X
11'-6"

KITCHEN
10'-6" X 11'-6"

ISLAND

DESK

MAST. BEDROOM
14'-0"
X
15'-4"

B.

H.

DESK

LIVING ROOM
21'-4"
X
13'-6"
(12' CEIL.)

H.

B.

BEDROOM 2
11'-6"
X
11'-8"

C.

U.

W.

D.

C.

C.

F.

P.

GARAGE
21'-4"
X
21'-8"

52'-0"

60'-0"

An EXCLUSIVE DESIGN
By Karl Kreeger

REFER TO PRICE CODE B

PLAN INFO:

• Main floor	1,787 sq. ft.
• Basement	1,787 sq. ft.
• Garage	484 sq. ft.
• Bedrooms	Three
• Bathrooms	2(Full), 1(Half)
• Foundation	Basement
▼ **Total living area**	**1,787 sq. ft.**

COMPACT BRICK DESIGN

*F*our bedrooms, one a spectacular master suite with an extra large bath, equip this plan for a large family or overnight guests. The centrally located family room merits a fireplace, a wetbar, and a dining room is provided for formal entertaining. An interesting kitchen and a nook, as well as two and one-half baths, are featured. The photographed home has been modified to suit individual tastes.

Design 22004

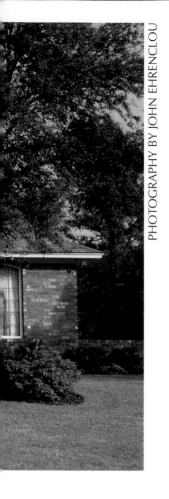

PHOTOGRAPHY BY JOHN EHRENCLOU

Design 22004

GARAGE
20'-6" X 21'-2"

UTILITY

NOOK
11'-0" X 10'-6"

PATIO

BATH

C   C

KITCHEN

MASTER BEDROOM
14'-8" X 13'-8"

FAMILY ROOM
23'-2" X 15'-4"

BATH

L

BATH

P

C

BAR

C

ENTRY

C   C

DINING
11'-0" X 12'-0"

PORCH

BEDROOM
10'-6" X 12'-6"

C

BEDROOM
11'-0" X 11'-6"

BEDROOM
12'-0" X 11'-0"

68'-6"

52'-0"

FLOOR PLAN

REFER TO PRICE CODE C

PLAN INFO:

• Main floor	2,070 sq. ft.
• Garage	474 sq. ft.
• Bedrooms	Four
• Bathrooms	#3(Full)
• Foundation	Slab
▼ **Total living area**	**2,070 sq. ft.**

TRADITIONAL BRICK GEM

*T*he unusual design of this kitchen provides the centerpiece for this thoroughly delightful floor plan. The kitchen is further enhanced by tiled hallways which surround it and delineate the adjacent living areas. The dining room, which opens onto the patio by large glass doors, includes both a built-in hutch and a display case. The large family room has a fireplace with its own wood storage and provides direct access to the sunspace. The master bedroom suite has a private patio, bay window, five-piece bath, separate vanity and a large, walk-in closet. The photographed home has been modified to suit individual tastes.

Design 10514

Design 10514

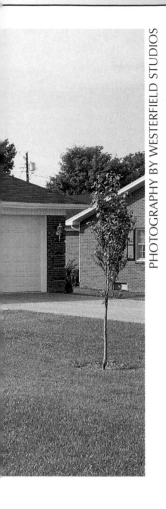

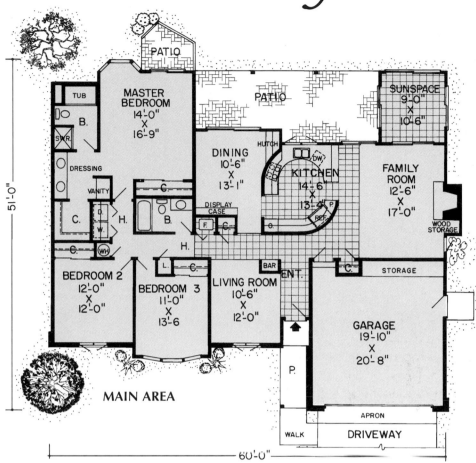

MAIN AREA

51'-0"

60'-0"

Key floor plan labels:
- PATIO
- PATIO
- SUNSPACE 9'-0" X 10'-6"
- TUB
- B.
- SHR.
- MASTER BEDROOM 14'-0" X 16'-9"
- DRESSING
- VANITY
- DINING 10'-6" X 13'-1"
- HUTCH
- KITCHEN 14'-6" X 13'-4"
- DW
- REF
- FAMILY ROOM 12'-6" X 17'-0"
- WOOD STORAGE
- C.
- D
- W.
- H.
- B.
- DISPLAY CASE
- F.
- G.
- O.
- WH
- BEDROOM 2 12'-0" X 12'-0"
- L.
- C.
- H.
- BEDROOM 3 11'-0" X 13'-6
- LIVING ROOM 10'-6" X 12'-0"
- BAR
- ENT.
- C.
- STORAGE
- GARAGE 19'-10" X 20'-8"
- P.
- APRON
- WALK
- DRIVEWAY

REFER TO PRICE CODE C

PLAN INFO:

• Main floor	1,870 sq. ft.
• Sun space	110 sq. ft.
• Garage	434 sq. ft.
• Bedrooms	Three
• Bathrooms	2(Full)
• Foundation	Crawl space
▼ **Total living area**	**1,980 sq. ft.**

AFFORDABLE TO BUILD

CLASSICALLY DESIGNED ONE LEVEL

Design 34043

*T*his convenient, one-level plan is perfect for the modern family with a taste for classic design. Traditional Victorian touches in this three-bedroom beauty include a romantic, railed porch and an intriguing breakfast tower just off the kitchen. You will love the step-saving arrangement of the kitchen between the breakfast and formal dining rooms. Enjoy the wide-open living room with sliders out to a rear deck, and the handsome master suite with its skylit, compartmentalized bath. Notice the convenient laundry location on the bedroom hall. The photographed home has been modified to suit individual tastes.

Slab/Crawlspace Option

An EXCLUSIVE DESIGN *By Karl Kreeger*

- Main floor   1,583 sq. ft.
- Basement   1,583 sq. ft.
- Garage   484 sq. ft.
- Bedrooms   Three
- Bathrooms   2(Full)
- Foundation   Basement, Slab, Crawl space
- ▼ **Total living area   1,583 sq. ft.**

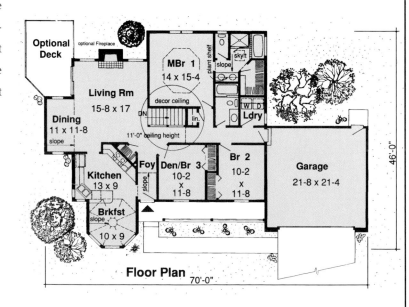

Floor Plan
70'-0"
46'-0"

PHOTOGRAPHY BY JOHN EHRENCLOU

MORE FOR LESS!

FRENCH PROVINCIAL BRICK DESIGN

Design 22020

With an exterior that expresses French Provincial charm, this single level design emphasizes elegance and offers a semi-circular dining area overlooking the patio. To pamper parents, the master bedroom annexes a long dressing area and private bath, while another bath serves the second and third bedrooms. A wood-burning fireplace furnishes the family room. The photographed home has been modified to suit individual tastes.

• Main floor	1,772 sq. ft.
• Garage	469 sq. ft.
• Bedrooms	Three
• Bathrooms	2(Full)
• Foundation	Slab
▼ Total living area	1,772 sq. ft.

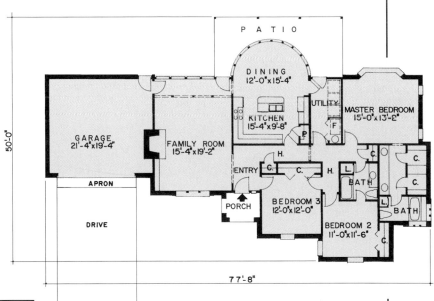

MAIN AREA

PRICE CODE C

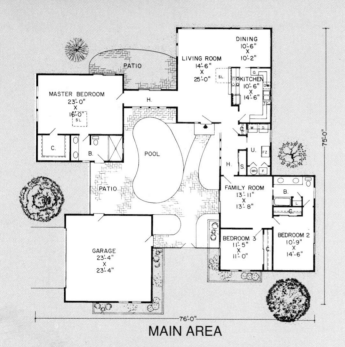

MAIN AREA

*C*reated for gracious living, this design is organized around a central courtyard complete with a pool. Secluded near one corner of the courtyard, the master bedroom suite is accented by a skylight, a spacious walk-in closet, and a bath to accommodate swimmers and sunbathers. The the living room, the dining room and kitchen occupy another corner. The well-placed kitchen easily serves the patio for comfortable outdoor entertaining. A family room and two more bedrooms complete the design.

• Main living area	2,194 sq. ft.
• Garage	576 sq. ft.
• Bedrooms	3
• Bathrooms	2(Full)
• Foundation	Crawl
▼ Total living area	**2,194 sq. ft.**

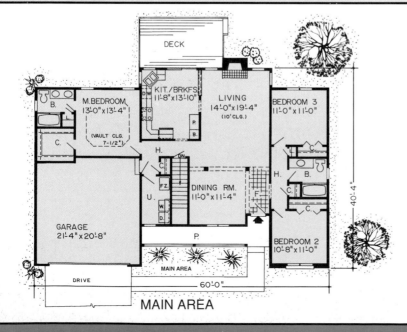

MAIN AREA

*H*ere's an inviting home with a distinctive difference. Active living areas are wide-open and centrally located. From the foyer, you'll enjoy a full view of the spacious dining, living, and kitchen areas in one sweeping glance. You can even see the deck adjoining the breakfast room. The difference in this house lies in the bedrooms. Each is a private retreat, away from active areas. The master suite at the rear of the house features a full bath with double sinks. Two additional bedrooms, off in their own wing, share a full bath and the quiet atmosphere that results from intelligent design.

• Main living area	1,575 sq. ft.
• Basement	1,575 sq. ft.
• Garage	475 sq. ft.
• Bedrooms	3
• Bathrooms	2(Full)
• Foundation	Basement, Crawl, Slab
▼ Total living area	**1,575 sq. ft.**

20

PRICE CODE B

Hate to climb stairs? This one-level gem will accommodate your family in style, and keep your housework to a minimum. Recessed ceilings add an elegant touch to the dining room and master suite. With half walls, skylights, and a handy rear deck off the sunny breakfast room, there's an airy feeling throughout the centrally-located active areas. You'll appreciate the convenience of built-in storage in the kitchen and fireplaced living room, and the huge bedroom closets that keep the clutter down. Look at the private master bath with its twin vanities, raised tub and walk-in shower. Don't you deserve a little luxury?

• Main living area	1,686 sq. ft.
• Basement	1,677 sq. ft.
• Garage	475 sq. ft.
• Bedrooms	3
• Bathrooms	2(Full)
• Foundation	Basement
▼ Total living area	1,686 sq. ft.

MAIN AREA

PRICE CODE B

ONE-LEVEL LIVING WITH A TWIST

Design 20083

Design 20156

An
EXCLUSIVE DESIGN
By Karl Kreeger

PRICE CODE A

MAIN AREA

*T*he elegant half-round windows flanking the clapboard-faced chimney hint at the comfortable atmosphere you'll find inside this easy-care Ranch. An open arrangement with the dining room combine with ten-foot ceilings to make the sunny living room seem even more spacious than its generous size. Glass on three sides overlooking the deck off the dining room adds an outdoor feeling to both rooms. And the compact kitchen, designed for efficiency, is just steps away. You'll appreciate the private location of the bedrooms, tucked away for a quiet atmosphere. The master suite is a special retreat, with its romantic window seat, compartmentalized bath and walk-in closet.

• Main living area	1,359 sq. ft.
• Basement	1,359 sq. ft.
• Garage	501 sq. ft.
• Bedrooms	3
• Bathrooms	2(Full)
• Foundation	Basement, Slab, Crawl
▼ Total living area	**1,359 sq. ft.**

MAIN AREA

*T*his striking exterior features vertical siding, shake shingles, and stone, to offset a large picture window. Inside, the kitchen has a built-in pantry, refrigerator, dishwasher and range, breakfast bar, an open-beamed ceiling with a skylight, plus a breakfast area with lots of windows. A formal dining room complements the living room, which has two open beams running through a sloped-ceiling. There is a laundry closet, and the foyer area also has a closet. Three bedrooms share a full bath. The master bedroom has an open-beamed, sloped-ceiling, a spacious bath area and a walk-in closet.

• Main living area	1,674 sq. ft.
• Basement	1,656 sq. ft.
• Garage	472 sq. ft.
• Bedrooms	3
• Bathrooms	2(Full)
• Foundation	B
▼ Total living area	**1,674 sq. ft.**

Design 10483

An
EXCLUSIVE DESIGN
By Karl Kreeger

PRICE CODE A

L ots of living is packed into this well-designed home which features a combined kitchen and dining room. The highly functional U-shaped kitchen includes a corner sink under double windows. Opening onto the dining room is the living room which is illuminated by both a front picture window and a skylight. A lovely fireplace makes this an inviting place to gather. The sleeping area of this home contains three bedrooms and two full baths, one of which is a private bath accessed only from the master bedroom.

• Main floor	1,025 sq. ft.
• Garage	403 sq. ft.
• Bedrooms	3
• Bathrooms	2(Full)
• Foundation	B
▼ **Total living area**	**1,025 sq. ft.**

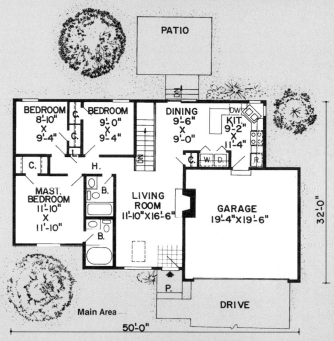

PRICE CODE B

An
EXCLUSIVE DESIGN
By Karl Kreeger

Design 20061

PRICE CODE A

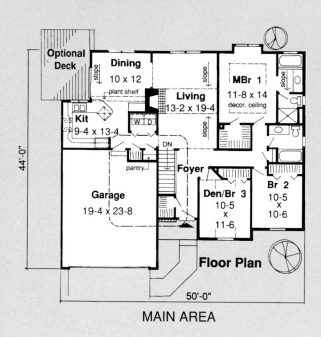

Optional Deck

Dining 10 x 12

plant shelf

Living 13-2 x 19-4 decor. ceiling

MBr 1 11-8 x 14 decor. ceiling

Kit 9-4 x 13-4

W D

DN

pantry

Foyer

Garage 19-4 x 23-8

Den/Br 3 10-5 x 11-6

Br 2 10-5 x 10-6

44'-0"

50'-0"

Floor Plan

MAIN AREA

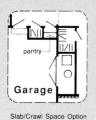

pantry

Garage

Slab/Crawl Space Option

Here's a pretty one-level home designed for carefree living. The central foyer divides active and quiet areas. Step back to a fireplaced living room with dramatic, towering ceilings and a panoramic view of the backyard. The adjoining dining room features a sloping ceiling crowned by a plant shelf, and sliders to an outdoor deck. Just across the counter, a handy, U-shaped kitchen features abundant cabinets, a window over the sink overlooking the deck, and a walk-in pantry. You'll find three bedrooms tucked off the foyer. Front bedrooms share a handy full bath, but the master suite boasts its own private bath with both shower and tub, a room-sized walk-in closet, and a bump-out window that adds light and space.

• Main living area	1,456 sq. ft.
• Basement	1,448 sq. ft.
• Garage	452 sq. ft.
• Bedrooms	3
• Bathrooms	2(Full)
• Foundation	Basement, Slab
▼ **Total living area**	**1,456 sq. ft.**

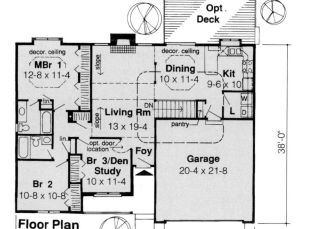

Opt. Deck

decor. ceiling

MBr 1 12-8 x 11-4

slope

decor. ceiling

Dining 10 x 11-4

Kit 9-6 x 10

W
L D

slope

Living Rm 13 x 19-4

DN

pantry

lin.

lin.

opt. door location

Foy

Br 3/Den Study 10 x 11-4

Br 2 10-8 x 10-8

Garage 20-4 x 21-8

38'-0"

Floor Plan

50'-0"

MAIN AREA

pantry

Slab/Crawl Space Option

Walk past the charming front porch, in through the foyer and you'll be struck by the exciting, spacious living room. Complete with high sloping ceilings and a beautiful fireplace flanked by large windows. The large master bedroom shows off a full wall of closet space, its own private bath, and an extraordinary decorative ceiling. Just down the hall are two more bedrooms and another full bath. Along with great counter space, the kitchen includes a double sink and an attractive bump-out window.

• Main living area	1,307 sq. ft.
• Basement	1,298 sq. ft.
• Garage	462 sq. ft.
• Bedrooms	3
• Bathrooms	2(Full)
• Foundation	Basement, Slab, Crawl
▼ **Total living area**	**1,307 sq. ft.**

Design 34011

Plenty of windows brighten this beautiful home with natural lighting and fresh air. More than enough closet space keeps clutter under control. A laundry room is located conveniently near all three bedrooms. The master suite features huge his-and-her walk-in closets and a private bath. Between the second and third bedroom is the second bathroom and linen closet. The family room is open to the dining area and kitchen. The kitchen is equipped with island counter and has access to an optional garage. Please indicate slab, crawl space or basement when ordering.

- Main living area 1,672 sq. ft.
- Optional Garage 566 sq. ft.
- Bedrooms 3
- Bathrooms 2(Full)
- Foundation Basement, Slab, Crawl
- ▼ Total living area 1,672 sq. ft.

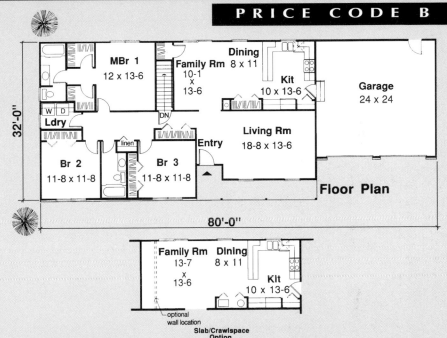

MBr 1
12 x 13-6

Family Rm
10-1
x
13-6

Dining
8 x 11

Kit
10 x 13-6

Garage
24 x 24

W D

Ldry

DN

linen

Entry

Living Rm
18-8 x 13-6

Br 2
11-8 x 11-8

Br 3
11-8 x 11-8

32'-0"

80'-0"

Floor Plan

Family Rm
13-7
x
13-6

Dining
8 x 11

Kit
10 x 13-6

optional
wall location

Slab/Crawlspace
Option

An EXCLUSIVE DESIGN
By Karl Kreeger

DETAILED CHARMER

Design 20161

PRICE CODE D

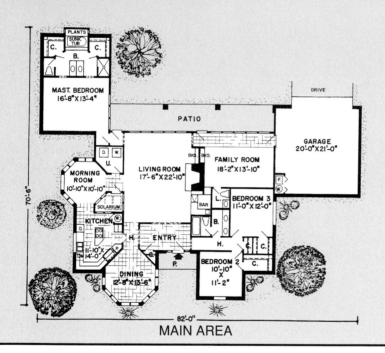

MAIN AREA

*T*iled floors unify the dining and food preparation areas of this masterful design. Located off the well-organized kitchen is a morning room that's perfect for an elegant brunch or some private time before the day begins. Highlighted by a solarium, this octagonal room opens onto the centrally-located living room that features built-in bookcases, a fireplace, and a wetbar. The family room design employs more tile accents and opens onto the patio. The secluded master bedroom suite features a sunken tub, a small greenhouse for the plant enthusiast, and roomy closets.

• Main living area	2,466 sq. ft.
• Garage	482 sq. ft.
• Bedrooms	3
• Bathrooms	2(Full), 1(Half)
• Foundation	Slab
▼ Total living area	2,466 sq. ft.

MAIN AREA

*P*laced behind the home and separate, so as not to detract from the rich traditional facade, the garage in this Colonial plan is attached by a roofed walkway. Brick and white pillars grace the exterior, while the interior floor plan speaks of modern luxury. The formal living room and dining room are placed to the left of the foyer, with the family room behind the living room having access to the terrace. To the right of the foyer are three bedrooms, one with a private bathroom.

• Main living area	2,014 sq. ft.
• Garage	576 sq. ft.
• Bedrooms	3
• Bathrooms	2(Full), 1(Half)
• Foundation	Basement, Slab
▼ Total living area	2,014 sq. ft.

The fireplace and sloped-ceiling in the family room offer something a bit out of the ordinary in this small home. The master bedroom is complete with a full bath and a dressing area. Bedrooms two and three share a full bath across the hall, and a half-bath is conveniently located adjacent to the kitchen. A bump-out bay window is shown in the spacious breakfast room, and a bay window with a window seat has been designed in the master bedroom. The screened porch off of the breakfast room is an inviting feature for meals outside.

• Main living area	1,688 sq. ft.
• Basement	1,688 sq. ft.
• Garage	489 sq. ft.
• Bedrooms	3
• Bathrooms	2(Full), 1(Half)
• Foundation	Basement
▼ Total living area	1,688 sq. ft.

PRICE CODE B

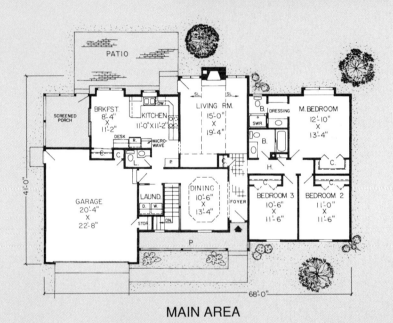

MAIN AREA

PRICE CODE C

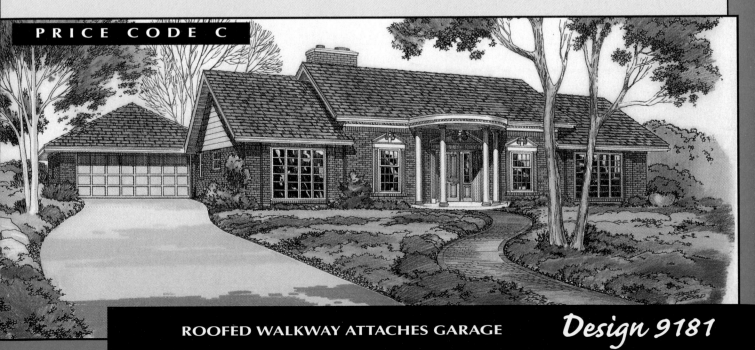

SKYLIGHT BRIGHTENS BEDROOM

An
EXCLUSIVE DESIGN
By Karl Kreeger

PRICE CODE B

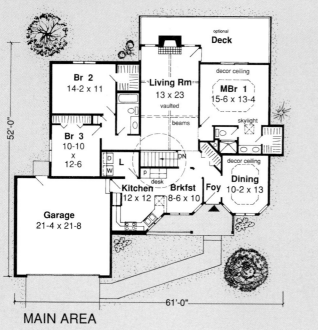

Br 2
14-2 x 11

Living Rm
13 x 23
vaulted
beams

optional
Deck

decor ceiling

MBr 1
15-6 x 13-4

skylight

Br 3
10-10
x
12-6

DN

decor ceiling

Dining
10-2 x 13

Kitchen
12 x 12

Brkfst
8-6 x 10

Foy

desk

D L
W
p

Garage
21-4 x 21-8

52'-0"

61'-0"

MAIN AREA

desk
p

Slab/Crawlspace
Option

Keep dry during the rainy season under the covered porch entry way of this gorgeous home. A foyer separates the dining room with a decorative ceiling from the breakfast area and the kitchen. Off the kitchen is the laundry room, conveniently located. The living room features a vaulted beamed ceiling and a fireplace. A full bath is located between the living room and two bedrooms, both with large closet.. On the other side of the living room is the master bedroom. The master bedroom has a decorative ceiling and a skylight above the entrance of its private bath. For those who enjoy outdoor living, an optional deck is offered, which is accessible through sliding glass doors.

• Main living area	1,698 sq. ft.
• Garage	484 sq. ft.
• Bedrooms	3
• Bathrooms	2(Full)
• Foundation	Basement, Slab
▼ **Total living area**	**1,698 sq. ft.**

56'-0"

Deck

Kitchen
12 x 11-4

Dining Rm
9 x 11-4

ov

pantry

W
D

Ldry

MBr 1
14-2 x 14-4

lin.

Living Rm
21-6 x 19-4
decor. beams

Br 3
12 x 12-6

Br 2
12 x 12-6

32'-0"

slope

MAIN AREA

The exterior of this ranch home is all wood with interesting lines. More than an ordinary ranch home, it has an expansive feeling to drive up to. The large living area has a stone fireplace and decorative beams. The kitchen and dining room lead to an outside deck. The laundry room has a large pantry, and is off the eating area. The master bedroom has a wonderful bathroom with a huge walk-in closet. In the front of the house, there are two additional bedrooms with a bathroom. This house offers one floor living and has nice big rooms.

• Main living area	1,792 sq. ft.
• Basement	864 sq. ft.
• Garage	928 sq. ft.
• Bedrooms	3
• Bathrooms	2(Full)
• Foundation	Basement
▼ **Total living area**	**1,792 sq. ft.**

Design 34055

An
EXCLUSIVE DESIGN
By Karl Kreeger

PRICE CODE B

*T*his great ranch features a front porch to sit and admire your view. A large living room and dining room flow together into one open space perfect for entertaining. The laundry room, which doubles as a mudroom, is off the kitchen and a back door entrance gives easy access to the outside. A master suite includes a private bathroom and the three additional bedrooms share a bathroom. A double-car garage is included in this plan.

- Main living area   1,527 sq. ft.
- Basement   1,344 sq. ft.
- Garage   425 sq. ft.
- Bedrooms   4
- Bathrooms   2(Full)
- Foundation   Basement, Slab, Crawl
- ▼ Total living area   1,527 sq. ft.

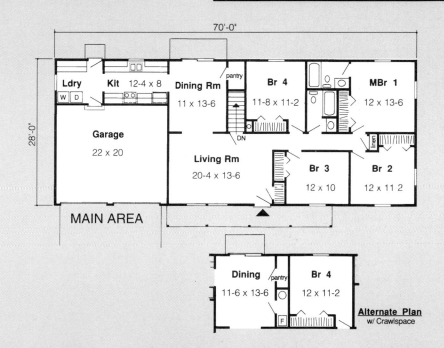

70'-0"

28'-0"

Ldry **Kit** 12-4 x 8   **Dining Rm** pantry **Br 4**   **MBr 1**
W D   11 x 13-6   11-8 x 11-2   12 x 13-6

Garage   linen
22 x 20   DN

Living Rm   **Br 3**   **Br 2**
20-4 x 13-6   12 x 10   12 x 11-2

MAIN AREA   ▲

Dining pantry   **Br 4**
11-6 x 13-6   12 x 11-2

F

Alternate Plan
w/ Crawlspace

PRICE CODE B

An
EXCLUSIVE DESIGN
By Karl Kreeger

DRAMATIC RANCH

Design 20198

PRICE CODE A

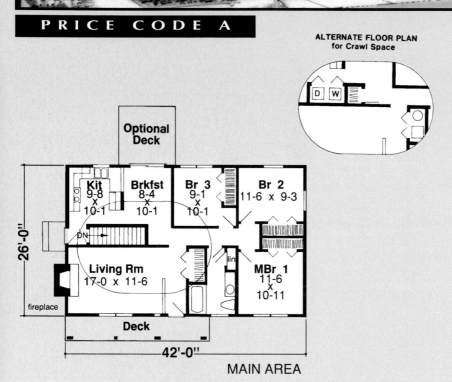

ALTERNATE FLOOR PLAN
for Crawl Space

D W

Optional Deck

| Kit | Brkfst | Br 3 | Br 2 |
| 9-8 x 10-1 | 8-4 x 10-1 | 9-1 x 10-1 | 11-6 x 9-3 |

DN

Living Rm
17-0 x 11-6

lin

MBr 1
11-6 x 10-11

fireplace

Deck

26'-0"

42'-0"

MAIN AREA

A central entry opens to a spacious living room with ample windows and a handy closet nearby. The kitchen features a dining area with sliding glass doors to the backyard and optional deck. A hallway separates three bedrooms and a full bath from the active areas. The laundry facilities are tucked behind double doors if you choose to build this without a basement.

• Main living area	1,092 sq. ft.
• Basement	1,092 sq. ft.
• Bedrooms	3
• Bathrooms	1(Full)
• Foundation	Basement, Slab, Crawl
▼ Total living area	**1,092 sq. ft.**

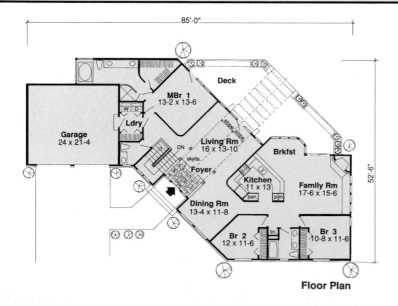

85'-0"

Deck

MBr 1
13-2 x 13-6

W D

Ldry

Garage
24 x 21-4

Living Rm
16 x 13-10

DN   skylts.

Foyer

Brkfst

Kitchen
11 x 13
pan.   pan.

Family Rm
17-6 x 15-6

Dining Rm
13-4 x 11-8

Br 2
12 x 11-6

lin

Br 3
10-8 x 11-6

52'-6"

Floor Plan

P icture yourself relaxing in the dappled sunlight of the partially covered deck that spans the rear of this sprawling home. Entertaining will be easy in this spectacular setting, whether you choose the large soaring living room off the vaulted skylit foyer, or the cozy family room. The kitchen easily serves every area, including the elegant formal dining room at the front of the house. The master suite, tucked off behind the garage, features private deck access and a magnificent bath.

• Main living area	2,084 sq. ft.
• Basement	2,084 sq. ft.
• Bedrooms	3
• Bathrooms	2(Full)
• Foundation	Basement, Crawl
▼ Total living area	**2,084 sq. ft.**

Design 34353

PRICE CODE A

*T*he L-shaped living and dining room arrangement is enhanced by bump-out windows, a fireplace and sliders to the backyard. The adjoining compact, galley-style kitchen easily serves the dining room and the rear entry is an added convenience. A hallway leads to the sleeping wing where there are three bedrooms and one and three-quarters baths.

- Main living area   1,268 sq. ft.
- Basement   1,248 sq. ft.
- Bedrooms   3
- Bathrooms   2(Full)
- Foundation   Basement, Slab, Crawl
- ▼ **Total living area**   **1,268 sq. ft.**

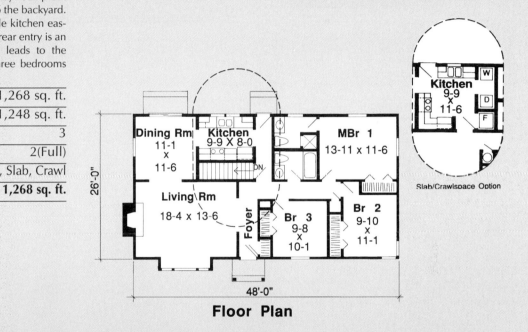

Kitchen 9-9 x 11-6

Slab/Crawlspace Option

Dining Rm 11-1 x 11-6

Kitchen 9-9 X 8-0

MBr 1 13-11 x 11-6

26'-0"

Living\Rm 18-4 x 13-6

Foyer

Br 3 9-8 x 10-1

Br 2 9-10 x 11-1

DN

48'-0"

Floor Plan

PRICE CODE C

Design 20451

POPULAR FOR THE 90'S

SINGLE LEVEL WITH FACADE EXTRAS

Design 24250

The design of this home allows for plenty of living space. This home makes use of custom, volume ceilings. The living room offers a sunk-in environment. The vaulted ceiling and fireplace give this room drama. The oversized windows framing the fireplace enhance the drama with natural light. The kitchen features a center island and eating nook. There is more than ample counter space, plus a double basin sink and all the amenities you could ask for. The formal dining room adjoins the kitchen allowing for easy entertaining. The spacious master suite enjoys a vaulted ceiling. Its lavish master bath allows for privacy and pampering. Cozy, comfortable, and peaceful are the feelings you get as you curl up on the window seat on a rainy afternoon to read a book. This suite is your own private get-away. The secondary bedrooms have large windows that view the front porch.

• Main floor	1,700 sq. ft.
• Bedrooms	Three
• Bathrooms	2(Full)
• Foundation	Basement, Crawl space
▼ **Total living area**	**1,700 sq. ft.**

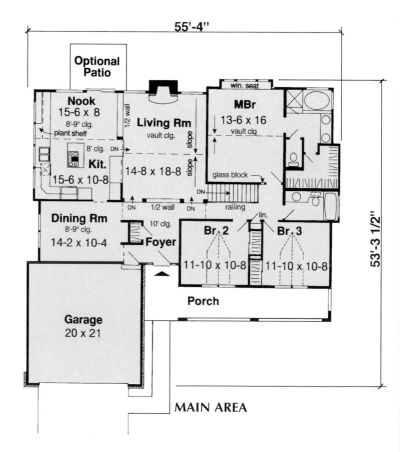

MAIN AREA

An EXCLUSIVE DESIGN
By Energetic Enterprises

PRICE CODE B

FIREPLACE IS CENTER OF CIRCULAR LIVING AREA

No. 10274

This plan features:

— Three bedrooms

— Two full baths

A dramatically positioned fireplace as a focal point for the main living area

The Kitchen, Dining and Living Rooms form a circle that allows work areas to flow into living areas

Sliding glass doors accessible to wood a Deck

A convenient Laundry Room located off the Kitchen

A double Garage providing excellent storage

Accessibility Features:

— Level entry way

— Wide doorways (32"-36" clear width)

— Chair height electrical controls/outlets

— Reinforced walls for installation of grab bars

FIRST FLOOR — 1,783 SQ. FT.
GARAGE — 576 SQ. FT.

TOTAL LIVING AREA:
1,783 SQ. FT.

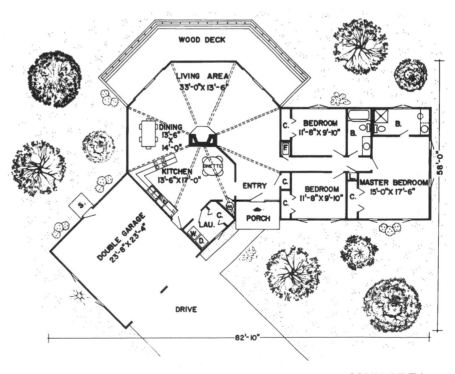

MAIN AREA

PRICE CODE A

GREAT ROOM FEATURES A FIREPLACE

No. 90105

■ This plan features:

— Three bedrooms

— Two full baths

■ A spacious Great Room with a cozy fireplace

■ A Kitchen with a pass through serving for convenience

■ A combination Mud Room/Laundry room, to make cleaning up a breeze

■ An optional basement, slab or crawl space foundation — please specify when ordering

MAIN AREA — 1,345 SQ. FT.

TOTAL LIVING AREA:
1,345 SQ. FT.

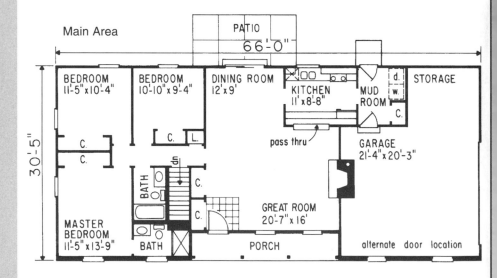

Main Area

66'-0"

30'-5"

PATIO

BEDROOM 11'-5"x10'-4"

BEDROOM 10'-10"x9'-4"

DINING ROOM 12'x9'

KITCHEN 11'x8'-8"

MUD ROOM

STORAGE

d. w.

C.

pass thru

GARAGE 21'-4"x20'-3"

C.

L.

BATH

C.

C.

GREAT ROOM 20'-7"x16'

MASTER BEDROOM 11'-5"x13'-9"

BATH

PORCH

alternate door location

PRICE CODE A

LARGE LIVING IN A SMALL SPACE

No. 24304

■ This plan features:

— Three bedrooms

— Two full baths

■ A sheltered entrance leads into an open Living Room with a corner fireplace and a wall of windows

■ A well-equipped Kitchen features a peninsula counter with a Nook, a laundry and clothes closet, and a built-in pantry

■ A Master Bedroom with a private bath

■ Two additional bedrooms that share full hall bath

MAIN FLOOR — 993 SQ. FT.
GARAGE — 987 SQ. FT.
OPTIONAL BASEMENT — 987 SQ. FT.

TOTAL LIVING AREA: 993 SQ. FT.

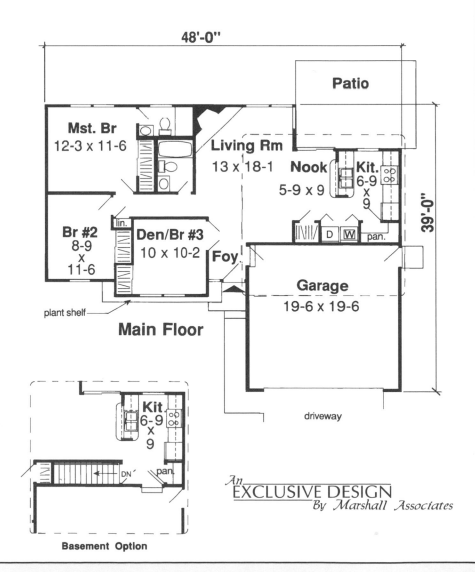

48'-0"

Patio

Mst. Br
12-3 x 11-6

Living Rm
13 x 18-1

Nook
5-9 x 9

Kit.
6-9 x 9

Br #2
8-9 x 11-6

Den/Br #3
10 x 10-2

Foy

D W pan.

Garage
19-6 x 19-6

39'-0"

plant shelf

Main Floor

driveway

Kit.
6-9 x 9

DN pan.

Basement Option

An EXCLUSIVE DESIGN *By* Marshall *Associates*

PRICE CODE D

No. 24588

This plan features:

— Three bedrooms

— Two full baths

Impressive entrance with a transom window leads into the open Foyer and Great Room

Central Great Room with a fireplace and a vaulted ceiling accented by columns

Large Kitchen with a work island, a walk-in pantry, a built-in desk and French doors to the Screen Porch

Convenient Garage entrance and laundry adjacent to the Kitchen

Master Suite with a vaulted ceiling above a triple window, a walk-in closet and a private bath

Two more bedrooms, one with a window seat, share a full bath

This plan is available with a Basement foundation only

MAIN FLOOR — 1,786 SQ. FT.
LOWER FLOOR — 718 SQ. FT.
BASEMENT — 1,044 SQ. FT.
GARAGE — 724 SQ. FT.

TOTAL LIVING AREA:
2,504 SQ. FT.

PLENTY OF ROOM INSIDE

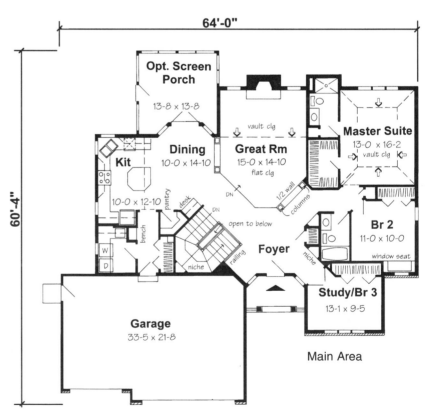

Main Area

No materials list available

An
EXCLUSIVE DESIGN
By Britt J. Willis

PRICE CODE B

ROOMS WITH A VIEW

No. 90954

■ This plan features:

— Three bedrooms

— Two full and one half baths

■ A vaulted foyer offering access to every area of the house

■ A Kitchen featuring a built-in pantry and desk, and a bay Nook for informal meals

■ A Master Suite with private access to the sun deck

FIRST FLOOR — 1,617 SQ. FT.
BASEMENT — 1,617 SQ. FT.
GARAGE — 471 SQ. FT.

TOTAL LIVING AREA:
1,617 SQ. FT.

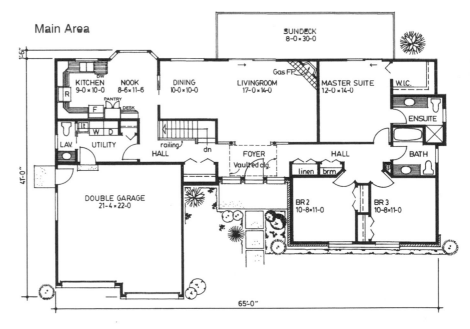

An
EXCLUSIVE DESIGN
By Westhome Planners, Ltd.

PRICE CODE C

UNIQUE OPEN QUALITY TO EVERY ROOM

No. 84040

■ This plan features:

— Three bedrooms

— Two full and one half baths

■ Angular windows and recessed ceilings, separating the island Kitchen from the formal Dining and Breakfast Rooms

■ Twelve foot ceilings in the soaring, sky-lit Living Room

■ A Master Suite enhanced by bump-out windows, a personal bath, and a huge, walk-in closet

■ An optional slab, crawl space or basement foundation available, please specify when ordering

FIRST FLOOR — 2,026 SQ. FT.
GARAGE — 545 SQ. FT.

TOTAL LIVING AREA: 2,026 SQ. FT.

No materials list available

Slab/Crawlspace Option

Main Area

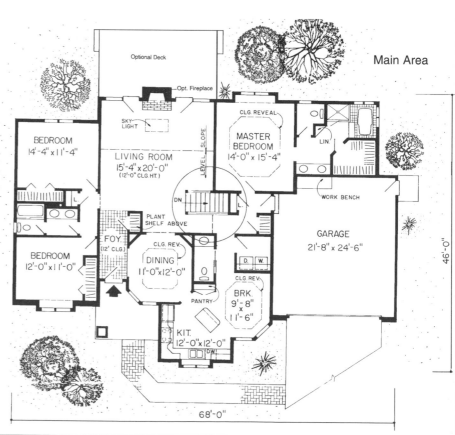

PRICE CODE A

FEATURES FOUND IN LARGE HOMES

No. 10509

■ This plan features:

— Three bedrooms

— Two full baths

■ A tiled Entry leading into a spacious Living Room

■ A Living Room/Dining area featuring a fireplace with an extended hearth flanked by glass windows and sliding doors

■ An efficient Kitchen with plenty of counter space and a food bar adjacent to the Living Room

■ An inviting Master Suite with a dressing area, a walk-in closet and a private bath

■ Two additional bedrooms, one with a built-in dressing table, sharing a full hall bath

MAIN FLOOR — 1,464 SQ. FT.
GARAGE — 528 SQ. FT.

TOTAL LIVING AREA:
1,464 SQ. FT.

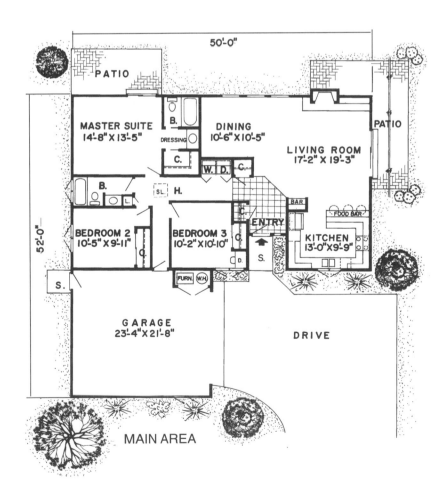

MAIN AREA

PRICE CODE C

RAMBLING RANCH

No. 24314

■ This plan features:

— Three bedrooms

— Two full baths

■ A cozy Living Room that flows into an elegant Dining Room with a vaulted ceiling

■ A well-appointed Kitchen that includes double sink and a walk-in pantry that conveniently serves the Dining Room and the Family Room's eating bar

■ A Family Room with direct access to the rear yard

■ A Master Suite with a lavish private bath and a walk-in closet

■ Two additional bedrooms that share a full hall bath

FIRST FLOOR — 1,850 SQ. FT.
GARAGE — 358 SQ. FT.

TOTAL LIVING AREA:
1,850 SQ. FT.

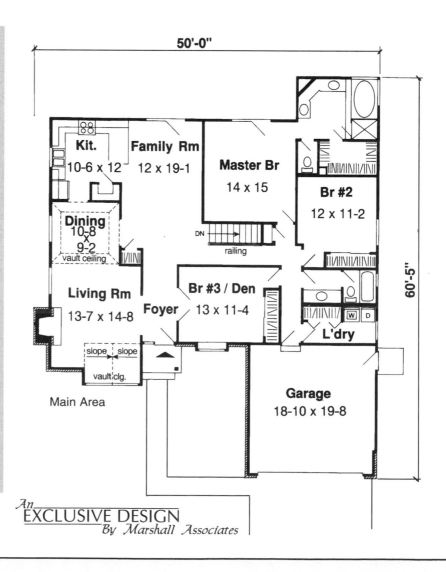

An
EXCLUSIVE DESIGN
By Marshall Associates

PRICE CODE C

No. 91627

This plan features:

— Three bedrooms

— Two full and one half baths

Impressive entrance leads into an octagonal Great Hall hub for all areas of the home

Elegant coved ceiling in the Living Room tops triple arched windows and a cozy fireplace

Formal Dining area with a decorative window and a built-in serving shelf

Ultimate Kitchen with an angled cooktop island serving the Nook, the Deck and the Family Room

Coved ceiling tops another fireplace between the views of the Deck in the Family Room

Plush Master Suite with a walk-in closet and a private bath with a double vanity and a spa tub

Two bedrooms share a full bath

This plan is available with a Basement foundation only

MAIN FLOOR — 2,097 SQ. FT.
GARAGE — 440 SQ. FT.

**TOTAL LIVING AREA:
2,097 SQ. FT.**

UNIQUE GREAT HALL GREETS GUESTS

Main Area

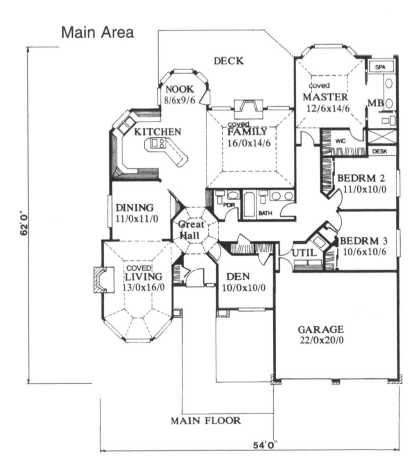

MAIN FLOOR

62'0"

54'0"

DECK

NOOK 8/6x9/6

KITCHEN

coved FAMILY 16/0x14/6

coved MASTER 12/6x14/6

SPA

MB

WIC

DESK

BEDRM 2 11/0x10/0

DINING 11/0x11/0

Great Hall

PDR

BATH

COVED LIVING 13/0x16/0

DEN 10/0x10/0

UTIL

BEDRM 3 10/6x10/6

GARAGE 22/0x20/0

An EXCLUSIVE DESIGN *By Mark Stewart*

PRICE CODE A

NO WASTED SPACE

No. 90412

- This plan features:
— Three bedrooms
— Two full baths
- A centrally located Great Room with a cathedral ceiling, exposed wood beams, and large areas of fixed glass
- The Living and Dining areas separated by a massive stone fireplace
- A secluded Master Suite with a walk-in closet and private Master Bath
- An efficient Kitchen with a convenient laundry area
- An optional basement, slab or crawl space foundation — please specify when ordering

MAIN AREA — 1,454 SQ. FT.

**TOTAL LIVING AREA:
1,454 SQ. FT.**

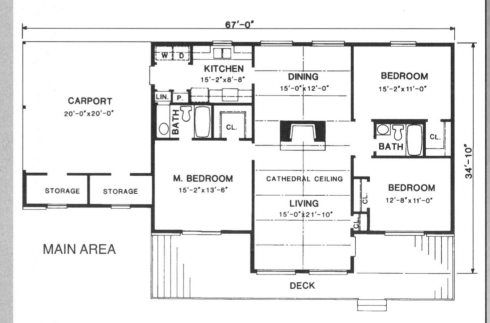

PRICE CODE A

CABIN IN THE COUNTRY

No. 90433

■ This plan features:

— Two bedrooms

— One full and one half baths

■ A screened porch for enjoyment of your outdoor surroundings

■ A combination Living and Dining area with cozy fireplace for added warmth

■ An efficiently laid out Kitchen with a built-in pantry

■ Two large bedrooms located at the rear of the home

■ An optional slab or crawl space foundation — please specify when ordering

FIRST FLOOR — 928 SQ. FT.
SCREENED PORCH — 230 SQ. FT.
STORAGE — 14 SQ. FT.

TOTAL LIVING AREA:
928 SQ. FT.

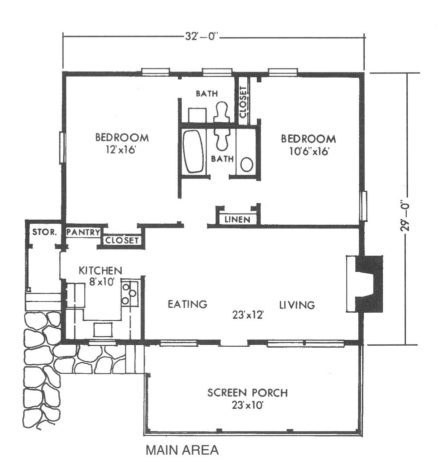

MAIN AREA

PRICE CODE A

YEAR ROUND LEISURE

No. 90630

This plan features:

— Three bedrooms

— Two full baths

A cathedral ceiling with exposed beams and a stone wall with heat-circulating fireplace in the Living Room

Three sliding glass doors leading from the Living Room to a large deck

A built-in Dining area that separates the Kitchen from the far end of the Living Room

A Master Suite with his and her closets and a private bath

Two additional bedrooms, one double sized, sharing a full hall bath

A crawl space foundation only

FIRST FLOOR — 1,207 SQ. FT.

TOTAL LIVING AREA: 1,207 SQ. FT.

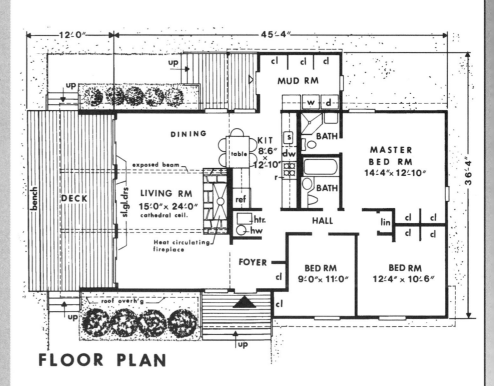

FLOOR PLAN

PRICE CODE A

FLEXIBLE PLAN CREATES MANY OPTIONS

No. 90324

■ This plan features:

— Two bedrooms with optional third bedroom/den

— Two full baths

■ A Great Room featuring vaulted ceiling, fireplace, and built-in bookcase

■ An eat-in Kitchen opening onto a partially enclosed deck through sliding doors

■ An L-shaped design of the Kitchen providing for easy meal preparation

■ A Master Bedroom with private bath, large walk-in closet, and window seat

FIRST FLOOR — 1,016 SQ. FT.

TOTAL LIVING AREA: 1,016 SQ. FT.

PRICE CODE A

PERFECT FOR A WATERSIDE SETTING

No. 90934

■ This plan features:

— Two bedrooms

— One full bath

■ An economical design

■ A covered sun deck adding outdoor living space

■ A mudroom/laundry area inside the side door, trapping dirt before it can enter the house

■ An open layout between the Living Room with fireplace, Dining Room and Kitchen

FIRST FLOOR — 884 SQ. FT.
WIDTH — 34'-0"
DEPTH — 28'-0"

TOTAL LIVING AREA:
884 SQ. FT.

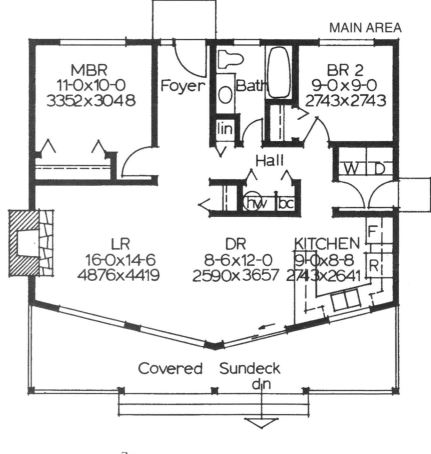

MAIN AREA

MBR
11-0x10-0
3352x3048

Foyer

Bath

BR 2
9-0x9-0
2743x2743

lin

Hall

W D

hw bc

LR
16-0x14-6
4876x4419

DR
8-6x12-0
2590x3657

KITCHEN
9-0x8-8
2743x2641

F
R

Covered Sundeck
dn

An
EXCLUSIVE DESIGN
By Westhome Planners, Ltd.

PRICE CODE C

*A*RCHITECTURAL DETAILING ADDS TO APPEAL

No. 24557

This plan features:

— Three bedrooms

— Two full and one half baths

Extensive detailing around exterior windows and doorways

A sloping ceiling in the Foyer

A formal Dining Room with columns on the half walls and a soffit detailed ceiling

A spacious Great Room with a fireplace

An expansive Kitchen that includes an island and joins a sunny Breakfast Nook

A pan vaulted ceiling in the Master Suite, with walk-in closet and private luxurious bath

Two additional bedrooms with ample closet space and a full bath

MAIN AREA — 2,110 SQ. FT.
BASEMENT — 2,096 SQ. FT.
GARAGE — 724 SQ. FT.

**TOTAL LIVING AREA:
2,110 SQ. FT.**

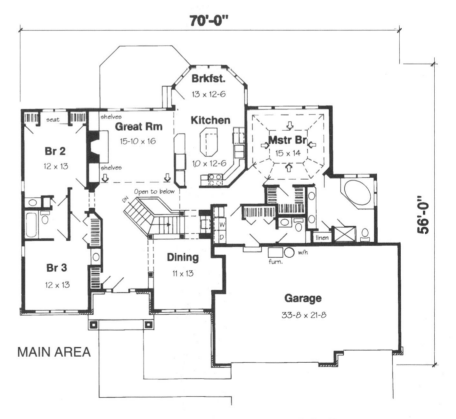

MAIN AREA

No materials list available

An
EXCLUSIVE DESIGN
By Britt J. Willis

PRICE CODE A

AN AFFORDABLE FLOOR PLAN

No. 91807

■ This plan features:

— Three bedrooms

— Two full baths

■ A covered porch entry

■ An old-fashioned hearth fireplace in the vaulted ceiling Living Room

■ An efficient Kitchen with U-shaped counter that is accessible from the Dining Room

■ A Master Bedroom with a large walk-in closet and private bath

■ This plan is available with a Slab or Crawlspace foundation — please specify when ordering

FIRST FLOOR — 1,410 SQ. FT.
GARAGE — 484 SQ. FT.

TOTAL LIVING AREA:
1,410 SQ. FT.

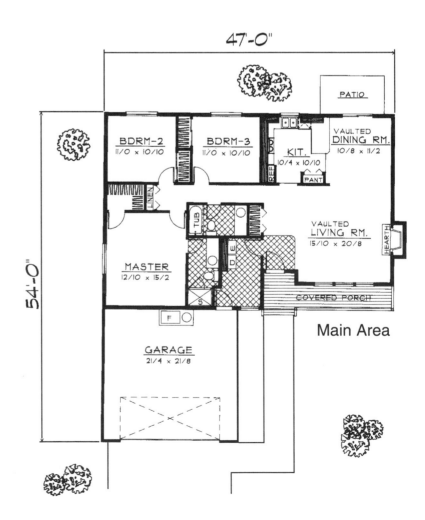

Main Area

PRICE CODE D

Dignified Traditional

No. 93049

This plan features:

— Four bedrooms

— Two full and one half baths

Dramatic columns defining the elegant Dining Room and framing the entrance to the large, spacious Great Room

A breakfast bar and work island in the gourmet Kitchen which also includes an abundance of counter and cabinet space

All bedrooms conveniently grouped at the opposite side of the home

A Master Suite with an enormous walk-in closet and a luxuriant Master Bath

Bedrooms two and three also have walk-in closets and share a full bath with a double vanity

MAIN FLOOR — 2,292 SQ. FT.
GARAGE — 526 SQ. FT.

**TOTAL LIVING AREA:
2,292 SQ. FT.**

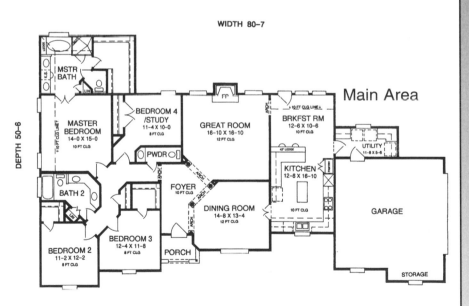

WIDTH 80–7

Main Area

DEPTH 50–6

MSTR BATH

MASTER BEDROOM 14-0 X 15-0 10 FT CLG

BEDROOM 4 /STUDY 11-4 X 10-0 8 FT CLG

GREAT ROOM 16-10 X 16-10 12 FT CLG

BRKFST RM 12-6 X 10-6 10 FT CLG

UTILITY 11-8 X 5-6

PWDR

BATH 2

FOYER 10 FT CLG

KITCHEN 12-6 X 16-10

GARAGE

BEDROOM 2 11-2 X 12-2 8 FT CLG

BEDROOM 3 12-4 X 11-8 8 FT CLG

DINING ROOM 14-8 X 13-4 12 FT CLG

PORCH

STORAGE

An
EXCLUSIVE DESIGN
By Belk Home Designs

No materials list available

PRICE CODE A

ONE LEVEL CONTEMPORARY

No. 24327

■ This plan features:

— Three bedrooms

— Two full baths

■ A vaulted ceiling and elegant fireplace in the Living Room

■ An open layout between the Living Room, Dining Room and Kitchen gives a more spacious feeling to these areas

■ A well-equipped Kitchen with a double sink and a peninsula counter that may be used as an eating bar

■ A Master Suite that includes a walk-in closet and a private bath with a double vanity

■ Two additional bedrooms that have ample closet space and share a full hall bath

MAIN AREA — 1,266 SQ. FT.
GARAGE — 443 SQ. FT.
BASEMENT — 1,266 SQ. FT.

TOTAL LIVING AREA:
1,266 SQ. FT.

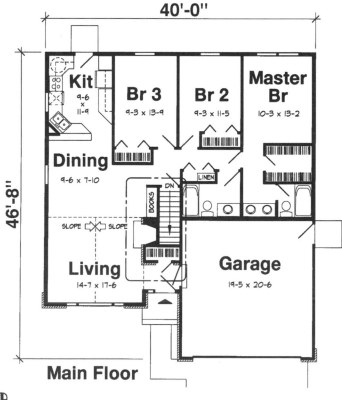

40'-0"

46'-8"

Kit
9-6 x 11-9

Br 3
9-3 x 13-9

Br 2
9-3 x 11-5

Master Br
10-3 x 13-2

Dining
9-6 x 7-10

LINEN

BOOKS

DN

SLOPE

Living
14-7 x 17-6

Garage
19-5 x 20-6

Main Floor

CRAWL ACCESS

D W

HW

FURN.

An EXCLUSIVE DESIGN
By Marshall Associates

No materials list available

PRICE CODE B

TRADITIONAL LINES ENHANCE PLAN

No. 92044

■ This plan features:

— Three bedrooms

— Two full baths

■ A formal entry with ten foot ceilings

■ An L-shaped Kitchen with an island eating bar

■ A two-car attached garage to make carrying groceries easier

■ A Master Bedroom with a large walk-in closet and luxury bath

FIRST FLOOR — 1,753 SQ. FT.
GARAGE — 528 SQ. FT.

TOTAL LIVING AREA:
1,753 SQ. FT.

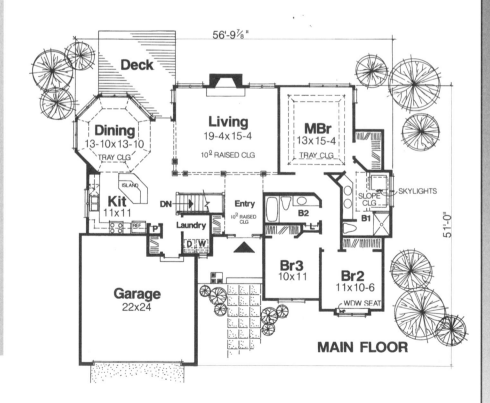

MAIN FLOOR

PRICE CODE A

AFFORDABLE RANCH

No. 34002

■ This plan features:

— Three bedrooms

— One full bath

■ Sidelight front door opens into the bright Living Room with a triple window

■ An efficient U-shaped Kitchen adjacent to the Garage and the laundry easily serves the Dining area with open counter space

■ Access to the Patio from the Dining Room, expands the living space outdoors

■ Roomy Master Bedroom and two additional bedrooms with spacious closets

■ This plan is available with a Basement, Slab or Crawlspace foundation. Please specify when ordering

MAIN FLOOR — 1,092 SQ. FT.
GARAGE — 473 SQ. FT.

TOTAL LIVING AREA:
1,092 SQ. FT.

Slab/crawlspace option

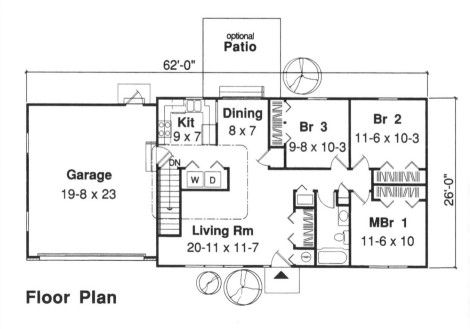

Floor Plan

PRICE CODE A

BUILT WITH A BUDGET

No. 90235

This plan features:

— Three bedrooms

— Two full baths

Easy-care tiled Entry into spacious Living Room with raised hearth fireplace and access to the Terrace

Formal Dining Room overlooking the rear yard adjoins the Living Room and the Kitchen

Eat-in, country Kitchen with a built-in pantry

Master Bedroom offers a double closet, a private bath and access to the Terrace

Two additional bedrooms share a full bath

This plan is available with a Basement foundation only

MAIN FLOOR — 1,267 SQ. FT.
GARAGE — 467 SQ. FT.
BASEMENT — 1,267 SQ. FT.

TOTAL LIVING AREA:
1,267 SQ. FT.

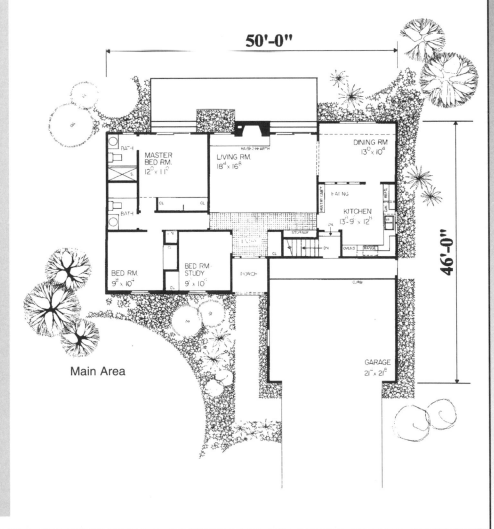

Main Area

PRICE CODE A

ABUNDANCE OF STORAGE SPACE

No. 91787

This plan features:

— Three bedrooms

— Two full baths

Front Porch shelters the entrance into an open layout of the Living and Dining Rooms and the Kitchen

Lovely bay window highlights the Living Room

Ultimate Kitchen with a walk-in pantry and a cooktop eating bar easily serves the Dining Room and the Deck

Private Master Suite offers a walk-in closet and a double vanity bath

Two additional bedrooms with walk-in closets share a full bath

This plan is available with a Crawlspace foundation only

MAIN FLOOR — 1,488 SQ. FT.
GARAGE/STORAGE — 606 SQ. FT.

**TOTAL LIVING AREA:
1,488 SQ. FT.**

FLOOR PLAN

WIDTH — 54'-0"
DEPTH — 60'-0"

PRICE CODE A

STRIKING ENTRYWAY

No. 20054

■ This plan features:

— Two bedrooms, with optional third bedroom/den

— Two full baths

■ A cathedral ceiling gracing the Living Room

■ A large Master Bedroom with an ample closet and a full Master Bath

■ A Dining Room with an attractive decorative ceiling

■ A modern Kitchen flowing into the Breakfast area

■ A conveniently located laundry area

MAIN AREA — 1,461 SQ. FT.
BASEMENT — 1,458 SQ. FT.
GARAGE — 528 SQ. FT.

TOTAL LIVING AREA:
1,461 SQ. FT.

An EXCLUSIVE DESIGN *By Karl Kreeger*

PRICE CODE A

LAYOUT PROMOTES QUIET LIVING

No. 91642

■ This plan features:

— Two bedrooms

— Two full baths

■ An covered Entry leading to the back of the home

■ Living/Dining area with built-in shelves, loads of windows and access to the back yard

■ An open Kitchen with an island cooktop adjacent to the laundry, the Garage and the Dining/Living area

■ A Master suite with a decorative window topped by a coved ceiling, an oversized closet and a private bath with a dressing table and a roll-in shower

■ A Den/Bedroom with a recessed window and a private bath

MAIN FLOOR — 1,295 SQ. FT.

TOTAL LIVING AREA:
1,295 SQ. FT.

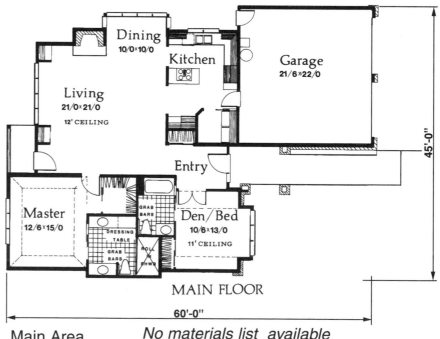

Main Area   *No materials list available*

An
EXCLUSIVE DESIGN
By Mark Stewart

PRICE CODE C

ENTERTAINING INDOORS AND OUT

No. 90001

■ This plan features:

— Four bedrooms

— Two full and one half baths

■ Gracious double doors lead into the Reception Foyer with a unique bridge over a moat to the Living Room

■ Huge, stone fireplace with a barbeque and a wood storage on the Terrace side, a concealed bar and French doors enhance this Living Room

■ Efficient Kitchen with an eating bar as part of the Family Room, highlighted by a corner fireplace

■ Sunken Master Bedroom suite with a decorative window topped by a cathedral ceiling, three closets and a private bath with a Roman tub

■ This plan is available with a Basement or Crawlspace foundation. Please specify when ordering

MAIN FLOOR — 2,177 SQ. FT.

TOTAL LIVING AREA:
2,177 SQ. FT.

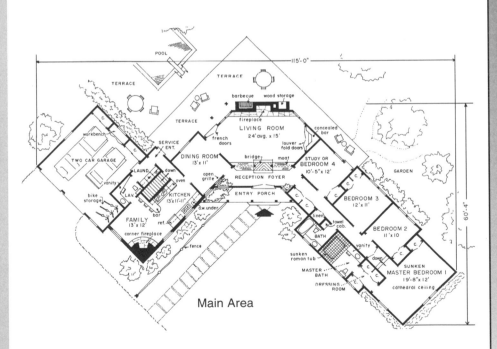

Main Area

PRICE CODE A

No. 24700

- ■ This plan features:
- — Three bedrooms
- — Two full baths
- ■ Front Porch entry leads into an open Living Room, accented by a hearth fireplace below a sloped ceiling
- ■ Efficient Kitchen with a peninsula counter convenient to the Laundry, Garage, Dining area and Deck
- ■ Master Bedroom accented by a decorative ceiling, a double closet and a private bath
- ■ Two additional bedrooms with decorative windows and ample closets share a full bath
- ■ This plan is available with a Basement, Slab, or Crawlspace foundation. Please specify when ordering

MAIN FLOOR — 1,312 SQ. FT.
BASEMENT — 1,293 SQ. FT.
GARAGE — 445 SQ. FT.

TOTAL LIVING AREA:
1,312 SQ. FT.

ARCHED WINDOWS HIGHLIGHT FACADE

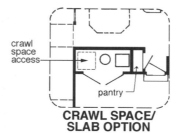

crawl space access

pantry

CRAWL SPACE/ SLAB OPTION

No materials list available

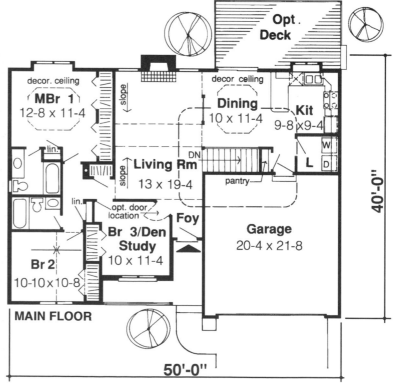

MAIN FLOOR

Opt. Deck

decor. ceiling
MBr 1
12-8 x 11-4

slope

decor. ceiling
Dining
10 x 11-4

Kit
9-8 x9-4

lin.

slope

Living Rm
13 x 19-4

DN

pantry

W
D
L

lin.

opt. door location

Foy

Br 3/Den Study
10 x 11-4

Garage
20-4 x 21-8

Br 2
10-10 x 10-8

40'-0"

50'-0"

PRICE CODE A

RANCH WITH EVERYTHING

No. 20187

■ This plan features:

— Three bedrooms

— Two full baths

■ A decorative ceiling in the elegant formal Dining Room

■ A well-appointed Kitchen with built-in pantry, ample counter space and peninsula island that separates the Kitchen from the Breakfast room

■ A Living Room, with easy access to the deck, made cozy by a fireplace

■ A Master Bedroom with private Master Bath and walk-in closet

■ Two additional bedrooms that share a full hall bath

MAIN AREA — 1,416 SQ. FT.
BASEMENT — 1,416 SQ. FT.
GARAGE — 484 SQ. FT.

TOTAL LIVING AREA:
1,416 SQ. FT.

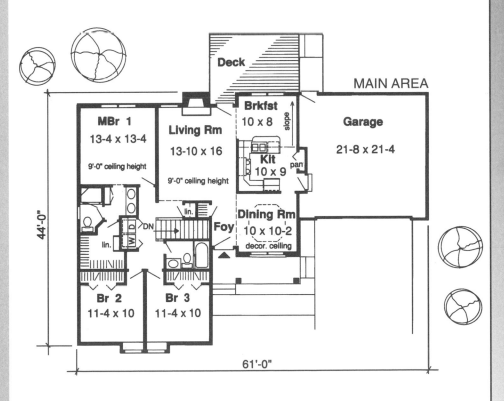

MAIN AREA

Deck

MBr 1
13-4 x 13-4
9'-0" ceiling height

Living Rm
13-10 x 16
9'-0" ceiling height

Brkfst
10 x 8

Garage
21-8 x 21-4

Kit
10 x 9

pan.

slope

DN

lin.

lin.

lin.

Foy

Dining Rm
10 x 10-2
decor. ceiling

Br 2
11-4 x 10

Br 3
11-4 x 10

44'-0"

61'-0"

An
EXCLUSIVE DESIGN
By Karl Kreeger

PRICE CODE B

CONVENIENT FLOOR PLAN

No. 24701

■ This plan features:

— Three bedrooms

— Two full baths

■ Central Foyer leads to Den/Guest room with arched window below vaulted ceiling and Living Room accented by two-sided fireplace

■ Efficient, U-shaped Kitchen with peninsula counter/breakfast bar serving Dining Room and adjacent Utility/Pantry

■ Master Suite features large walk-in closet and private bath with double vanity and whirlpool tub

■ Two additional bedrooms with ample closet space share full bath

MAIN FLOOR — 1,625 SQ. FT.
BASEMENT — 1,625 SQ. FT.
FOUNDATION — BASEMENT, SLAB OR CRAWL SPACE

**TOTAL LIVING AREA :
1,625 SQ. FT.**

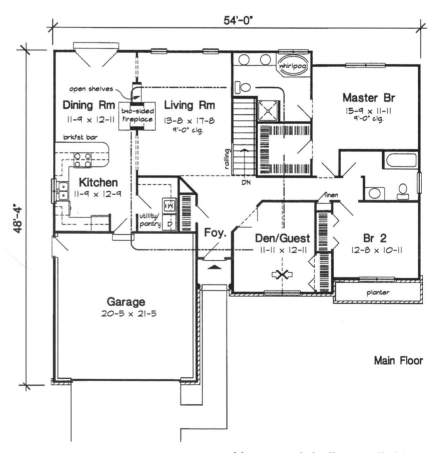

Main Floor

No materials list available

PRICE CODE A

MAGNIFICENT MASTER SUITE

No. 90987

This plan features:

— Two bedrooms

— Two full baths

Covered walkway leads into the Foyer and the expansive Living/Dining Room area enhanced by a bay window and a built-in china cupboard

■ Efficient Kitchen with a cooktop island, a built-in pantry, a desk, and a glass eating Nook with access to the Sundeck

■ Ultimate Master Suite with a large walk-in closet, a gas fireplace, a whirlpool bath and access to the Sundeck

Second bedroom with a large closet adjacent to the full bath

This plan is available with a Basement foundation only

MAIN FLOOR — 1,355 SQ. FT.
GARAGE — 475 SQ. FT.
BASEMENT — 1,341 SQ. FT.

TOTAL LIVING AREA:
1,355 SQ. FT.

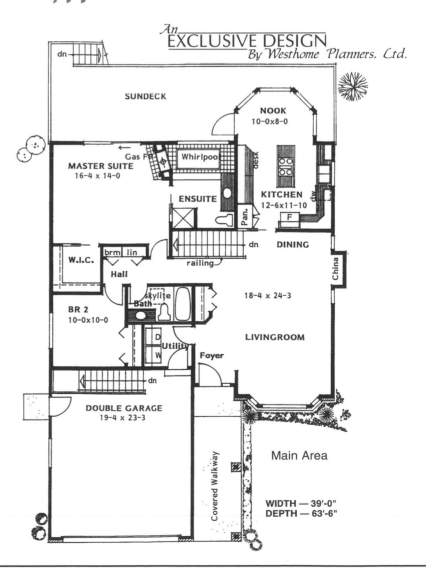

An
EXCLUSIVE DESIGN
By Westhome Planners, Ltd.

SUNDECK

NOOK
10-0x8-0

MASTER SUITE
16-4 x 14-0

Gas F

Whirlpool

ENSUITE

KITCHEN
12-6x11-10

DINING

W.I.C.

brm lin

Hall

railing

dn

China

skylite
Bath

BR 2
10-0x10-0

18-4 x 24-3

LIVINGROOM

Utility

Foyer

DOUBLE GARAGE
19-4 x 23-3

Covered Walkway

Main Area

WIDTH — 39'-0"
DEPTH — 63'-6"

PRICE CODE C

BREEZEWAY CONNECTS ANGLED GARAGE

No. 90011

This plan features:

— Three bedrooms

— Three full baths

A sunken Living Room with a fireplace and sliding glass doors to a covered porch

A step up from the Living Room to the Dining Room with a built-in china cabinet and sliding glass doors to the covered porch

A well-equipped Kitchen with a breakfast/snack bar adjoining the Family Room

A Master Bedroom with a private Master Bath and more than ample closet space

A glazed hot house for the plant enthusiast

A private Den right off breezeway

FIRST FLOOR — 1,867 SQ. FT.
BASEMENT — 1,020 SQ. FT.
GARAGE — 485 SQ. FT.

TOTAL LIVING AREA:
1,867 SQ. FT.

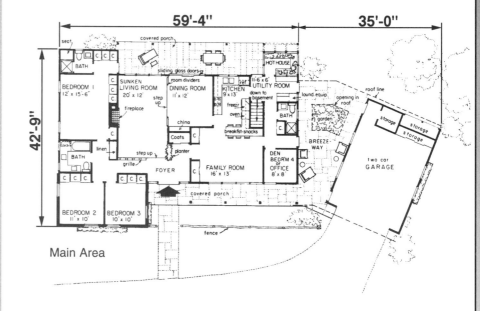

Main Area

PRICE CODE B

No. 20220

- This plan features:
- — Three bedrooms
- — Two full baths
- A large front palladium window that gives this home great curb appeal, and allows a view of the front yard from the Living Room
- A vaulted ceiling in the Living Room, adding to the architectural interest and the spacious feel of the room
- Sliding glass doors in the Dining Room that lead to a wood deck
- A built-in pantry, double sink and breakfast bar in the efficient Kitchen
- A Master Suite that includes a walk-in closet and a private bath with a double vanity
- Two additional bedrooms that share a full hall bath

MAIN AREA —1,568 SQ. FT.
BASEMENT — 1,568 SQ. FT.
GARAGE — 509 SQ. FT.

TOTAL LIVING AREA:
1,568 SQ. FT.

TRADITIONAL RANCH

No materials list available

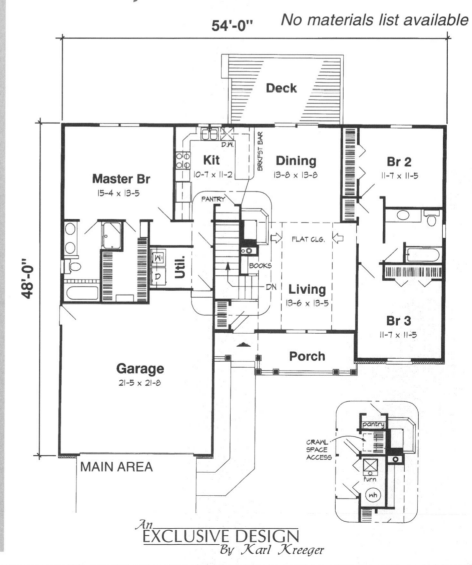

An
EXCLUSIVE DESIGN
By Karl Kreeger

PRICE CODE A

VICTORIAN ACCENTS ENHANCE APPEAL

No. 92702

This plan features:

— Three bedrooms

— Two full baths

Entry Porch into the Foyer leads to the Dining area and the Living Room

A corner window and a hearth fireplace topped by a sloped ceiling highlight the Living Room with access to the rear yard

Efficient, U-shaped Kitchen with a wonderful corner window, a built-in pantry and a Dining area

Private Master Bedroom suite with a sloped ceiling, a walk-in closet and a private bath with a raised tub

Two more bedrooms with ample closet space, one with a great bay window, share a full bath

This plan is available with a Slab foundation only

MAIN FLOOR — 1,198 SQ. FT.
GARAGE — 431 SQ. FT.

TOTAL LIVING AREA: 1,198 SQ. FT.

No materials list available

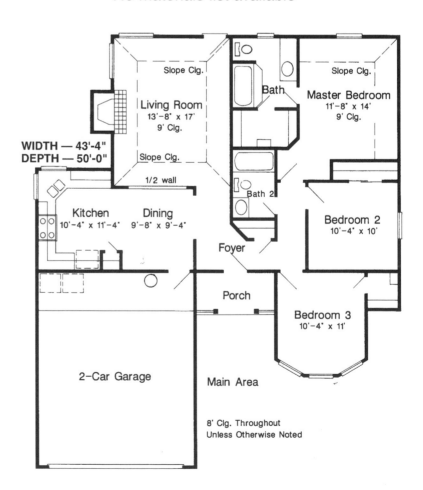

WIDTH — 43'-4"
DEPTH — 50'-0"

Slope Clg.

Living Room
13'-8" x 17'
9' Clg.

Bath

Master Bedroom
11'-8" x 14'
9' Clg.

Slope Clg.

Slope Clg.

1/2 wall

Bath 2

Kitchen
10'-4" x 11'-4"

Dining
9'-8" x 9'-4"

Foyer

Bedroom 2
10'-4" x 10'

Porch

Bedroom 3
10'-4" x 11'

2-Car Garage

Main Area

8' Clg. Throughout
Unless Otherwise Noted

PRICE CODE D

ATTRACTIVE FIELDSTONE AND VERTICAL SIDING

No. 90109

■ This plan features:

— Four bedrooms

— Two full and one half baths

■ Double door entry framed with glass leads into the formal Living Room with a sloped ceiling

■ Convenient Family Room with a sliding glass door to the Patio

■ L-shaped Kitchen with a peninsula counter/eating bar hub for the Breakfast area, Family Room, Dining and Utility areas

■ Master Bedroom suite enhanced by a walk-in closet, a private bath and an optional Den access

■ Three additional bedrooms share a double vanity bath

■ This plan is available with a Basement or Crawlspace foundation. Please specify when ordering

MAIN FLOOR — 2,305 SQ. FT.
GARAGE — 530 SQ. FT.

TOTAL LIVING AREA:
2,305 SQ. FT.

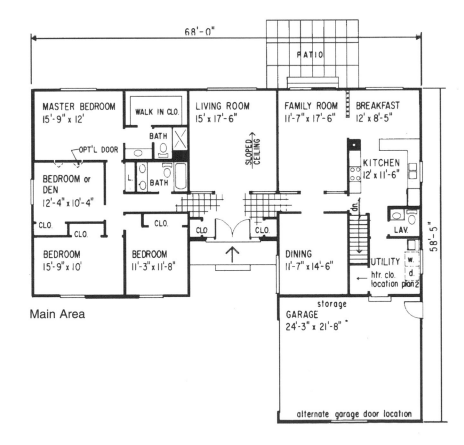

Main Area

PRICE CODE C

TRADITIONAL BRICK WITH DETAILING

No. 92536

This plan features:

—Three bedrooms

—Two full baths

Covered entry leads into the Foyer, the formal Dining Room and the Den

Expansive Den with a decorative ceiling over a hearth fireplace and sliding glass doors to the rear yard

Country Kitchen with a built-in pantry, double ovens and a cooktop island easily serves the Breakfast area and Dining Room

Private Master Bedroom suite with a decorative ceiling, a walk-in closet, a double vanity and a whirlpool tub

Two additional bedrooms share a full bath

This plan is available with a Slab or Crawlspace foundation. Please specify when ordering

MAIN FLOOR — 1,869 SQ. FT.
GARAGE — 484 SQ. FT.

**TOTAL LIVING AREA:
1,869 SQ. FT.**

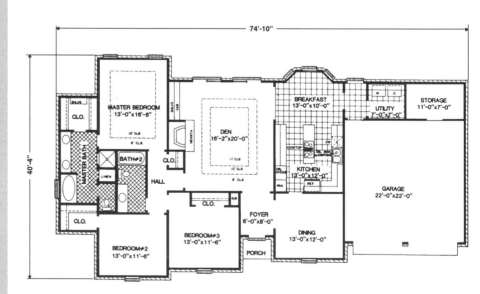

Main Area

COMPACT SOUTHERN TRADITIONAL

No. 93035

■ This plan features:

— Four bedrooms

— Two full and one half baths

■ An entrance flanked by columns and imposing gables, accented with dentil molding

■ An angled Foyer, drawing the eye to an arched passage in the Living Room

■ A large Kitchen/Family Room combination with an octagonal shaped breakfast area

■ A Master Bedroom that is entered through angled double doors and has a cathedral ceiling

■ A Master Bath with his-and-her vanities and walk-in closets

FIRST FLOOR — 2,545 SQ. FT.
GARAGE — 436 SQ. FT.

TOTAL LIVING AREA:
2,545 SQ. FT.

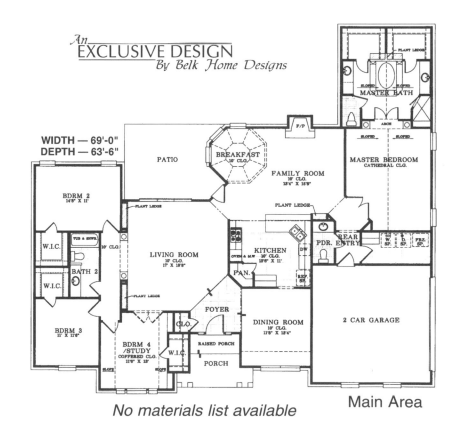

An
EXCLUSIVE DESIGN
By Belk Home Designs

WIDTH — 69'-0"
DEPTH — 63'-6"

No materials list available

Main Area

PRICE CODE A

PERFECT FOR FIRST TIME BUYERS

No. 93048

■ This plan features:

— Three bedrooms

— Two full baths

■ An efficiently designed Kitchen with a corner sink, ample counter space and a peninsula counter

■ A sunny Breakfast Room with a convenient hide-away laundry center

■ An expansive Family Room that includes a corner fireplace and direct access to the Patio

■ A private Master Suite with a walk-in closet and a double vanity Bath

■ Two additional bedrooms, both with walk-in closets, that share a full hall bath

MAIN FLOOR — 1,310 SQ. FT.
GARAGE — 449 SQ. FT.

TOTAL LIVING AREA:
1,310 SQ. FT.

An
EXCLUSIVE DESIGN
By Belk Home Designs

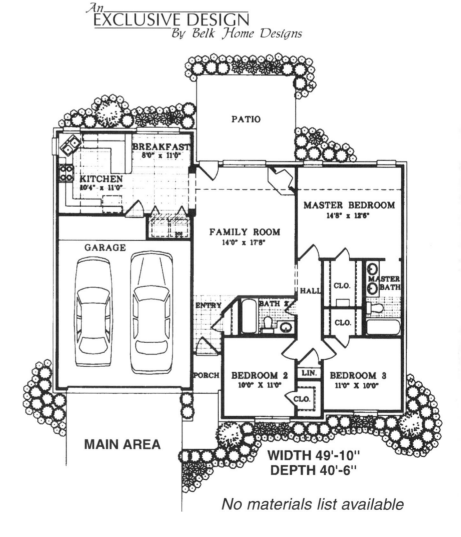

WIDTH 49'-10"
DEPTH 40'-6"

No materials list available

PRICE CODE A

COMFORT AND STYLE

No. 90990

■ This plan features:

— Two bedrooms with possible third bedroom/den

— Two full baths

■ An unfinished daylight basement, providing possible space for family recreation

■ A Master Suite complete with private bath and skylight

■ A large Kitchen including an eating nook

■ A sundeck that is easily accessible from the Master Suite, Nook and the Living/Dining area

FIRST FLOOR — 1,423 SQ. FT.
BASEMENT — 1,423 SQ. FT.
GARAGE — 399 SQ. FT.
WIDTH — 46'-0"
DEPTH — 52'-0"

TOTAL LIVING AREA:
1,423 SQ. FT.

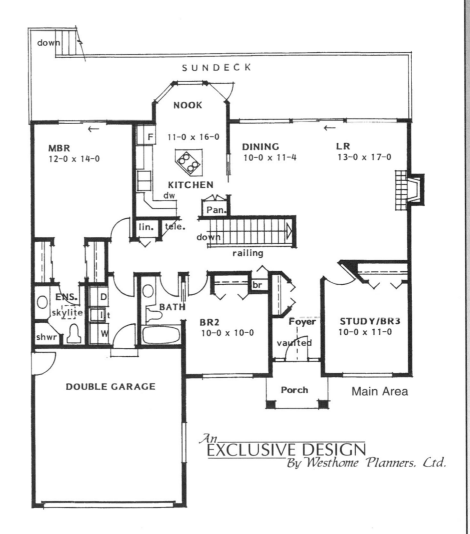

An
EXCLUSIVE DESIGN
By Westhome Planners. Ltd.

PRICE CODE A

HALF-ROUND WINDOW GRACES ATTRACTIVE EXTERIOR

No. 90395

■ This plan features:

— Three bedrooms

— Two full baths

■ Soaring ceilings in the Kitchen, Living Room, Dining, and Breakfast Rooms

■ An efficient, well-equipped Kitchen with a pass-through to the Dining room

■ Built-in bookcases flanking the fireplace in the Living Room

■ A Master Suite with a private Master Bath and walk-in closet

FIRST FLOOR — 1,452 SQ. FT.

TOTAL LIVING AREA:
1,452 SQ. FT.

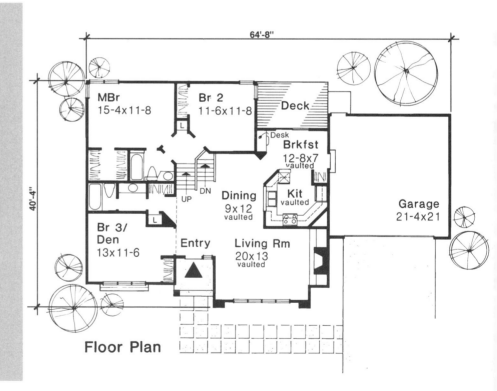

Floor Plan

PRICE CODE C

No. 92244

This plan features:

— Four bedrooms

— Two full and one half baths

Covered Porch and a bright Entry open to the expansive Living Room

Living Room crowned by a cathedral ceiling above a hearth fireplace, flanked by full windows

Formal Dining Room across from the Gallery

Hub Kitchen with a cooktop island/snackbar and a built-in pantry easily serves the Breakfast area, the Patio and Dining Room

Private Master Suite with an expansive view and a plush bath with a double vanity and a large walk-in closet

Three additional bedrooms with ample closets, share a full bath

This plan is available with a Slab foundation only

MAIN FLOOR — 2,009 SQ. FT.
GARAGE — 660 SQ. FT.

**TOTAL LIVING AREA:
2,009 SQ. FT.**

CATHEDRAL CEILING ADDS INSPIRATION

MAIN FLOOR

No materials list available

PRICE CODE D

ARCHES ACCENT ELEVATION

No. 93056

This plan features:

— Four bedrooms

— Two full and one half baths

Arched portico entrance leads into the raised Foyer, Dining and Living Rooms

Expansive Living Room with plant ledges and a wall of windows overlooks the Patio

Arched window below a sloped ceiling in the Dining Room

Ultimate Kitchen with a walk-in pantry and a peninsula snackbar that services the glass, octagon Breakfast area and the Family Room with a cozy fireplace

Double door entrance to the Master Bedroom suite with a cathedral ceiling, a lavish Master Bath with a garden tub and two walk-in closets

This plan is available with a Slab or Crawlspace foundation — please specify when ordering

MAIN FLOOR — 2,517 SQ. FT.
GARAGE — 443 SQ. FT.

**TOTAL LIVING AREA:
2,517 SQ. FT.**

Main Area

WIDTH — 69'-0"
DEPTH — 63'-6"

An
EXCLUSIVE DESIGN
By Belk Home Designs

PRICE CODE A

BE IN TUNE WITH THE ELEMENTS

No. 24240

This plan features:

— Two bedrooms

— Two full baths

Cozy front porch to enjoy three seasons

A simple design allowing breezes to flow from front to back, heat to rise to the attic and cool air to settle

A fireplaced Living Room

A formal Dining Room next to the Kitchen

A compact Kitchen with a handy pantry

A rear entrance with a covered porch

A Master Suite with a private bath

MAIN AREA — 964 SQ. FT.

TOTAL LIVING AREA:
964 SQ. FT.

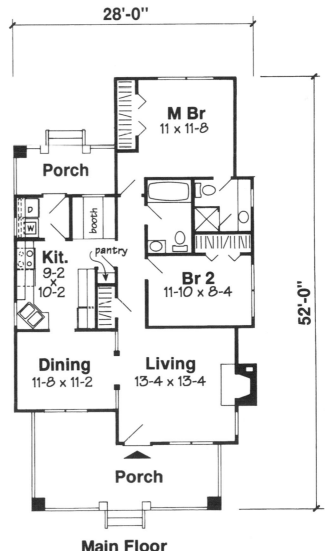

28'-0"

52'-0"

M Br
11 x 11-8

Porch

booth

pantry

Kit.
9-2 x 10-2

Br 2
11-10 x 8-4

Dining
11-8 x 11-2

Living
13-4 x 13-4

Porch

Main Floor

PRICE CODE D

SPECTACULAR EXPANDABLE STUCCO

No. 93236

This plan features:

— Three bedrooms

— Two full baths

Large Living Room with a huge fireplace flanked by windows and access to the Wood Deck

Efficient, country Kitchen with a cooktop island/eating bar, and a glass Breakfast area

Spacious Master Suite with a tray ceiling, access to the Wood Deck, a huge walk-in closet and a plush bath with a corner garden tub

Two additional bedrooms with ample closets share a full bath

Optional second floor plan with a fourth bedroom and a full bath

This plan is available with a Basement, Slab or Crawlspace foundation. Please specify when ordering

FIRST FLOOR — 2,068 SQ. FT.
SECOND FLOOR —
477 SQ. FT.
BASEMENT — 2,055 SQ. FT.
GARAGE — 548 SQ. FT.

**TOTAL LIVING AREA:
2,515 SQ. FT.**

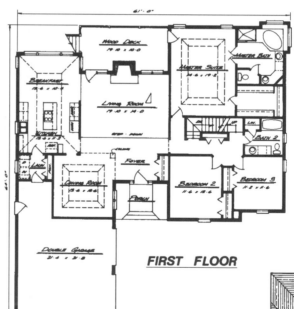

FIRST FLOOR

No materials list available

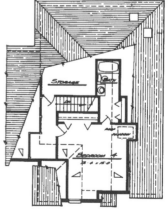

SECOND FLOOR

An EXCLUSIVE DESIGN
By Jannis Vann & Associates, Inc.

PRICE CODE C

COZY HOMESTEAD

No. 24651

- This plan features:
— Three bedrooms
— Two full baths

- Multi-paned windows and a country porch

- A spacious Living Room, enhanced by the natural light and the fireplace with built-in bookshelves flanking one side

- An efficient U-shaped Kitchen, located next to the Dining Room, with a walk-in pantry, double sink and a Breakfast Nook

- A convenient first floor Laundry Room

- Private Master Suite with a whirlpool tub, separate shower, walk-in closet and tray ceiling

- Two additional bedrooms are located at the opposite side of the home and share a full hall bath with a skylight

MAIN AREA — 1,821 SQ. FT.
BASEMENT — 742 SQ. FT.
GARAGE — 1,075 SQ. FT.

**TOTAL LIVING AREA:
1,821 SQ. FT.**

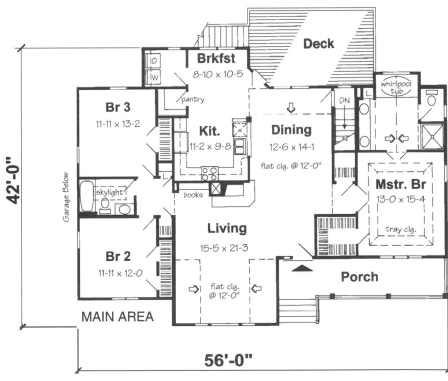

No materials list available

An
EXCLUSIVE DESIGN
By Plan One Homes, Inc.

PRICE CODE A

YOU'VE GOT THE CHOICE

No. 99241

■ This plan features:

— Three bedrooms

— Two full baths

■ A galley-style Kitchen with easy access to both the formal Dining Room, with built-in china closet, and the eating Nook, with a sunny bay

■ A spacious Gathering Room with a raised hearth fireplace

■ A Master Bedroom with a walk-in closet, and a private bath

■ Two additional bedrooms served by a full hall bath

FIRST FLOOR — 1,366 SQ. FT.
BASEMENT — 1,281 SQ. FT.
GARAGE — 484 SQ. FT.

TOTAL LIVING AREA:
1,366 SQ. FT.

WIDTH — 65'-0"
DEPTH — 37'-4"

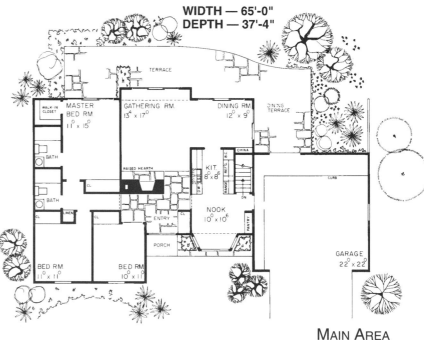

MAIN AREA

PRICE CODE B

No. 91651

■ This plan features:

— Three bedrooms

— Two full baths

■ A vaulted ceiling enhancing the window alcove in the Living Room and corner windows in the Dining area

■ An efficient Kitchen with a peninsula sink serving the Family room and the eating Nook, with a laundry room and access to the Porch

■ A Master suite with an over-sized closet and a private bath with a roll-in shower

■ A Den/Bedroom and a second bedroom sharing a full hall bath

■ Accessibility Features:

— Level entry way

— Wide doorways (32"-36" clear width)

— Chair height electrical controls/outlets

— Reinforced walls for installation of grab bars

MAIN LIVING AREA — 1,653 SQ. FT.

**TOTAL LIVING AREA:
1,653 SQ. FT.**

YOURS FOR A LIFETIME

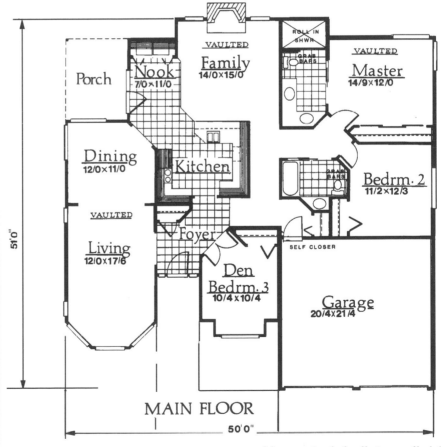

MAIN FLOOR

No materials list available

An
EXCLUSIVE DESIGN
By Mark Stewart

PRICE CODE A

SMALL RANCH WITH BIG SPACES

No. 99731

■ This plan features:

— Three bedrooms

— Two full baths

■ Covered Porch leads into a Living/Dining Room with a corner fireplace and a sliding glass door to the Deck

■ Efficient, U-shaped Kitchen with an eating bar adjoins the Dining Room and Garage with a laundry

■ Quiet Master Suite offers a walk-in closet and a dressing area

■ Two additional bedrooms share a full bath

■ This plan is available with a Crawlspace foundation only

MAIN FLOOR — 1,255 SQ. FT.
GARAGE — 516 SQ. FT.

TOTAL LIVING AREA:
1,255 SQ. FT.

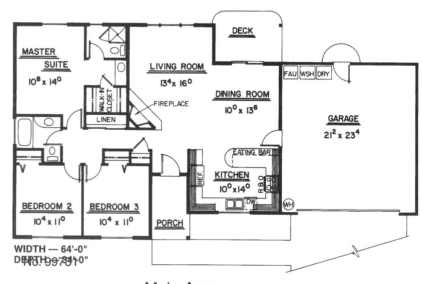

Main Area

PRICE CODE B

BONUS ROOM CROWNS PLAN

No. 99900

This plan features:

— Three bedrooms

— Two full baths

A optional Bonus Room over the double garage, giving that little extra space for a relatively low cost

A spacious, secluded Master Suite, accented by a walk-in closet and a full bath

Two additional bedrooms, equally roomy, with good sized closets

A cozy Family Room, warmed by a gas fireplace

A Kitchen and Nook area with a snack bar for informal eating

A combined Living Room and Dining Room that are well-placed to one side, next to the front Entry

FIRST FLOOR — 1,592 SQ. FT.
OPT. SECOND FLOOR — 275 SQ. FT.
GARAGE — 462 SQ. FT.

TOTAL LIVING AREA:
1,592 SQ. FT.

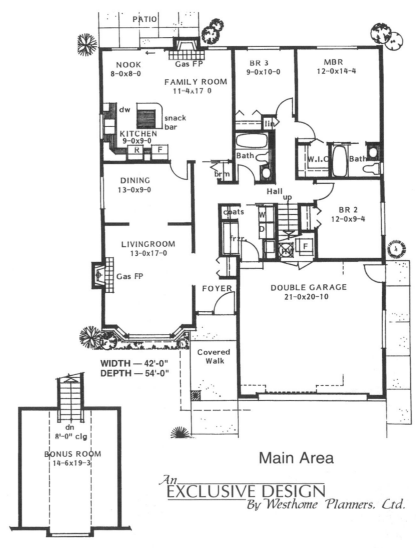

WIDTH — 42'-0"
DEPTH — 54'-0"

Main Area

An
EXCLUSIVE DESIGN
By Westhome Planners, Ltd.

PRICE CODE D

TRADITIONAL RANCH

No. 92404

This plan features:

— Three bedrooms

— Two full baths

A tray ceiling in the Master Suite that is equipped with his-and-her walk-in closets and a private Master Bath with a cathedral ceiling

A formal Living Room with a cathedral ceiling

A decorative tray ceiling in the elegant formal Dining Room

A spacious Family Room with a vaulted ceiling and a fireplace

A modern, well-appointed Kitchen with snack bar and bayed Breakfast area

Two additional bedrooms that share a full hall bath each having a walk-in closet

FIRST FLOOR — 2,275 SQ. FT.
BASEMENT — 2,207 SQ. FT.
GARAGE — 512 SQ. FT.

TOTAL LIVING AREA:
2,275 SQ. FT.

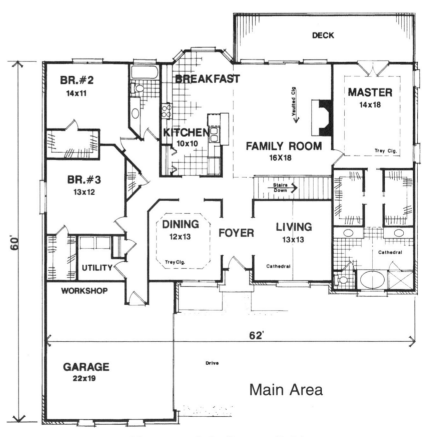

Main Area

No materials list available

PRICE CODE A

No. 24241

This plan features:

— Three bedrooms

— Two full baths

A covered Porch, welcoming visitors

A spacious Living Room with a fireplace, adding to the warmth and elegance of the room

A formal Dining Room with a convenient, built-in china cabinet

Ample cabinets, counters and a built-in pantry in the well-appointed Kitchen

A Master Suite with a private bath

■ Two additional bedrooms, one with a walk-in closet, that share a full hall bath

A typical bungalow design, allowing the heat to collect in the attic space while keeping the house cool in the summer months

MAIN AREA — 1,174 SQ. FT.

TOTAL LIVING AREA:
1,174 SQ. FT.

QUIET SUMMER HIDE-A-WAY

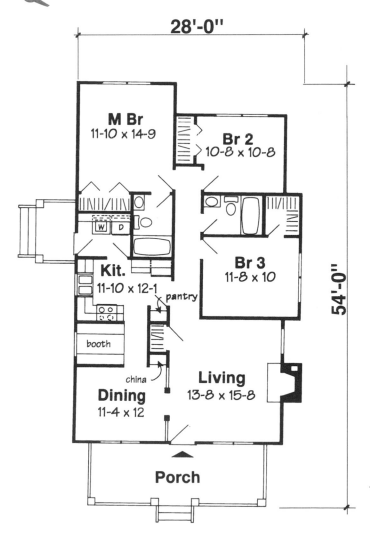

28'-0"

54'-0"

M Br
11-10 x 14-9

Br 2
10-8 x 10-8

Br 3
11-8 x 10

Kit.
11-10 x 12-1

W D

pantry

booth

china

Living
13-8 x 15-8

Dining
11-4 x 12

Porch

Main Floor

PRICE CODE A

GREAT ROOM IS HUB OF THE HOME

No. 93015

This plan features:

— Three bedrooms

— Two full baths

Sheltered porch leads into the Entry with arches and a Great Room

Spacious Great Room with a ten foot ceiling above a wall of windows and rear yard access

Efficient Kitchen with a built-in pantry, a laundry closet and a Breakfast area accented by a decorative window

Bay of windows enhances the Master Bedroom suite with a double vanity bath and a walk-in closet

Two additional bedrooms with ample closets, share a full bath

This plan is available with a Slab foundation only

MAIN FLOOR — 1,087 SQ. FT.

**TOTAL LIVING AREA:
1,087 SQ. FT.**

No materials list available

An EXCLUSIVE DESIGN
By Belk Home Designs

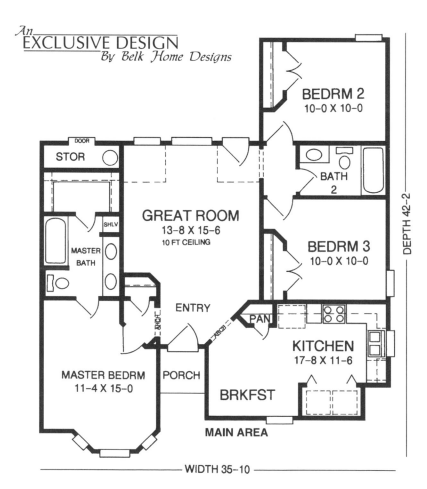

PRICE CODE A

INVITING PORCH HAS DUAL FUNCTIONS

No. 91021

This plan features:

— Three bedrooms

— Two full baths

An inviting, wrap-around porch Entry with sliding glass doors leading right into a bayed Dining Room

A Living Room with a cozy feeling, enhanced by the fireplace

An efficient Kitchen opening to both Dining and Living Rooms

A Master Suite with a walk-in closet and private Master Bath

An optional basement, slab or crawl space foundation — please specify when ordering

FIRST FLOOR — 1,295 SQ. FT.
GARAGE — 384 SQ. FT.

TOTAL LIVING AREA:
1,295 SQ. FT.

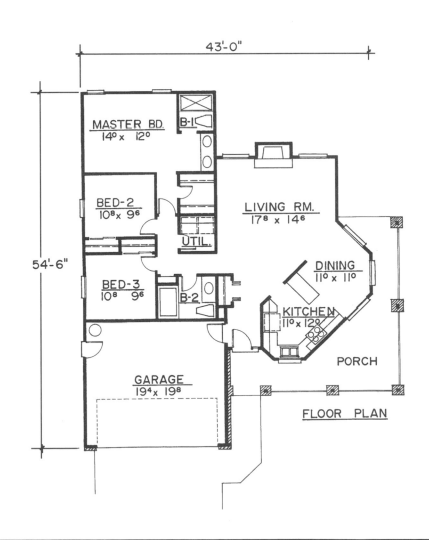

FLOOR PLAN

PRICE CODE A

PRIVATE MASTER SUITE

No. 92523

■ This plan features:

— Three bedrooms

— Two full baths

■ A spacious Great Room enhanced by a vaulted ceiling and fireplace

■ A well-equipped Kitchen with windowed double sink

■ A secluded Master Suite with decorative ceiling, private Master Bath, and walk-in closet

■ Two additional bedrooms sharing hall bath

FIRST FLOOR — 1,293 SQ. FT.
GARAGE — 400 SQ. FT.

TOTAL LIVING AREA:
1,293 SQ. FT.

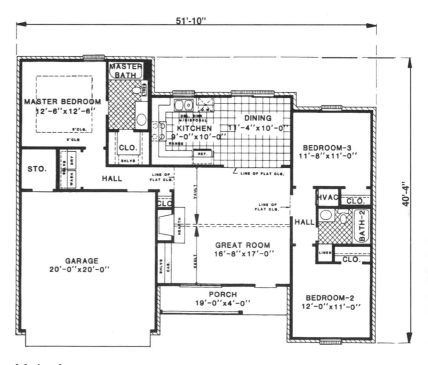

Main Area

PRICE CODE A

INVITING PORCH ADORNS AFFORDABLE HOME

No. 90682

■ This plan features:

— Three bedrooms

— Two full baths

■ A large and spacious Living Room that adjoins the Dining Room for ease in entertaining

■ A private bedroom wing offering a quiet atmosphere

■ A Master Bedroom with his-n-her closets and a private bath

■ An efficient Kitchen with a walk-in pantry

MAIN AREA — 1,160 SQ. FT.
LAUNDRY/MUDROOM — 83 SQ. FT.
GARAGE — 380 SQ. FT.

TOTAL LIVING AREA: 1,243 SQ. FT.

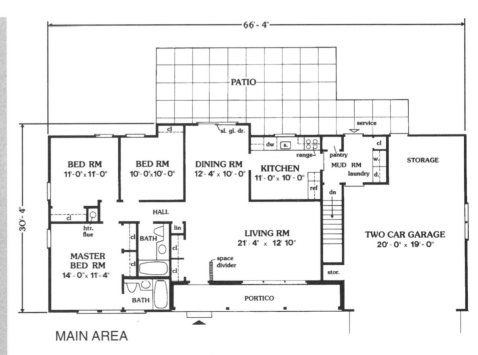

MAIN AREA

PRICE CODE D

VAULTED CEILINGS AND SKYLIGHTS

No. 98733

■ This plan features:

— Three bedrooms

— Two full baths

■ A sheltered entrance leading to a large Living Room topped by a vaulted ceiling and enhanced by a large bay window and a fireplace

■ A formal Dining Room with arched openings and a vaulted ceiling

■ A cook top island/eating bar and a walk-in pantry adding to the efficiency of the Kitchen that is open to the Nook

■ A privately situated Master Suite including an ultra bath, his-n-her walk-in closets and direct access to the side porch that is equipped with a hot tub

■ Two additional bedrooms with bay windows sharing a hall bath that includes two skylights

MAIN FLOOR — 2,496 SQ. FT.
GARAGE — 827 SQ. FT.

TOTAL LIVING AREA:
2,496 SQ. FT.

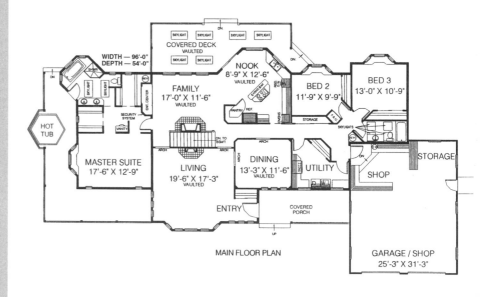

MAIN FLOOR PLAN

PRICE CODE A

STEP-SAVING ONE FLOOR LIVING

No. 24320

- This plan features:
— Three bedrooms
— Two full baths

- A covered entrance leads to the Foyer and opens into the Living, Breakfast and Kitchen areas

- A fireplace and corner windows in Living area

- A galley Kitchen offers a breakfast bar, a built-in pantry and easy access to the covered Porch and Garage

- The Master Bedroom features a double closet and a private bath

- Two additional bedrooms sharing a full hall bath

MAIN AREA — 1,235 SQ. FT.
GARAGE — 425 SQ. FT.

**TOTAL LIVING AREA:
1,235 SQ. FT.**

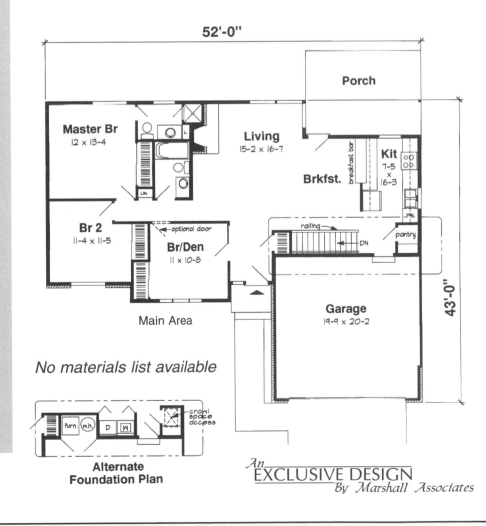

52'-0"

43'-0"

Porch

Master Br
12 x 13-4

Living
15-2 x 16-7

Kit
7-5 x 16-3

Brkfst.

breakfast bar

Br 2
11-4 x 11-5

optional door

Br/Den
11 x 10-8

railing

DN

pantry

Garage
19-9 x 20-2

Main Area

No materials list available

furn. w.h. D W

crawl space access

**Alternate
Foundation Plan**

An
EXCLUSIVE DESIGN
By Marshall Associates

PRICE CODE A

ENERGY EFFICIENT

No. 90130

This plan features:

— Three bedrooms

— Two full baths

A galley-style Kitchen efficiently laid out to accommodate a busy life style

A Great Room with an open area for Dining space giving a feeling of spaciousness

A Master Bedroom with ample closet space and private full bath

Two additional bedrooms that share a full hall bath

An optional basement or crawl space foundation — please specify when ordering

FIRST FLOOR — 1,118 SQ. FT.

TOTAL LIVING AREA: 1,118 SQ. FT.

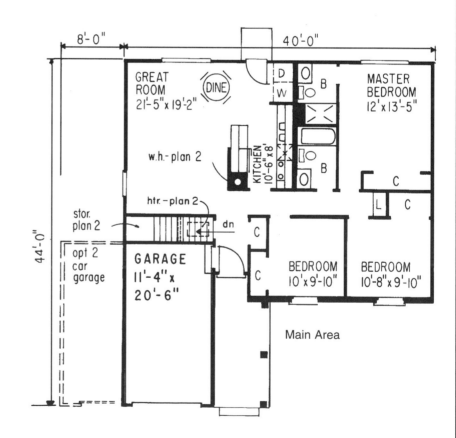

Main Area

PRICE CODE B

AN ENERGY EFFICIENT HOME

No. 90165

■ This plan features:

— Three bedrooms

— Two full baths

■ A step-saving ranch layout with the bedrooms situated on one side of the home

■ A U-shaped Kitchen equipped with a peninsula counter/eating bar, double sink, and laundry area

■ A Great Room that may include a fireplace, open to the Dining Area enhancing spaciousness

■ A roomy Master Bedroom equipped with a walk-in closet and private Bath

■ Two additional bedrooms, one as a Den possibility, that share a full hall bath

MAIN AREA — 1,605 SQ. FT.
GARAGE — 445 SQ. FT.

TOTAL LIVING AREA:
1,605 SQ. FT.

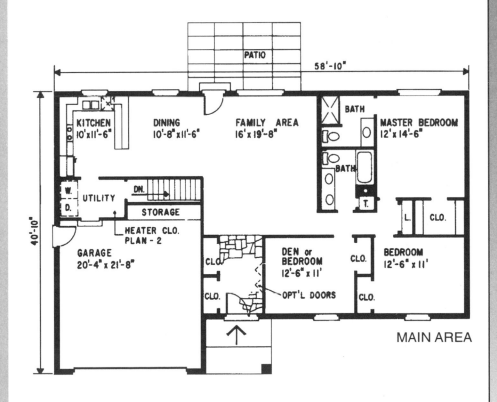

MAIN AREA

PRICE CODE A

DINING IN A GREENHOUSE BAY

No. 90620

This plan features:

— Three bedrooms

— Two full baths

Covered entrance into a bright Foyer highlighted by a skydome

Formal Living Room accented by a heat-circulating fireplace and sliding glass doors to the Terrace

Greenhouse Dining Room feels like eating outdoors

Efficient Kitchen with a peninsula counter and a bay window Dinette area convenient to the Laundry and Garage

Comfortable Master Bedroom with a private bath and walk-in closet

Two additional bedrooms share a full bath

This plan is available with a Basement or Slab foundation. Please specify when ordering

MAIN FLOOR — 1,476 SQ. FT.
BASEMENT — 1,475 SQ. FT.
GARAGE — 480 SQ. FT.

**TOTAL LIVING AREA:
1,476 SQ. FT.**

PRICE CODE B

ZONED FOR PRIVACY

No. 91506

■ This plan features:

— Three bedrooms

— Two full baths

■ A sun-catching bay window accentuating the Living/Dining combination

■ A fireplace in the Family Room that spreads its warmth through the angular, efficient Kitchen and Nook

■ Sliding glass doors in the Nook leading to a rear patio

■ A Master Suite with a private bath equipped with a step-in shower

■ Two additional bedrooms that share a full hall bath

FIRST FLOOR — 1,546 SQ. FT.
GARAGE — 423 SQ. FT.

TOTAL LIVING AREA:
1,546 SQ. FT.

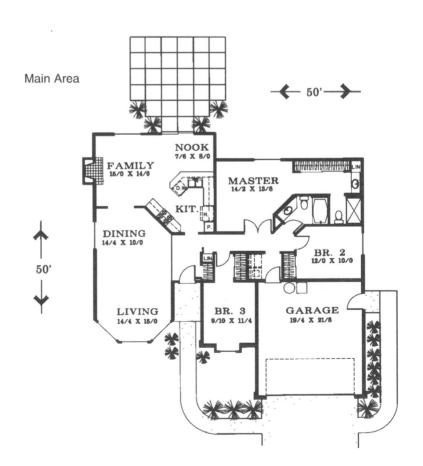

Main Area

50'

50'

FAMILY 15/0 X 14/0

NOOK 7/6 X 8/0

MASTER 14/2 X 13/8

KIT.

DINING 14/4 X 10/0

BR. 2 12/0 X 10/0

LIVING 14/4 X 15/0

BR. 3 9/10 X 11/4

GARAGE 19/4 X 21/8

PRICE CODE E

DISTINCTIVE EXPANDABLE BRICK

No. 93206

This plan features:

— Four bedrooms

— Two and half baths

Arched entrance with decorative glass leads into two-story Foyer

Formal Dining Room with tray ceiling above decorative window

Efficient Kitchen with island cooktop , built-in desk , pantry easily serves Breakfast area

Master Bedroom wing topped by tray ceiling with French door to Patio, huge private bath with garden tub, two walk-in closets and vanities

Three additional bedrooms with ample closets share laundry and full bath

Second Floor optional space for Storage and huge Future Bedroom with full bath

FIRST FLOOR — 2,577 SQ. FT.
OPT. SECOND FLOOR — 68 SQ. FT.
BASEMENT — 2,561 SQ. FT.
GARAGE — 560 SQ. FT.
FOUNDATION — BASEMENT ONLY

**TOTAL LIVING AREA:
2,645 SQ. FT.**

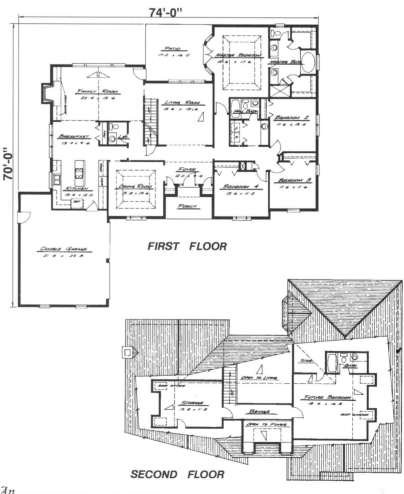

FIRST FLOOR

SECOND FLOOR

An
EXCLUSIVE DESIGN
By Jannis Vann & Associates, Inc.

PRICE CODE C

SPACIOUS SMALLER HOME

No. 98743

■ This plan features:

— Three bedrooms

— Two full baths

■ A vaulted ceiling in the richly illuminated Foyer, which presents three choices of direction

■ An eye-catching Great Room with a vaulted ceiling, a corner fireplace and a bank of windows on the rear wall showering the room with light

■ An efficient U-shaped Kitchen with an angled eating bar, built-in pantry and a double sink that views the Great Room

■ A luxurious Master Suite that includes a roomy walk-in closet, access to the rear deck and a private bath

■ A Mini-Master Suite that includes a walk-in closet with a vanity right outside and private access to the hall bath

■ A third bedroom that shares the use of the hall bath

MAIN FLOOR — 1,958 SQ. FT.

TOTAL LIVING AREA: 1,958 SQ. FT.

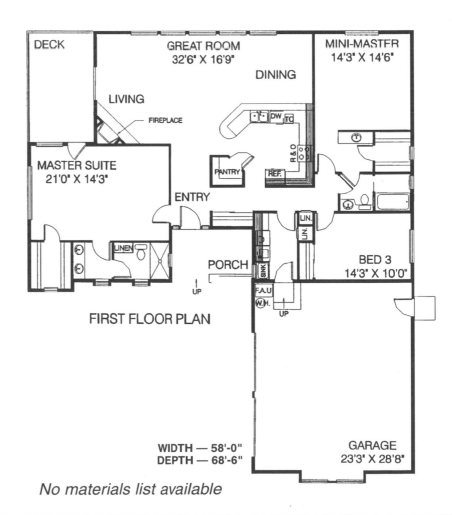

DECK

GREAT ROOM
32'6" X 16'9"

MINI-MASTER
14'3" X 14'6"

DINING

LIVING

FIREPLACE

DW

R&O

MASTER SUITE
21'0" X 14'3"

PANTRY

REF.

ENTRY

LIN.

LINEN

LIN.

PORCH

BED 3
14'3" X 10'0"

SINK

UP

F.A.U

W.H.

UP

FIRST FLOOR PLAN

WIDTH — 58'-0"
DEPTH — 68'-6"

GARAGE
23'3" X 28'8"

No materials list available

PRICE CODE C

UNDERSTATED ELEGANCE

No. 99627

■ This plan features:

— Three bedrooms

— Two full baths

■ Double door entrance into the Foyer with two closets and a formal Living Room beyond

■ Expansive Living Room with a decorative ceiling above a hearth fireplace and an alcove of glass with access to the Terrace

■ Spacious Family Room with a media wall, and a fireplace

■ U-shaped Kitchen with a glass Dinette area and Laundry nearby

■ Master Bedroom suite with a recessed window, two closets, and a whirlpool tub

■ Two additional bedrooms

■ This plan is available with a Basement, Slab or Crawlspace foundation. Please specify when ordering

MAIN FLOOR — 2,083 SQ. FT.
BASEMENT — 1,242 SQ. FT.
GARAGE & STORAGE — 473 SQ. FT.

TOTAL LIVING AREA:
2,083 SQ. FT.

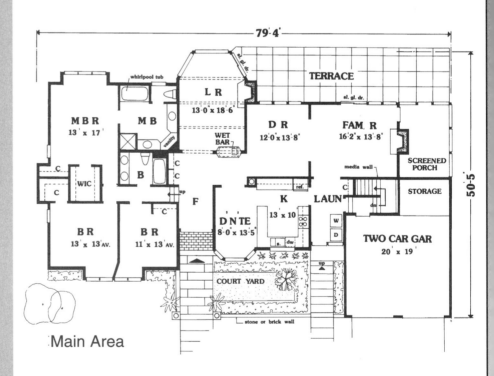

Main Area

PRICE CODE B

No. 93702

This plan features:

— Three bedrooms

— Two full baths

An open floor plan giving the appearance of spaciousness even through the home is small in square footage

A sheltered entrance that leads to a short Foyer with a coat closet

A large front window adding to the elegance of the Dining Room

A tray ceiling in the Living Room which is also enhanced by a fireplace

An octagonal Kitchen including a dining bar and open to the Breakfast Room

A large and private Master Bedroom with an oversized walk-in closet

A secondary bedroom located at the front of the house with a vaulted ceiling and a circle-topped window

MAIN FLOOR — 1,605 SQ. FT.
GARAGE — 436 SQ. FT.

TOTAL LIVING AREA:
1,605 SQ. FT.

AN OPEN PLAN

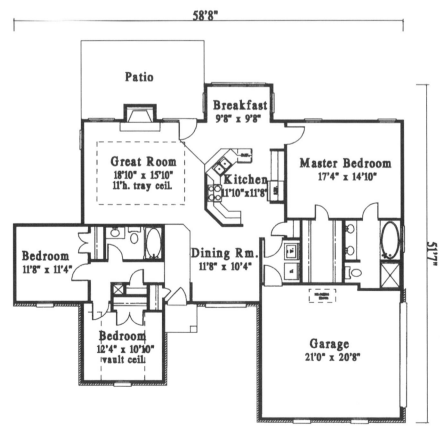

Main Level Floor Plan
8' Ceilings

No materials list available

PRICE CODE B

*L*ARGE PLAN IN A SMALL PACKAGE

No. 93062

■ This plan features:

— Three bedrooms

— Two full baths

■ Porch and Entry lead into an open layout with sloped ceilings for the Dining, Living and Breakfast rooms

■ Living Room accented by a cozy fireplace, plant ledges

■ Efficient Kitchen with an angled counter/eating bar, a Bright Breakfast Room, a built-in pantry, a Utility area and a Garage

■ Master Bedroom suite features a decorative window, a walk-in closet and an upscale Master Bath with a whirlpool tub and a double vanity

■ This plan is available with a Slab or Crawlspace foundation — please specify when ordering

MAIN FLOOR — 1,575 SQ. FT.
GARAGE — 474 SQ. FT.
PORCH — 41 SQ. FT.

TOTAL LIVING AREA:
1,575 SQ. FT.

Main Area

WIDTH 55–6

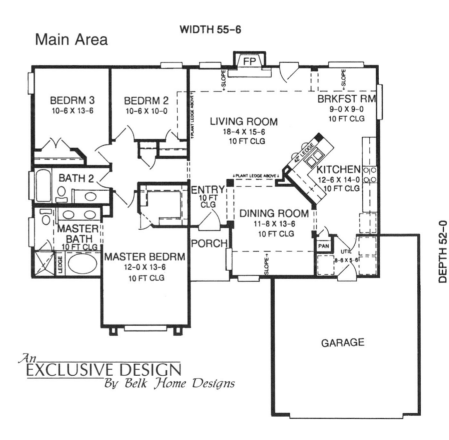

DEPTH 52–0

An
EXCLUSIVE DESIGN
By Belk Home Designs

PRICE CODE A

DELIGHTFUL, COMPACT HOME

No. 34003

■ This plan features:

— Three bedrooms

— Two full baths

■ A fireplaced Living Room brightened by a wonderful picture window

■ A counter island featuring double sinks separating the Kitchen and Dining areas

■ A Master Bedroom that includes a private Master Bath and double closets

■ Two additional bedrooms with ample closet spacethat share a full bath

FIRST FLOOR — 1,146 SQ. FT.

TOTAL LIVING AREA: 1,146 SQ. FT.

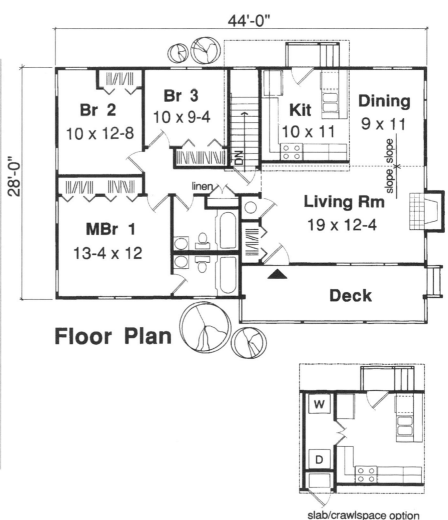

44'-0"

28'-0"

Br 2
10 x 12-8

Br 3
10 x 9-4

Kit
10 x 11

Dining
9 x 11

DN

linen

MBr 1
13-4 x 12

Living Rm
19 x 12-4

Deck

Floor Plan

W

D

slab/crawlspace option

PRICE CODE A

A COMPACT HOME

No. 93018

This plan features:

— Three bedrooms

— Two full baths

Siding with brick wainscoting distinguishing the elevation

A large Family Room with a corner fireplace and direct access to the outside

An arched opening leading to the Breakfast Area

A bay window illuminating the Breakfast Area with natural light

An efficiently designed, U-shaped Kitchen with ample cabinet and counter space

A Master Suite with a private Master Bath

Two additional bedrooms that share a full hall bath

FIRST FLOOR — 1,142 SQ. FT.
GARAGE — 428 SQ. FT.

TOTAL LIVING AREA:
1,142 SQ. FT.

No materials list available

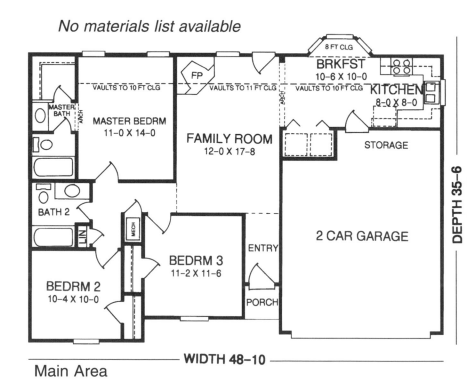

Main Area

An EXCLUSIVE DESIGN
By Belk Home Designs

PRICE CODE D

SUITABLE FOR TODAY'S LIFESTYLE

No. 93253

■ This plan features:

   Four bedrooms

— Two full and one half baths

■ A large Family Room with a fireplace and access to the patio

■ A Breakfast Area that flows directly into the Family Room

■ A well-appointed Kitchen equipped with an eating bar, double sinks, built-in pantry and an abundance of counter and cabinet space

■ A Master Suite with a decorative ceiling and a private Bath

■ Three additional bedrooms that share a full bath

MAIN AREA — 2,542 SQ. FT.
GARAGE — 510 SQ. FT.

TOTAL LIVING AREA: 2,542 SQ. FT.

No materials list available

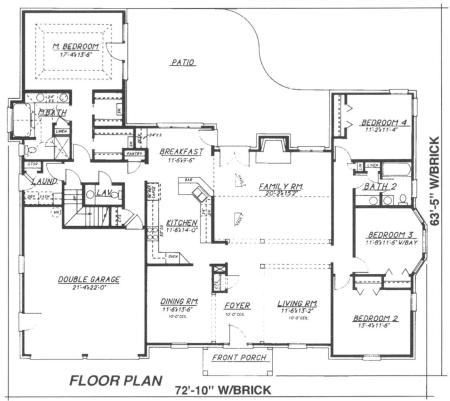

FLOOR PLAN

72'-10" W/BRICK

An
EXCLUSIVE DESIGN
By Jannis Vann & Associates, Inc.

PRICE CODE E

ANGLED FOR EXCITEMENT

No. 90653

■ This plan features:

— Four bedrooms

— Two full and one half baths

■ A Family Room that is hexagonal in shape with soaring cathedral ceiling and two-way fireplace

■ A Living Room that is enhanced by the other side of the two-way fireplace

■ A conveniently arranged Kitchen, flanked by a sunny Dining Room and a dinette

■ A Master Bedroom with a walk-in closet and private bath

■ Three additional bedrooms that share a full hall bath

FIRST FLOOR — 2,601 SQ. FT.

**TOTAL LIVING AREA:
2,601 SQ. FT.**

FLOOR PLAN

PRICE CODE D

INDOOR/OUTDOOR UNITY

No. 91011

■ This plan features:

— Three bedrooms

— Two full baths

■ A luxurious Master Suite, complete with a spa and a private deck

■ A sunken Living Room with a glass wall opening into the formal Dining Room

■ Expansive windows and sliders in the island Kitchen, Nook and Family Room which has a fireplace

■ An optional basement, slab or crawl space foundation — please specify when ordering

FIRST FLOOR — 2,242 SQ. FT.
GARAGE — 736 SQ. FT.

TOTAL LIVING AREA:
2,242 SQ. FT.

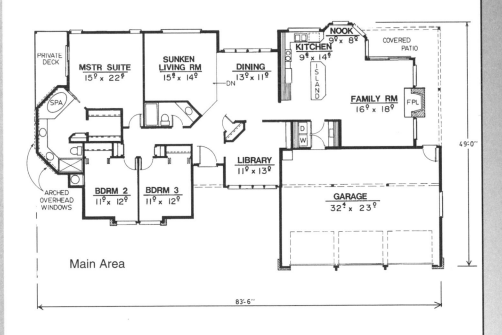

Main Area

PRICE CODE B

COMPACT HOME DESIGN

No. 10455

■ This plan features:

— Three bedrooms

— Two full baths

■ An airlock Entry that saves energy

■ A Living Room with an entire wall of windows, fireplace, built-in bookcases, and a wetbar

■ A step-saver Kitchen with an abundance of storage and a convenient peninsula

■ A Master Bedroom with separate vanities and walk-in closets

MAIN AREA — 1,643 SQ. FT.
GARAGE — 500 SQ. FT.

**TOTAL LIVING AREA:
1,643 SQ. FT.**

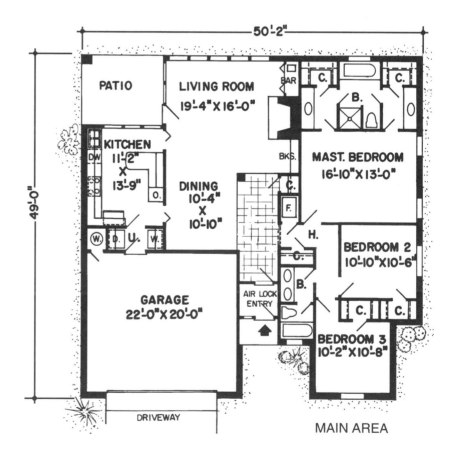

MAIN AREA

PRICE CODE E

RELAX ON THE VERANDA

No. 91749

This plan features:

— Four bedrooms

— Three full and one half baths

A wrap-around veranda

A sky-lit Master Suite with elevated custom spa, twin basins, a walk-in closet, and an extra vanity outside the bathroom

A vaulted ceiling in the Den

A fireplace in both the Family Room and the formal Living Room

An efficient Kitchen with a peninsula counter and a double sink

Two additional bedrooms with walk-in closets, served by a compartmentalized bath

A Guest Suite with a private bath

MAIN AREA — 3,051 SQ. FT.
GARAGE — 646 SQ. FT.

**TOTAL LIVING AREA:
3,051 SQ. FT.**

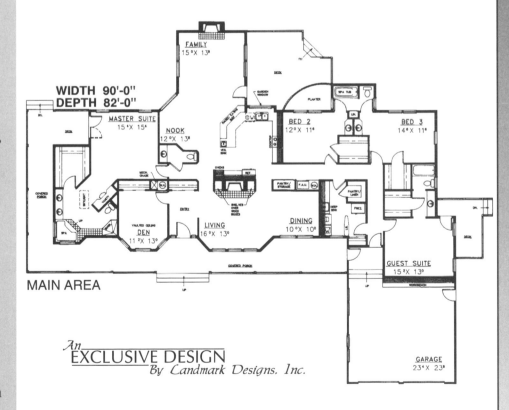

WIDTH 90'-0"
DEPTH 82'-0"

MAIN AREA

An
EXCLUSIVE DESIGN
By Landmark Designs, Inc.

PRICE CODE B

No. 93104

This plan features:

— Three bedrooms

— Two full baths

Sheltered entrance surrounded by glass leads into the Foyer and the expansive Great Room

Windows surround a cozy fireplace in the Great Room topped by a vaulted ceiling

Well-appointed Kitchen with loads of counter and storage space, and a snackbar serving the bright Dining area with access to the rear yard

French doors lead into the Master Bedroom Suite with a huge walk-in closet and a double vanity bath

Two additional bedrooms with ample closets, share a full bath

This plan is available with a Basement foundation only

MAIN FLOOR — 1,756 SQ. FT.
BASEMENT — 1,756 SQ. FT.
GARAGE — 536 SQ. FT.

**TOTAL LIVING AREA:
1,756 SQ. FT.**

UNIQUE BRICK AND SHAKE SIDING

An EXCLUSIVE DESIGN *By Ahmann Design Inc.*

DINING ROOM
15'-0" X 12'-0"

MASTER BEDROOM
14'-0" X 16'-0"

GREAT ROOM
16'-0" X 22'-0"

BEDROOM #2
13'-0" X 11'-0"

KITCHEN
15'-0" X 11'-0"

FOYER

BEDROOM #3
12'-0" X 11'-0"

2 CAR GARAGE
22'-0" X 24'-0"

MAIN FLOOR

No materials list available

WIDTH — 58'-0"
DEPTH — 55'-0"

PRICE CODE C

SMART STUCCO

No. 93228

- This plan features:
  - — Three bedrooms
  - — Two full baths
- A large Living Area with a warm fireplace
- A formal Dining Room conveniently located off the kitchen for entertaining ease
- A double sink, ample cabinet and counter area, a built-in pantry and direct access to a sun deck in the Kitchen/Breakfast Room
- A wonderful Master Suite with private five piece Bath and a walk-in closet
- Two additional bedrooms that share a full hall bath
- A Loft Area with three skylights that will become a special area, customized for the family's needs

FIRST FLOOR — 1,678 SQ. FT.
LOFT — 282 SQ. FT.
BASEMENT — 836 SQ. FT.
GARAGE — 784 SQ. FT.
DECK — 288 SQ. FT.

TOTAL LIVING AREA:
1,960 SQ. FT.

SECOND FLOOR

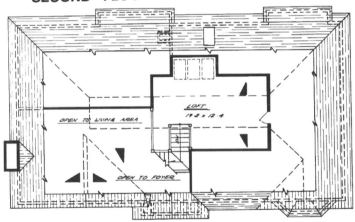

An
EXCLUSIVE DESIGN
By Jannis Vann & Associates, Inc.

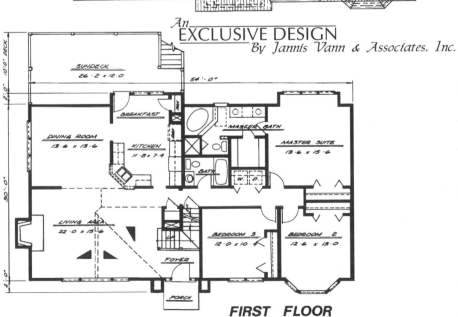

FIRST FLOOR

PRICE CODE D

No. 93059

This plan features:

— Four bedrooms

— Two full and one half baths

Sheltered Porch and an open Foyer lead into the Dining and Living Rooms with ten foot ceilings

Open, efficient Kitchen with an island counter/serving bar, a walk-in pantry, a built-in desk, a Utility room and a Garage

Spacious Keeping/Breakfast Rooms adjoin the Kitchen and access the Covered Porch

Private Master Bedroom suite with his-n-her closets and a Master Bath with two vanities and a corner whirlpool tub

Walk-in closet in the Study/Bedroom offers options

This plan is available with a Slab or Crawlspace foundation — please specify when ordering

MAIN FLOOR — 2,559 SQ. FT.
GARAGE — 544 SQ. FT.
PORCH — 77 SQ. FT.

TOTAL LIVING AREA:
2,559 SQ. FT.

UNIQUE KEEPING ROOM

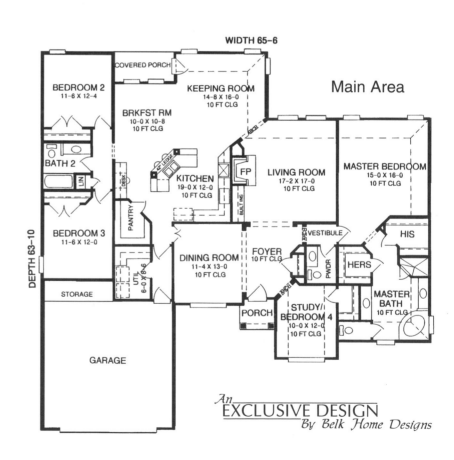

Main Area

An
EXCLUSIVE DESIGN
By Belk Home Designs

PRICE CODE A

COMPACT AND OPEN CABIN

No. 84020

■ This plan features:

— Three bedrooms

— One full bath

■ An open Living Room leading into an efficient Kitchen

■ Three bedrooms, with ample closets, sharing a full hall bath

■ A full basement option or a separate washer and dryer area

MAIN FLOOR — 768 SQ. FT.

TOTAL LIVING AREA:
768 SQ. FT.

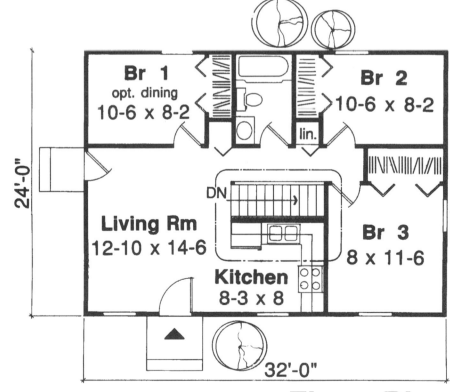

Br 1
opt. dining
10-6 x 8-2

Br 2
10-6 x 8-2

lin.

24'-0"

Living Rm
12-10 x 14-6

DN

Br 3
8 x 11-6

Kitchen
8-3 x 8

32'-0"

Floor Plan

No materials list available

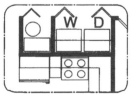

Slab/Crawlspace Option

PRICE CODE B

TODAY'S LIVING IN MIND

No. 93133

This plan features:

— Three bedrooms

— Two full baths

■ A large Foyer leading to the bright and spacious Living Room

■ A large open Kitchen with a central work island complete with extra storage space

■ A handy Laundry Room with a pantry and garage access

■ A Master Suite with a bay windowed sitting area and French doors, as well as a private Master Bath that includes an oversized tub, corner shower and room-sized walk-in closet

■ Two additional front bedrooms that share a full bath

■ A tandem garage with space for a third car, boat or just extra work and storage space

FIRST FLOOR — 1,761 SQ. FT.
BASEMENT — 1,761 SQ. FT.
GARAGE — 658 SQ. FT.

TOTAL LIVING AREA:
1,761 SQ. FT.

No materials list available

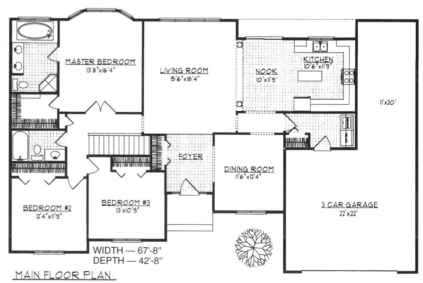

MAIN FLOOR PLAN

WIDTH — 67'-8"
DEPTH — 42'-8"

An
EXCLUSIVE DESIGN
By Ahmann Design Inc.

PRICE CODE B

BUILT-IN BEAUTY

No. 91507

■ This plan features:

— Three bedrooms

— Two full baths

■ A sky-lit Foyer

■ A bump-out window enhancing the wide-open arrangement in the Living/Dining Room

■ An efficient island Kitchen with a built-in pantry, and a corner double sink

■ An informal Family Room with a lovely fireplace

■ A Master Suite with elegant double doors, and a luxurious private Master Bath

■ Two additional bedrooms flanking the laundry area

■ An optional basement or crawl space foundation — please specify when ordering

FIRST FLOOR — 1,687 SQ. FT.
GARAGE — 419 SQ. FT.

TOTAL LIVING AREA:
1,687 SQ. FT.

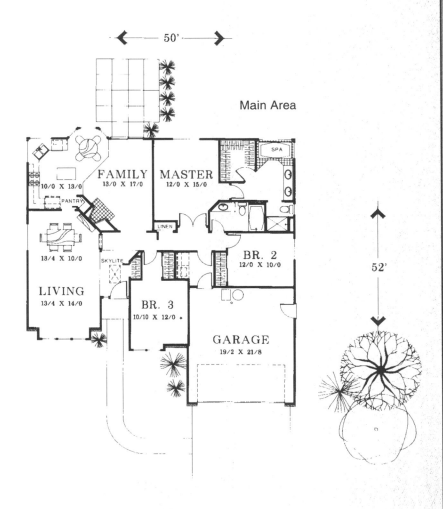

Main Area

50'

52'

FAMILY 13/0 X 17/0

MASTER 12/0 X 15/0

SPA

10/0 X 13/0

PANTRY

LINEN

13/4 X 10/0

BR. 2 12/0 X 10/0

SKYLITE

LIVING 13/4 X 14/0

BR. 3 10/10 X 12/0

GARAGE 19/2 X 21/8

PRICE CODE A

BASIC LIVING DESIGN

No. 91342

■ This plan features:

— Three bedrooms

— Two full baths

■ A handicapped Master Bath plan is available

■ Vaulted Great Room, Dining Room and Kitchen areas

■ A Kitchen accented with angles and an abundance of cabinets for storage

■ A Master Bedroom with an ample sized wardrobe, large covered private deck, and private bath

MAIN AREA — 1,345 SQ. FT.
WIDTH — 47'-8"
DEPTH — 56'-0"

TOTAL LIVING AREA:
1,345 SQ. FT.

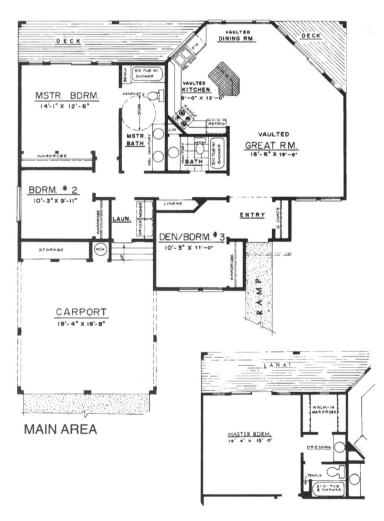

MAIN AREA

ALTERNATE BATH

PRICE CODE B

PORCH INSPIRES ROCKING CHAIR RELAXING

No. 90409

■ This plan features:

— Three bedrooms

— Two full baths

■ A massive fireplace separating Living and Dining Rooms

■ An isolated Master Suite with a walk-in closet and compartmentalized bath

■ A galley-type Kitchen between the Breakfast Room and Dining Room

■ An optional basement, slab or crawl space foundation — please specify when ordering

MAIN AREA — 1,670 SQ. FT.

TOTAL LIVING AREA:
1,670 SQ. FT.

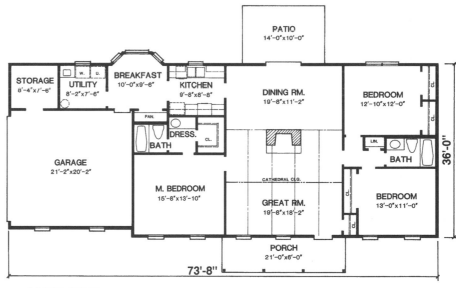

MAIN AREA

PRICE CODE A

P*LENTY OF EXTERIOR INTEREST*

No. 91063

■ This plan features:

— Three bedrooms

— Two full baths

■ Vaulted ceilings and an open interior creating a spacious feeling

■ A private Master Bedroom with a generous closet and Master Bath

■ Two additional bedrooms sharing the second full bath

■ A Kitchen with ample storage, countertops, and a built-in pantry

MAIN AREA — 1,207 SQ. FT.
GARAGE — 440 SQ. FT.

**TOTAL LIVING AREA:
1,207 SQ. FT.**

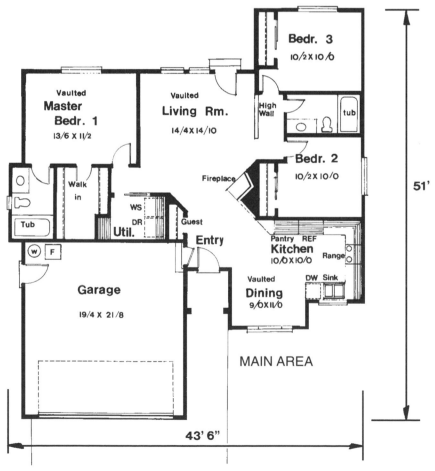

No materials list available

PRICE CODE B

VAULTED CEILINGS ADD SPACE

No. 92309

■ This plan features:

— Three bedrooms

— Two full baths

■ An covered entry leading into a tiled hall, the Kitchen/Dining Room, and the Great Room

■ An oversized Great Room highlighted by a raised, hearth fireplace, built-in shelves, a vaulted ceiling and a sliding glass door to a Wood Deck

■ An island cooktop Kitchen with a vaulted ceiling, offering laundry facilities and a decorative, box window in the Dining area

■ A plush Master Suite with a double vanity bath and a walk-in closet

■ Two additional bedrooms, one with a vaulted ceiling sharing a full hall bath

MAIN FLOOR — 1,544 SQ. FT.
GARAGE — 440 SQ. FT.

TOTAL LIVING AREA:
1,544 SQ. FT.

An
EXCLUSIVE DESIGN
By Gary Clayton

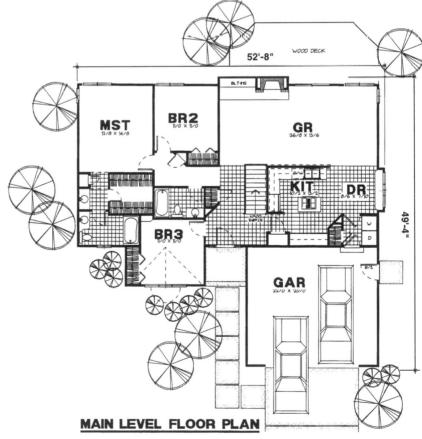

MAIN LEVEL FLOOR PLAN

No materials list available

PRICE CODE B

EXTERIOR ADDS DRAMA

No. 91349

- This plan features:
- — Two bedrooms
- — Two full baths
- A vaulted ceiling entry
- A Living Room with a vaulted ceiling, accented by a bay window and an optional fireplace
- A garden window, eating bar, and an abundance of storage space in the efficient Kitchen
- A Master Bedroom with its own bath, a double sink vanity and a walk-in closet
- A Library with a vaulted ceiling option and a window seat

MAIN AREA — 1,694 SQ. FT.

TOTAL LIVING AREA:
1,694 SQ. FT.

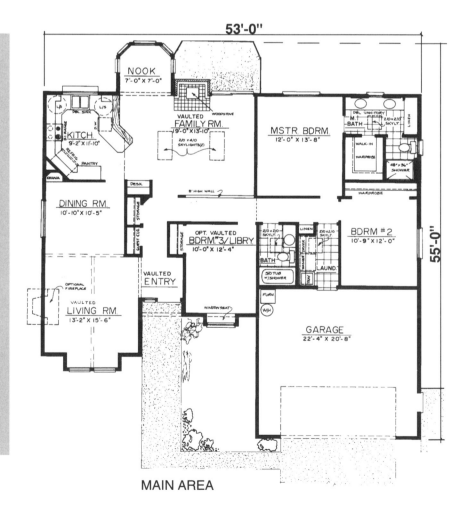

MAIN AREA

PRICE CODE B

COUNTRY STYLE AND CHARM

No. 91731

■ This plan features:

— Three bedrooms

— Two full baths

■ Brick accents, front facing gable, and railed wrap-around covered porch

■ A built-in range and oven in a dog-leg shaped Kitchen

■ A Nook with garage access for convenient unloading of groceries and other supplies

■ A bay window wrapping around the front of the formal Living Room

■ A Master Suite with French doors opening to the deck

MAIN AREA — 1,775 SQ. FT.
GARAGE — 681 SQ. FT.
WIDTH — 51'-6"
DEPTH — 65'-0"

TOTAL LIVING AREA:
1,775 SQ. FT.

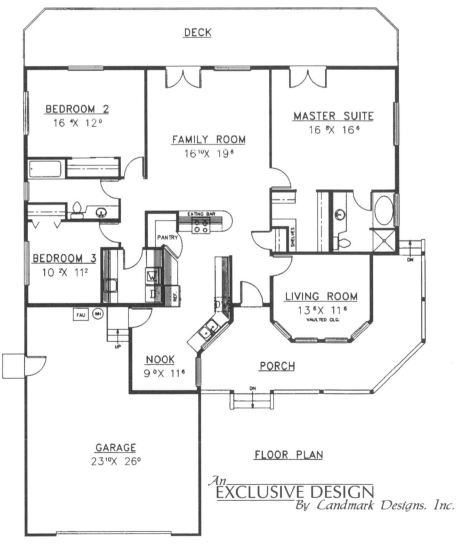

An
EXCLUSIVE DESIGN
By Landmark Designs, Inc.

PRICE CODE A

INEXPENSIVE RANCH DESIGN

No. 20062

■ This plan features:

— Three bedrooms

— Two full baths

■ A large picture window brightening the Breakfast area

■ A well planned Kitchen

■ A Living Room which is accented by an open beam across the sloping ceiling and wood burning fireplace

■ A Master Bedroom with an extremely large bath area

FIRST FLOOR — 1,500 SQ. FT.
BASEMENT — 1,500 SQ. FT.
GARAGE — 482 SQ. FT.

TOTAL LIVING AREA:
1,500 SQ. FT.

An
EXCLUSIVE DESIGN
By Karl Kreeger

MAIN AREA

PRICE CODE B

EXCITING CEILINGS ADD IMPACT

No. 20191

■ This plan features:

— Three bedrooms

— Two full baths

■ A brick hearth fireplace in the Living Room

■ An efficient Kitchen, with an island and double sinks, that flows into the Dining Room, which features a decorative ceiling

■ A private Master Suite with a decorative ceiling and a Master Bath

■ Two additional bedrooms that share a full bath

MAIN AREA — 1,606 SQ. FT.
BASEMENT — 1,575 SQ. FT.
GARAGE — 545 SQ. FT.

**TOTAL LIVING AREA:
1,606 SQ. FT.**

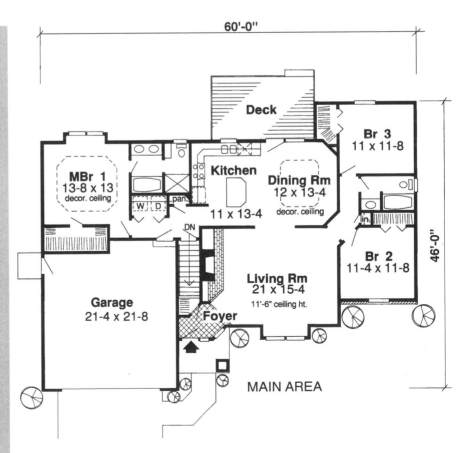

MAIN AREA

An
EXCLUSIVE DESIGN
By Karl Kreeger

PRICE CODE C

LOTS OF ROOM FOR ENTERTAINING

No. 91761

This plan features:

— Three bedrooms

— Two full baths

An open floor plan that is spacious and easy to adapt for wheelchair accessibility

A Kitchen, with an eating bar, that flows into the Family Room; allowing for continued conversation between the two rooms

Direct access to the wood deck from the Family Room that features a vaulted ceiling with skylights

A Master Suite enhanced by a private bath with a skylight and direct access to the wood deck

A combination Living Room/Dining Room making entertaining easy

Two additional bedrooms that share a full hall bath

MAIN AREA — 2,072 SQ. FT.
GARAGE — 585 SQ. FT.
WIDTH — 60'-0"
DEPTH — 70'-0"

TOTAL LIVING AREA:
2,072 SQ. FT.

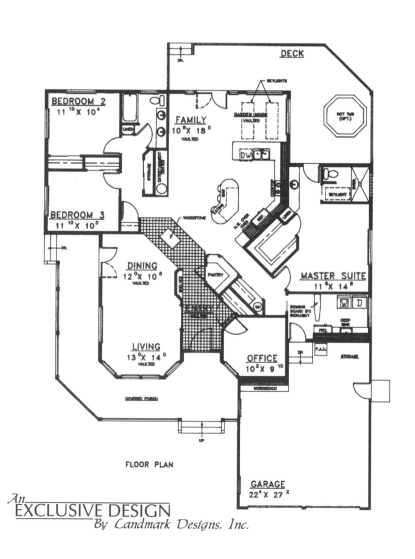

FLOOR PLAN

An
EXCLUSIVE DESIGN
By Landmark Designs, Inc.

PRICE CODE C

L-SHAPED BUNGALOW WITH TWO PORCHES

No. 90407

This plan features:

— Three bedrooms

— Two full baths

■ A Master Suite with a lavish Master Bath including a garden tub, shower, his-n-her vanities and separate walk-in closets

Two additional bedrooms having ample closet space and sharing a full hall bath

A large Family Room accentuated by a fireplace

A U-shaped Kitchen with a built-in pantry, double sink and ample storage and counter space

A sunny, bay Breakfast Nook for informal eating

An optional basement, slab or crawl space foundation — please specify when ordering

FIRST FLOOR — 1,950 SQ. FT.

TOTAL LIVING AREA: 1,950 SQ. FT.

PRICE CODE B

LIGHT AND AIRY DESIGN

No. 10745

■ This plan features:

— Three bedrooms

— Two full baths

■ An open plan with cathedral ceilings

■ A fireplaced Great Room flowing into the Dining Room

■ A Master Bedroom with a private Master Bath

■ An efficient Kitchen, with Laundry area and pantry in close proximity

MAIN AREA — 1,643 SQ. FT.
BASEMENT — 1,643 SQ. FT.
GARAGE — 484 SQ. FT.

TOTAL LIVING AREA:
1,643 SQ. FT.

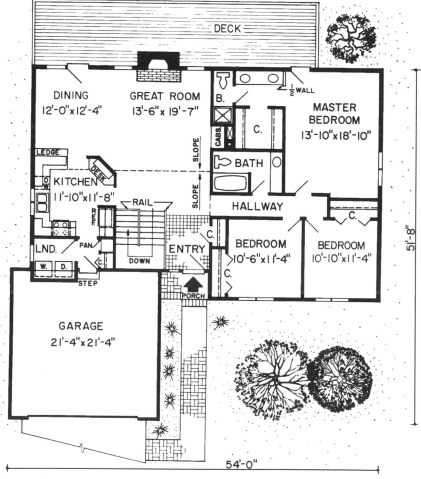

MAIN AREA

RANCH PROVIDES GREAT KITCHEN AREA

No. 34054

■ This plan features:

— Three bedrooms

— Two full baths

■ A Dining Room with sliding glass doors to the backyard

■ Access to the Garage through the laundry room

■ A Master Bedroom with a private full bath

■ An two-car Garage

FIRST FLOOR — 1,400 SQ. FT.
BASEMENT — 1,400 SQ. FT.
GARAGE — 528 SQ. FT.

**TOTAL LIVING AREA:
1,400 SQ. FT.**

MAIN AREA

50'-0"

28'-0"

Garage
22 x 24

W D
L
Kit
Dining
9 x 13
Br 2
11-6 x 13
Br 3
10-6 x 13

DN
pantry

Living Rm
19 x 14

MBr 1
11-6 x 14

W D
L
Kit
10 x 13
Dining
9 x 13
F

Alternate Plan
w/ Crawlspace

PRICE CODE B

GRACEFUL PORCH ENHANCES CHARM

No. 90106

■ This plan features:

— Three bedrooms

— Two full baths

■ A formal Living Room sheltered by a railed porch

■ A hobby area including laundry facilities

■ A Kitchen, Dining, and Family Room in a "three in one" design

■ An optional basement, slab or crawl space foundation — please specify when ordering

MAIN AREA — 1,643 SQ. FT.

TOTAL LIVING AREA: 1,643 SQ. FT.

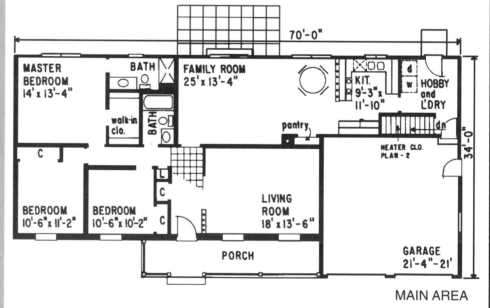

MAIN AREA

PRICE CODE A

DETAILED RANCH DESIGN

No. 90360

- This plan features:
- — Three bedrooms
- — Two full baths
- A Breakfast area with a vaulted ceiling and access to the deck
- An efficient Kitchen with built-in pantry and appliances
- A Master bedroom with private bath and ample closet space
- A large Great Room with a vaulted ceiling and cozy fireplace

MAIN AREA — 1,283 SQ. FT.

TOTAL LIVING AREA:
1,283 SQ. FT.

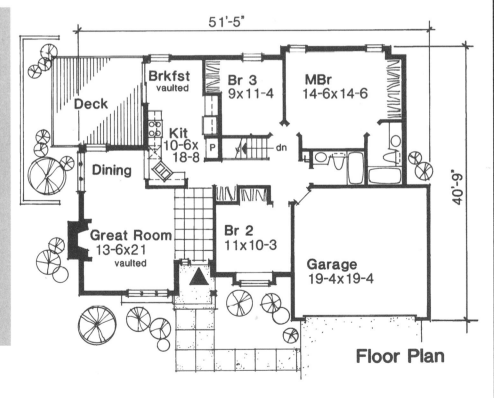

Floor Plan

PRICE CODE A

CATHEDRAL CEILING IN LIVING ROOM AND MASTER SUITE

No. 24402

■ This plan features:

— Three bedrooms

— Two full baths

■ A spacious Living Room with a cathedral ceiling and elegant fireplace

■ A Dining Room that adjoins both the Living Room and the Kitchen

■ An efficient Kitchen, with double sinks, ample cabinet space and peninsula counter that doubles as an eating bar

■ A convenient hallway laundry center

■ A Master Suite with a cathedral ceiling and a private Master Bath

MAIN AREA — 1,346 SQ. FT.
GARAGE — 449 SQ. FT.

TOTAL LIVING AREA:
1,346 SQ. FT.

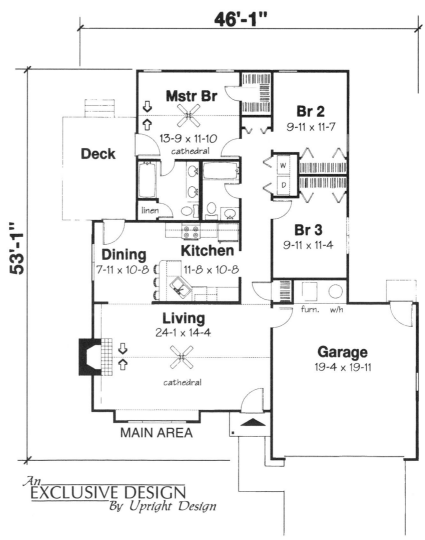

An
EXCLUSIVE DESIGN
By Upright Design

No materials list available

PRICE CODE B

PLENTY OF NATURAL LIGHT

No. 24317

■ This plan features:

— Three bedrooms

— Two full baths

■ A generous use of windows throughout the home, creating a bright living space

■ A center work island and a built-in pantry in the Kitchen

■ A sunny Eating Nook for informal eating and a formal Dining Room for entertaining

■ A large Living Room, with a cozy fireplace to add atmosphere to the room as well as warmth

■ A Master Bedroom with a private bath and double closets

■ Two additional bedrooms that share a full, compartmented hall bath

MAIN AREA — 1,620 SQ. FT.

**TOTAL LIVING AREA:
1,620 SQ. FT.**

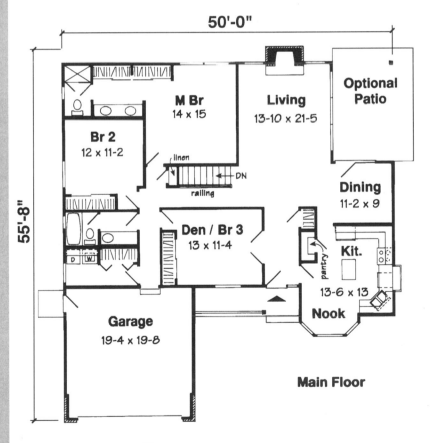

50'-0"

55'-8"

Br 2
12 x 11-2

M Br
14 x 15

Living
13-10 x 21-5

Optional Patio

linen

DN

railing

Den / Br 3
13 x 11-4

Dining
11-2 x 9

Kit.

pantry

13-6 x 13

Garage
19-4 x 19-8

Nook

Main Floor

An
EXCLUSIVE DESIGN
By Marshall Associates

PRICE CODE B

EASY LIVING WITH A HINT OF DRAMA

No. 90676

■ This plan features:

— Three bedrooms

— Two full baths

■ A cathedral ceiling in the Living Room with exposed beams and a heat-circulating fireplace

■ A formal Dining Room conveniently located next to the Kitchen and having sliding glass doors to the covered Porch

■ Bedrooms located in a separate wing for added privacy and quiet

■ A Master Bedroom with two walk-in closets and a private Master Bath

■ Two additional Bedrooms that have ample closet space and share a full hall bath

FIRST FLOOR — 1,575 SQ. FT.
GARAGE — 400 SQ. FT.

TOTAL LIVING AREA: 1,575 SQ. FT.

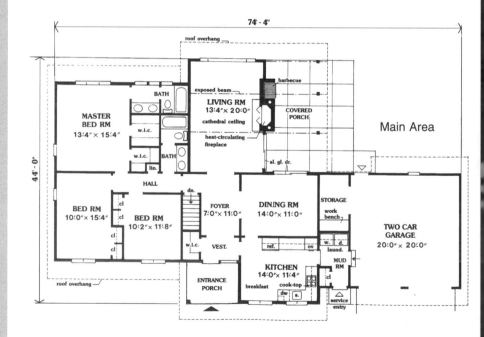

PRICE CODE B

RAILING DIVIDES LIVING SPACES

No. 10596

■ This plan features:

— Three bedrooms

— Two full baths

■ A one-level design with a sunken, fireplaced Living Room

■ A wall of windows bringing natural light into the two back bedrooms

■ An island Kitchen flowing easily into a sunny Breakfast Room

MAIN AREA — 1,740 SQ. FT.
BASEMENT — 1,377 SQ. FT.
GARAGE — 480 SQ. FT.

TOTAL LIVING AREA: 1,740 SQ. FT.

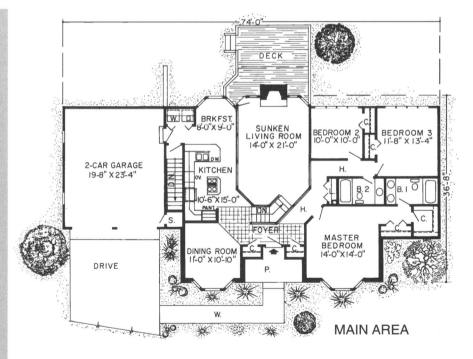

MAIN AREA

An EXCLUSIVE DESIGN
By Karl Kreeger

PRICE CODE B

CASUAL LIVING INSIDE AND OUT

No materials list available

No. 92703

This plan features:

— Three bedrooms

— Two full baths

A Living Room with a ten foot ceiling and a cozy corner fireplace

An enormous Dining Area that is able to handle even the largest family dinners

A large rear Porch that is perfect for outdoor dining

A conveniently placed Laundry Room

His-n-her walk-in closets and a double vanity in the Master Bath

Secondary bedrooms that share a full hall bath with a double vanity

MAIN AREA — 1,772 SQ. FT.

TOTAL LIVING AREA: 1,772 SQ. FT.

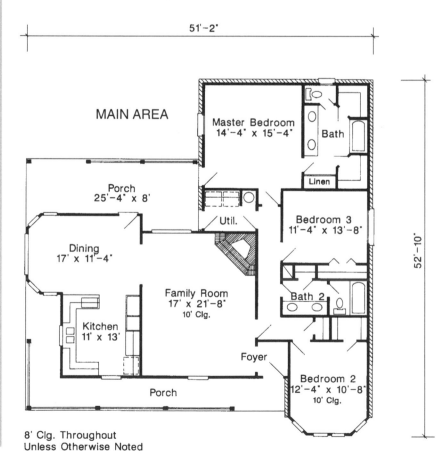

MAIN AREA

Master Bedroom
14'-4" x 15'-4"

Bath

Linen

Bedroom 3
11'-4" x 13'-8"

Porch
25'-4" x 8'

Util.

Dining
17' x 11'-4"

Family Room
17' x 21'-8"
10' Clg.

Bath 2

Kitchen
11' x 13'

Foyer

Porch

Bedroom 2
12'-4" x 10'-8"
10' Clg.

51'-2"

52'-10"

8' Clg. Throughout
Unless Otherwise Noted

PRICE CODE A

QUAINT STARTER HOME

No. 92400

■ This plan features:

— Three bedrooms

— Two full baths

■ A vaulted ceiling giving an airy feeling to the Dining and Living Rooms

■ A streamlined Kitchen with a comfortable work area, a double sink and ample cabinet space

■ A cozy fireplace in the Living Room

■ A Master Suite with a large closet, French doors leading to the patio and a private bath

■ Two additional bedrooms sharing a full bath

MAIN AREA — 1,050 SQ. FT.

TOTAL LIVING AREA:
1,050 SQ. FT.

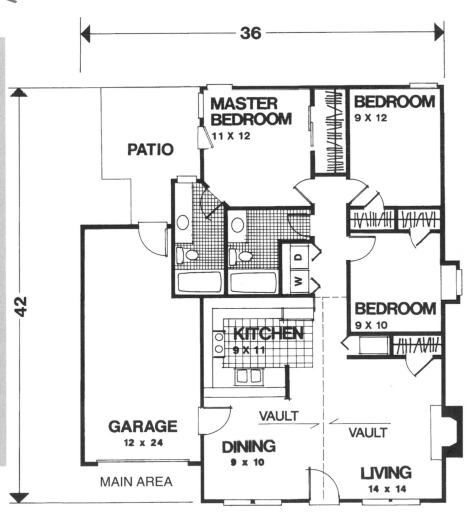

No materials list available

PRICE CODE B

No. 20116

This plan features:

— Three bedrooms

— Two full baths

Slender columns and brick detailing lending a Georgian flavor to the facade

An entry that opens upon a formal Living Room, equipped with a focal point fireplace, elegant arched windows, and high ceilings

A bay window enhancing the formal Dining Room

A U-shaped Kitchen with a double sink and ample work space

A tray ceiling, crowning a lovely and private Master Suite, enhanced by a double vanitied Bath and a walk-in closet

Two additional bedrooms, with walk-in closets, convenient to the full hall bath

MAIN AREA — 1,677 SQ. FT.
BASEMENT — 1,653 SQ. FT.
GARAGE — 520 SQ. FT.

TOTAL LIVING AREA:
1,677 SQ. FT.

GEORGIAN GRACE

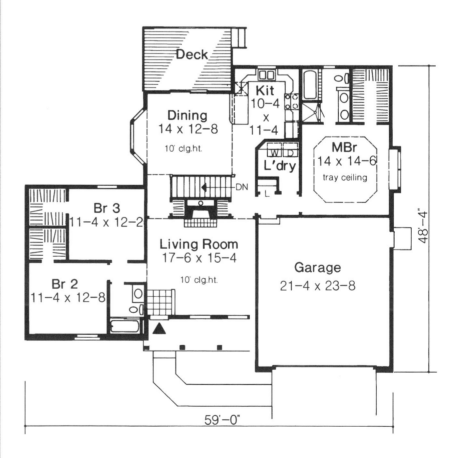

An
EXCLUSIVE DESIGN
By Karl Kreeger

PRICE CODE A

ARCHED WINDOW ENHANCES FACADE

No. 99345

■ This plan features:

— Three bedrooms

— Two full baths

■ A Great Room and Dining area with vaulted ceilings

■ A Great Room with a fabulous fireplace

■ A Kitchen and sunny Breakfast area with access to a rear deck

■ A Master Suite with a private full bath and one wall of closet space

MAIN AREA — 1,325 SQ. FT.

TOTAL LIVING AREA:
1,325 SQ. FT.

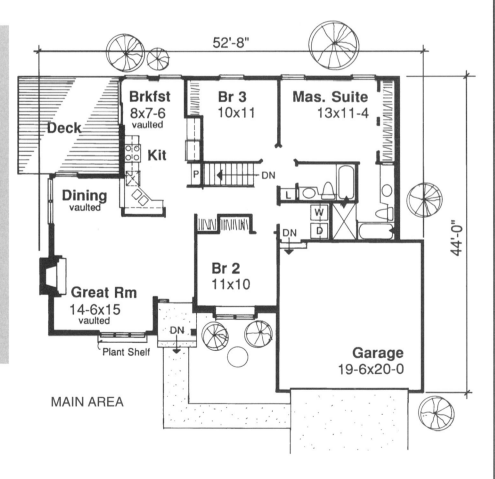

MAIN AREA

PRICE CODE C

COZY TRADITIONAL WITH STYLE

No. 99208

- This plan features:
- — Three bedrooms
- — Two full baths
- A convenient one-level design
- A galley-style Kitchen that shares a snack bar with the spacious Gathering Room
- A focal point fireplace making the Gathering Room warm and inviting
- An ample Master Suite with a luxury Bath which includes a whirlpool tub and separate Dressing Room
- Two additional bedrooms, one that could double as a Study, located at the front of the house

FIRST FLOOR — 1,830 SQ. FT.
BASEMENT — 1,830 SQ. FT.

TOTAL LIVING AREA:
1,830 SQ. FT.

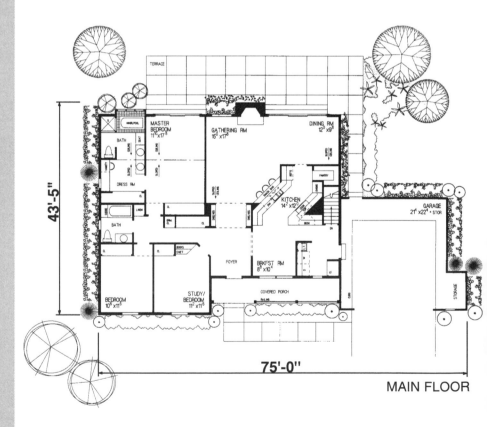

MAIN FLOOR

PRICE CODE A

COUNTRY RANCH

No. 91797

■ This plan features:

— Three bedrooms

— Two full baths

■ A railed and covered wrap-around porch, adding charm to this country-styled home

■ A high vaulted ceiling in the Living Room

■ A smaller Kitchen with ample cupboard and counter space, that is augmented by a large pantry

■ An informal Family Room with access to the wood deck

■ A private Master Suite with a spa tub and a walk-in closet

■ Two family bedrooms that share a full hall bath

■ A shop and storage area in the two-car garage

MAIN AREA — 1,485 SQ. FT.
GARAGE — 701 SQ. FT.
WIDTH — 63'-0"
DEPTH — 51'-6"

TOTAL LIVING AREA:
1,485 SQ. FT.

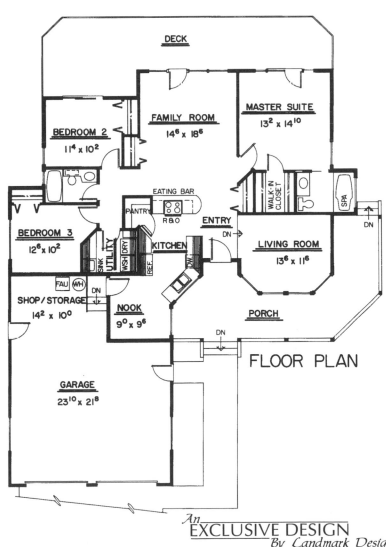

FLOOR PLAN

An
EXCLUSIVE DESIGN
By Landmark Designs, Inc.

PRICE CODE C

MODERATE RANCH WITH EXCITING FEATURES

No. 90441

■ This plan features:

— Three bedrooms

— Two full baths

■ A large Great Room with a vaulted ceiling and a stone fireplace with bookshelves on either side

■ A spacious Kitchen with ample cabinet space, conveniently located next to the large Dining Room

■ A Master Suite having a large bath with a garden tub, double vanity and a walk-in closet

■ Two other large bedrooms, each with a walk-in closet and access to the full bath

■ An optional basement, slab or crawl space foundation — please specify when ordering

MAIN AREA — 1,811 SQ. FT.

TOTAL LIVING AREA:
1,811 SQ. FT.

MAIN AREA

ANOTHER NICE RANCH DESIGN

No. 90354

■ This plan features:

— Three bedrooms

— Two full baths

■ A vaulted ceiling in the Great Room that includes a fireplace and access to the rear deck

■ Double door entrance into the Den/third bedroom

■ A Kitchen and breakfast area with a vaulted ceiling and an efficient layout

■ A Master Suite crowned by a vaulted ceiling, and pampered by a private bath and dressing area

■ A full hall bath that serves the two additional bedrooms

MAIN AREA — 1,360 SQ. FT.

TOTAL LIVING AREA:
1,360 SQ. FT.

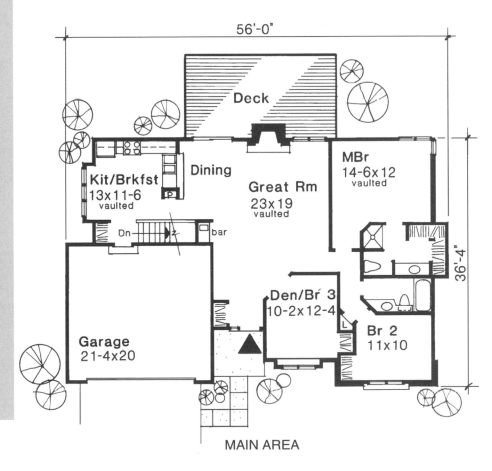

MAIN AREA

PRICE CODE B

ANGLED CONTEMPORARY

No. 99633

This plan features:

— Three bedrooms

— Two full and one half baths

An angled shape that allows the house to be rotated on a site to give optimum orientation

A spacious Foyer that opens to the Living Room

A heat-circulating fireplace in the Living Room

Sliding glass doors in the Living Room and the Dining Room that lead to a partially covered terrace

A cathedral ceiling in the Family Room which also has a heat-circulating fireplace

A Master Suite with a cathedral ceiling and private bath with double vanity and whirlpool tub

Two additional bedrooms share a full hall bath with a double vanity and whirlpool tub

MAIN AREA — 1,798 SQ. FT.
BASEMENT — 1,715 SQ. FT.
GARAGE — 456 SQ. FT.

TOTAL LIVING AREA:
1,798 SQ. FT.

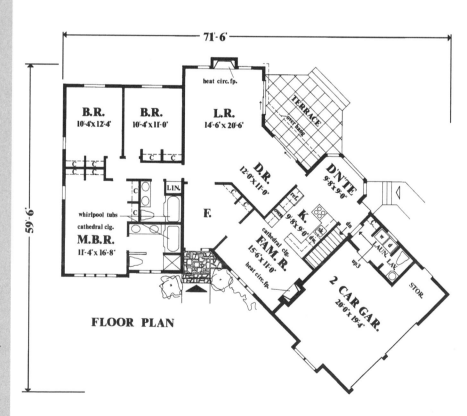

FLOOR PLAN

PRICE CODE B

COUNTRY CHARM

No. 99635

■ This plan features:

— Three bedrooms

— Two and one half baths

■ A large heat-circulating fireplace

■ A Master Bedroom with a private bath including a separate stall shower and whirlpool tub

■ A comfortable lifestyle by separating the formal and informal areas

■ Access to the Garage through the mudroom, which contains laundry facilities and extra closet space

MAIN AREA — 1,650 SQ. FT.
GARAGE — 491 SQ. FT.

TOTAL LIVING AREA: 1,650 SQ. FT.

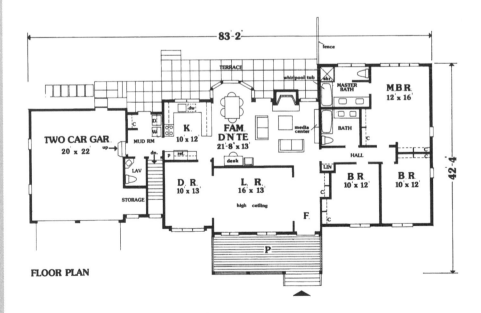

FLOOR PLAN

PRICE CODE D

BRICK DESIGN HAS STRIKING EXTERIOR

No. 10549

■ This plan features:

— Three bedrooms

— Three full and one half baths

■ A circle-head window that sets off a striking exterior

■ A Master Bedroom including a sloping ceiling, large closet space, and a private bath with both a tub and shower

■ A Great Room with impressive open-crossed beams and a wood-burning fireplace

■ A Kitchen with access to the Dining Room and Breakfast Room

FIRST FLOOR — 2,280 SQ. FT.
BASEMENT — 2,280 SQ. FT.
GARAGE — 528 SQ. FT.

TOTAL LIVING AREA:
2,280 SQ. FT.

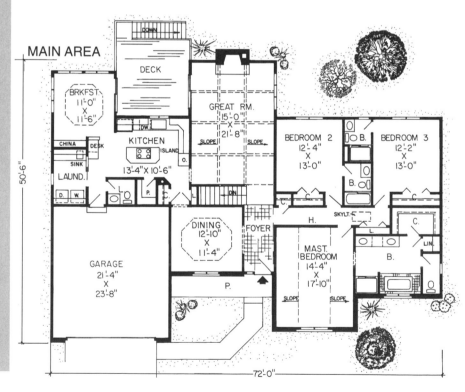

An
EXCLUSIVE DESIGN
By Karl Kreeger

PRICE CODE B

COMPACT AND APPEALING

An
EXCLUSIVE DESIGN
By Karl Kreeger

No. 20075

■ This plan features:

— Three bedrooms

— Two full baths

■ A fireplaced Living Room and formal Dining Room with extra wide doorways

■ A centrally-located Kitchen for maximum convenience

■ A Master Bedroom with a vaulted ceiling and a private Master Bath and walk-in closet

MAIN AREA — 1,682 SQ. FT.
BASEMENT — 1,682 SQ. FT.
GARAGE — 484 SQ. FT.

TOTAL LIVING AREA:
1,682 SQ. FT.

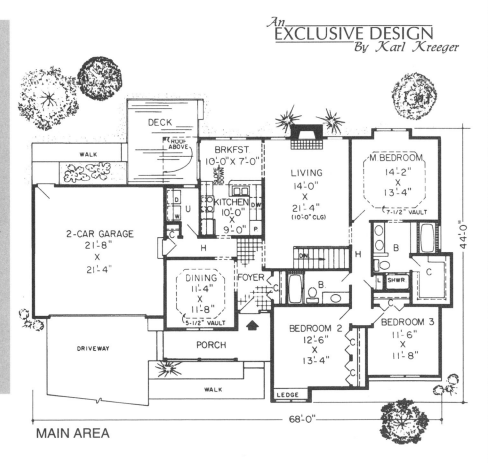

MAIN AREA

PRICE CODE B

WINDOW BOXES ADD ROMANTIC CHARM

No. 90684

■ This plan features:

— Three bedrooms

— Two full and one half baths

■ A spacious Living Room and formal Dining Room combination that is perfect for entertaining

■ A Family Room with a large fireplace and an expansive glass wall that overlooks the patio

■ An informal Dining bay, convenient to both the Kitchen and the Family Room

■ An efficient and well-equipped Kitchen, with a peninsula counter dividing it from the Family Room

■ A Master Bedroom with his-n-her closets and a private Master Bath

MAIN AREA — 1,590 SQ. FT.
BASEMENT — 900 SQ. FT.

TOTAL LIVING AREA:
1,590 SQ. FT.

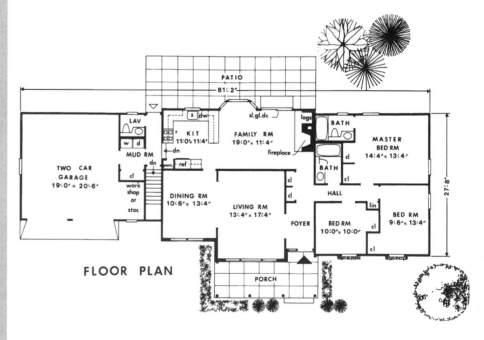

FLOOR PLAN

PRICE CODE A

EXPANSIVE, NOT EXPENSIVE

No. 90623

■ This plan features:

— Three bedrooms

— Two full baths

■ A Master Suite with his and her closets and a private Master Bath

■ Two additional bedrooms that share a full hall closet

■ A pleasant Dining Room that overlooks a rear garden

■ A well-equipped Kitchen with a built-in planning corner and eat-in space

■ A basement foundation only

FIRST FLOOR — 1,474 SQ. FT.

TOTAL LIVING AREA: 1,474 SQ. FT.

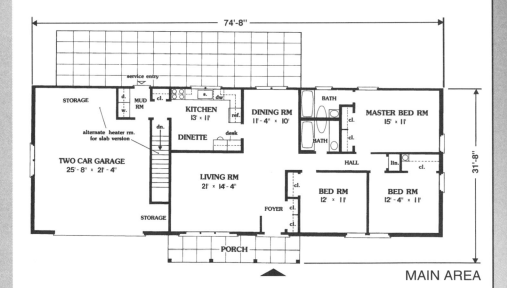

MAIN AREA

PRICE CODE B

COLONIAL RANCH

No. 9864

- This plan features:
— Three bedrooms
— Two baths
- A Master Bedroom complete with a full bath, walk-in closet and dressing area
- A fireplaced Living Room with access through glass sliders to deck
- A functional Kitchen separated from the Family Room by a cooking peninsula

FIRST FLOOR — 1,612 SQ. FT.
BASEMENT — 1,612 SQ. FT.
GARAGE, UTILITY ROOM AND
STORAGE — 660 SQ. FT.

TOTAL LIVING AREA:
1,612 SQ. FT.

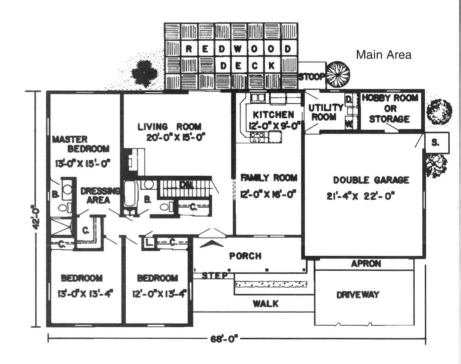

Main Area

PRICE CODE A

PERFECT FIRST HOME

No. 92704

This plan features:

— Three bedrooms

— Two full baths

A front porch with turned posts and railing, and a corner box window

■ A large Living Room with an 11 foot ceiling, sloping towards the sliding glass doors to the rear yard

■ A cathedral ceiling in the Dining Area, with a view of the porch through an elegant window

■ A corner double sink below the corner box window in the efficient Kitchen

A secluded Master Bedroom that includes a private bath and a walk-in closet

Two additional bedrooms that share a full hall bath

MAIN AREA — 1,078 SQ. FT.
GARAGE — 431 SQ. FT.

**TOTAL LIVING AREA:
1,078 SQ. FT.**

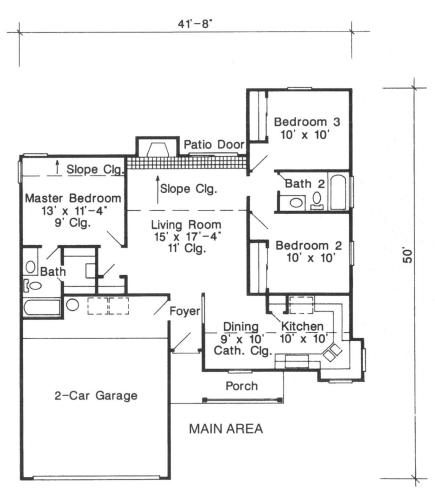

No materials list available

PRICE CODE A

NOSTALGIA RETURNS

No. 99321

■ This plan features:

— Three bedrooms

— Two full baths

■ A half-round transom window with quarter-round detail and a vaulted ceiling in the Great Room

■ A cozy corner fireplace which brings warmth to the Great Room

■ A vaulted ceiling in the Kitchen/Breakfast area

■ A Master Suite with a walk-in closet and a private Master Bath

■ Two additional bedrooms which share a full hall bath

MAIN AREA — 1,368 SQ. FT.

TOTAL LIVING AREA:
1,368 SQ. FT.

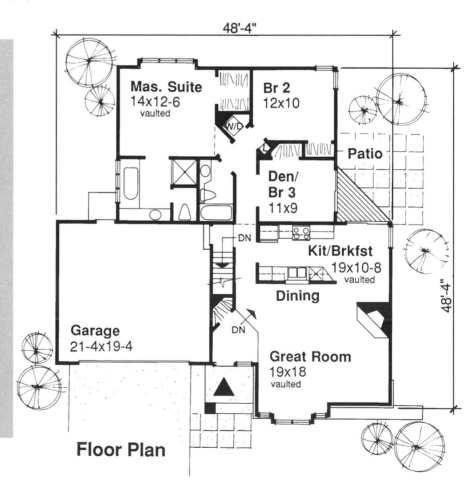

Floor Plan

PRICE CODE A

ONE STORY COUNTRY HOME

No. 99639

■ This plan features:

— Three bedrooms

— Two full baths

■ A Living Room with an imposing, high ceiling that slopes down to a normal height of eight feet, focusing on the decorative heat-circulating fireplace at the rear wall

■ An efficient Kitchen that adjoins the Dining Room that views the front Porch

■ A Dinette Area for informal eating in the Kitchen that can comfortably seat six people

■ A Master Suite arranged with a large dressing area that has a walk-in closet plus two linear closets and space for a vanity

■ Two family bedrooms that share a full hall bath

MAIN AREA — 1,367 SQ. FT.
BASEMENT — 1,267 SQ. FT.
GARAGE — 431 SQ. FT.

TOTAL LIVING AREA:
1,367 SQ. FT.

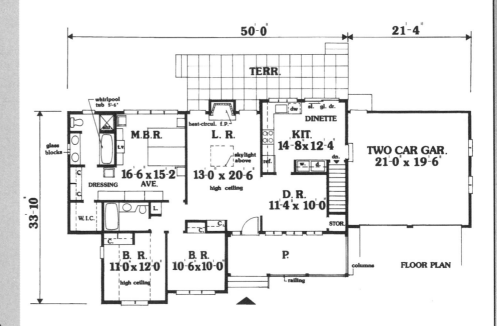

PRICE CODE A

CAREFREE COMFORT

No. 90692

■ This plan features:

— Three bedrooms

— Two full baths

■ Cedar shingle siding and flower boxes

■ A heat-circulating fireplace

■ A central Foyer separating active areas from the bedroom wing

■ A sunny Living Room with an arched window, fireplace, and soaring cathedral ceilings

■ A formal Dining Room adjoining the Living Room

MAIN AREA — 1,492 SQ. FT.

TOTAL LIVING AREA:
1,492 SQ. FT.

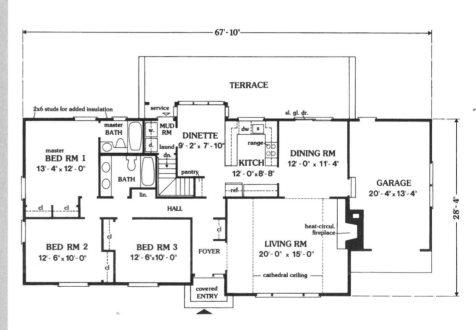

FLOOR PLAN

PRICE CODE A

SOARING CEILINGS ADD SPACE AND DRAMA

No. 90288

■ This plan features:

— Two bedrooms (with optional third bedroom)

— Two full baths

■ A sunny Master Suite with a sloping ceiling, private terrace entry, and luxurious garden bath with an adjoining Dressing Room

■ A Gathering Room with a fireplace, study and formal Dining Room, flowing together for a more spacious feeling

■ A convenient pass-through that adds to the efficiency of the galley Kitchen and adjoining Breakfast Room

MAIN AREA — 1,387 SQ. FT.

**TOTAL LIVING AREA:
1,387 SQ. FT.**

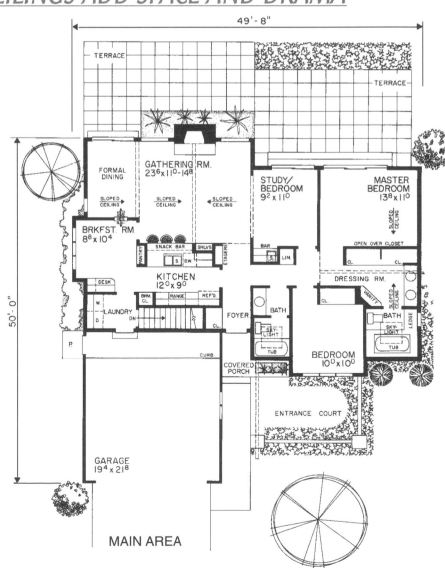

MAIN AREA

PRICE CODE D

STRIKING FACADE OF STONE AND WOOD

No. 10570

■ This plan features:

— Four bedrooms

— Two full baths

■ Recessed entrance leads into the tiled Foyer, and bright, expansive Living Room with a skylight and a double fireplace below a sloped ceiling

■ Ideal Kitchen with a work island, a cooktop snackbar, a walk-in pantry and a tiled Dining area with a built-in china cabinet, skylights and wall of windows overlooking the Deck

■ Master Bedroom suite with a corner fireplace, a walk-in closet and a plush bath with two vanities and a raised, tiled tub below the skylight

■ This plan is available with a basement foundation only

MAIN FLOOR — 2,450 SQ. FT.
BASEMENT — 2,450 SQ. FT
GARAGE — 739 SQ. FT.

TOTAL LIVING AREA:
2,450 SQ. FT.

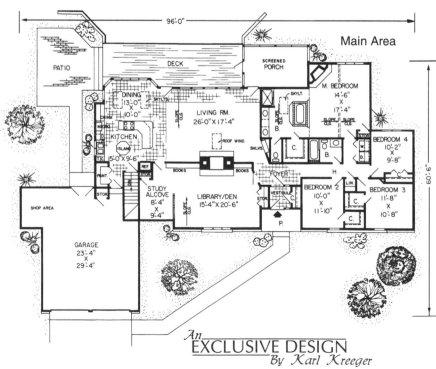

An
EXCLUSIVE DESIGN
By Karl Kreeger

PRICE CODE B

ABUNDANCE OF CLOSET SPACE

No. 20204

■ This plan features:

— Three bedrooms

— Two full baths

■ Roomy walk-in closets in all the bedrooms

■ A Master Bedroom with decorative ceiling and a private full bath

■ A fireplaced Living Room with sloped ceilings and sliders to the deck

■ An efficient Kitchen with plenty of cupboard space and a pantry

MAIN AREA — 1,532 SQ. FT.
GARAGE — 484 SQ. FT.

TOTAL LIVING AREA:
1,532 SQ. FT.

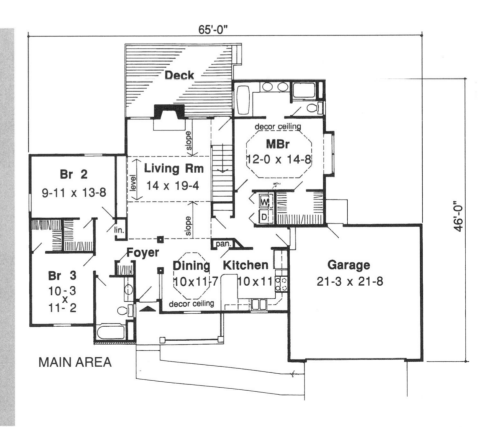

MAIN AREA

An
EXCLUSIVE DESIGN
By Karl Kreeger

PRICE CODE B

FOYER ISOLATES BEDROOM WING

No. 20087

■ This plan features:

— Three bedrooms

— Two full baths

■ A Living Room complete with a window wall, flanking a massive fireplace

■ A Dining Room with recessed ceilings and a pass-through for convenience

■ A Master Suite tucked behind the two-car garage for maximum noise protection

■ A spacious Kitchen with built-ins and access to the two-car garage

MAIN AREA —1,568 SQ. FT.
BASEMENT — 1,568 SQ. FT.
GARAGE — 484 SQ. FT.

TOTAL LIVING AREA:
1,568 SQ. FT.

An
EXCLUSIVE DESIGN
By Karl Kreeger

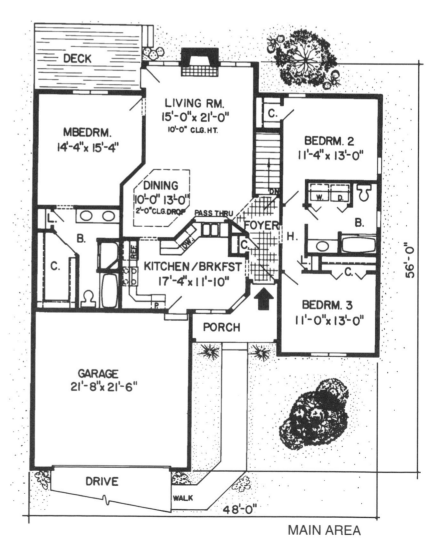

MAIN AREA

PRICE CODE C

FOR THE EMPTY-NESTER

No. 98316

■ This plan features:

— Two bedrooms, possible third

— Two full baths

■ A Great Room with a 13′ ceiling and access to the Lanai

■ An island Kitchen with a built-in pantry, desk, and an open layout to the Breakfast area

■ A Master Suite with his and her walk-in closets and a private Master Bath

■ A Den that can function as a third bedroom

FIRST FLOOR — 1,859 SQ. FT.
GARAGE — 393 SQ. FT.

TOTAL LIVING AREA:
1,859 SQ. FT.

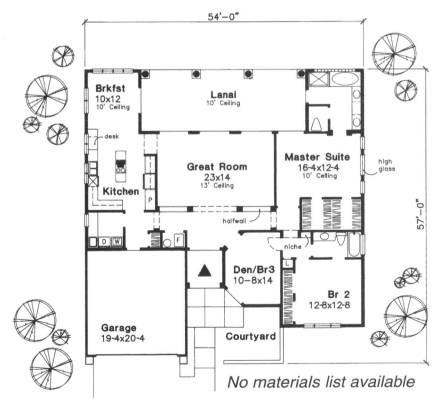

Floor Plan

No materials list available

PRICE CODE A

AFFORDABLE LIVING

No. 24303

This plan features:

— Three bedrooms

— Two full baths

A sheltered entrance into a roomy Living Room, graced with a large front window

A formal Dining Room flowing from the Living Room, allowing for ease in entertaining

A well-appointed U-shaped Kitchen with double sinks and adequate storage

A Master Bedroom equipped with a full Bath

Two additional bedrooms that share a full hall bath complete with a convenient laundry center

A covered Patio, tucked behind the garage, perfect for a cook out or picnic

MAIN AREA — 984 SQ. FT.
BASEMENT — 960 SQ. FT.
GARAGE — 280 SQ. FT.
OPT. 2-CAR GARAGE — 400 SQ. FT.

TOTAL LIVING AREA:
984 SQ. FT.

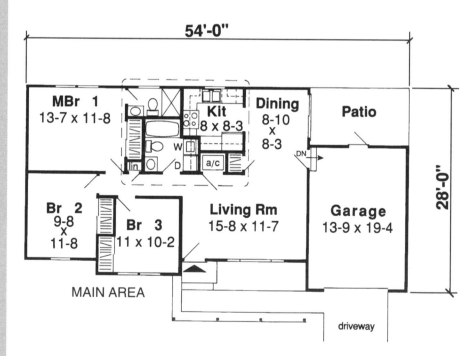

MAIN AREA

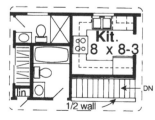

Basement Option

An EXCLUSIVE DESIGN
By Marshall Associates

PRICE CODE A

CHAMPAGNE STYLE ON A SODA-POP BUDGET

No. 24302

■ This plan features:

— Three bedrooms

— Two full baths

■ Multiple gables, circle-top windows, and a unique exterior setting this delightful Ranch apart in any neighborhood

■ Living and Dining Rooms flowing together to create a very roomy feeling

■ Sliding doors leading from the Dining Room to a covered patio

■ A Master Bedroom with a private Bath

MAIN AREA — 988 SQ. FT.
BASEMENT — 988 SQ. FT.
GARAGE — 280 SQ. FT
OPTIONAL 2-CAR GARAGE — 384 SQ. FT.

TOTAL LIVING AREA:
988 SQ. FT.

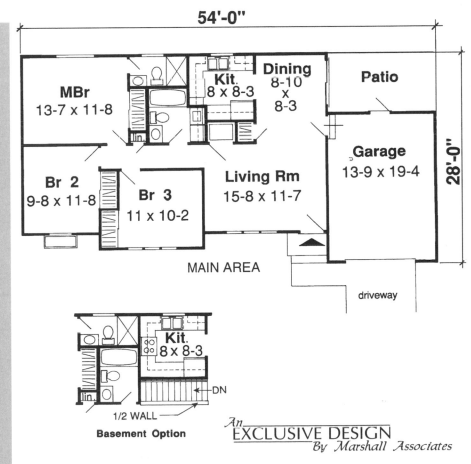

54'-0"

28'-0"

MBr
13-7 x 11-8

Kit.
8 x 8-3

Dining
8-10
x
8-3

Patio

Garage
13-9 x 19-4

Br 2
9-8 x 11-8

Br 3
11 x 10-2

Living Rm
15-8 x 11-7

MAIN AREA

driveway

Kit.
8 x 8-3

DN

1/2 WALL

Basement Option

An
EXCLUSIVE DESIGN
By Marshall Associates

PRICE CODE A

CAPTIVATING SUN-CATCHER

No. 99303

■ This plan features:

— Two bedrooms

— Two full baths

■ A glass-walled Breakfast Room adjoining the vaulted-ceiling Kitchen

■ A fireplaced, vaulted ceiling Living Room that flows from the Dining Room

■ A greenhouse window over the tub in the luxurious Master Bath

■ Two walk-in closets and glass sliders in the Master Bedroom

MAIN AREA — 1,421 SQ. FT.

TOTAL LIVING AREA:
1,421 SQ. FT.

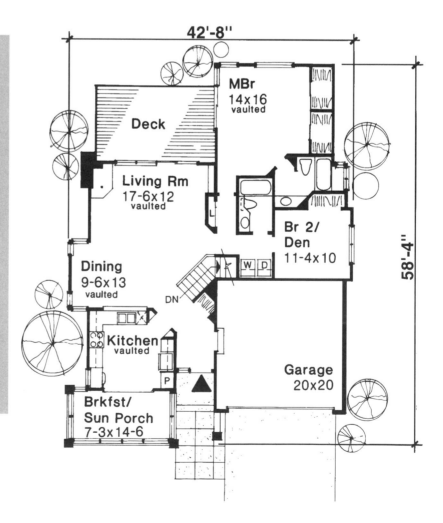

PRICE CODE B

EASY ONE FLOOR LIVING

No. 99216

■ This plan features:

— Three bedrooms

— Two full baths

■ Living areas conveniently grouped in the right half of the home for everyday activities

■ A Gathering Room with a sloped ceiling and a fireplace

■ A Kitchen designed for easy cooking with a closet pantry, plenty of counter space, and cupboards

■ A third bedroom making a perfect home office or study

MAIN AREA — 1,521 SQ. FT.
BASEMENT — 1,521 SQ. FT.

TOTAL LIVING AREA:
1,521 SQ. FT.

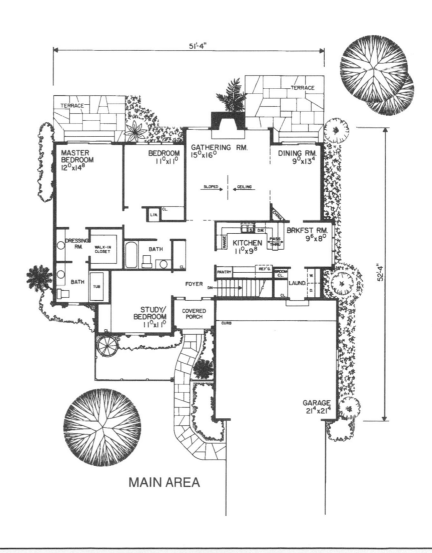

MAIN AREA

PRICE CODE A

DESIGNED FOR INFORMAL LIFE STYLE

No. 90325

■ This plan features:

— Two bedrooms

— One full bath

■ A Great Room and Kitchen accented by vaulted ceilings

■ A conveniently arranged L-shaped food preparation center

■ A Dining Room overlooking a deck through sliding doors

■ A Great Room highlighted by a corner fireplace

■ A Master Bedroom including a separate vanity and dressing area

FIRST FLOOR — 988 SQ. FT.
BASEMENT — 988 SQ. FT.
GARAGE — 400 SQ. FT.

TOTAL LIVING AREA:
988 SQ. FT.

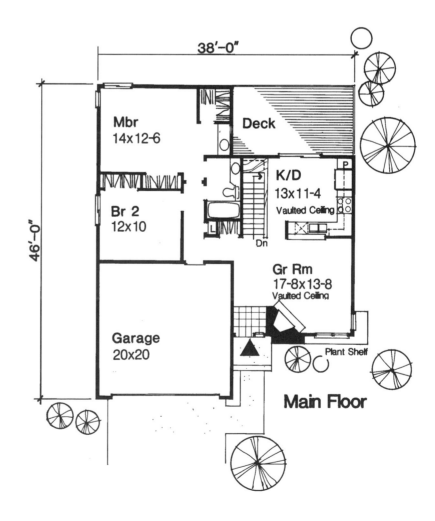

Main Floor

PRICE CODE A

OPEN LIVING AREA, PLUS TRADITIONAL STYLING

No. 90107

■ This plan features:

— Two bedrooms

— Two full baths

■ A Great Room concept that combines the Kitchen, Dining and Living Rooms

■ An efficient U-shaped Kitchen, equipped with a double sink and plenty of cupboard and counter space

■ A Dining Room that has direct access to the rear patio, expanding living spaces in warmer months

■ A Master Bedroom with a walk-in closet and a private bath

■ A second bedroom that has use of the full hall bath

■ A two-car garage with plenty of storage space

■ An optional basement, slab or crawl space foundation — please specify when ordering

MAIN AREA — 1,092 SQ. FT.

**TOTAL LIVING AREA:
1,092 SQ. FT.**

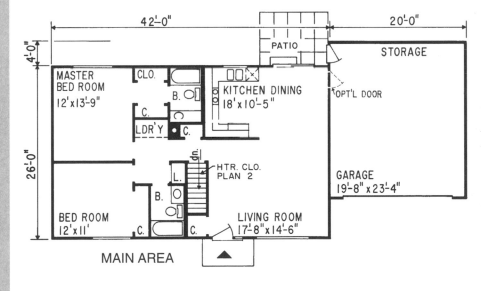

PRICE CODE A

SMALL YET COMFORTABLE HOME

No. 90146

■ This plan features:

— Three bedrooms

— Two full baths

■ A tiled Foyer area with a convenient coat closet

■ A L-shaped open layout between the Living Room and the Dining Room allowing for entertaining ease

■ An eat-in Kitchen with double sinks and adequate counter and storage area

■ A secluded Master Bedroom that includes a full bath

■ An optional basement or crawl space foundation — please specify when ordering

MAIN AREA— 1,500 SQ. FT.

**TOTAL LIVING AREA:
1,500 SQ. FT.**

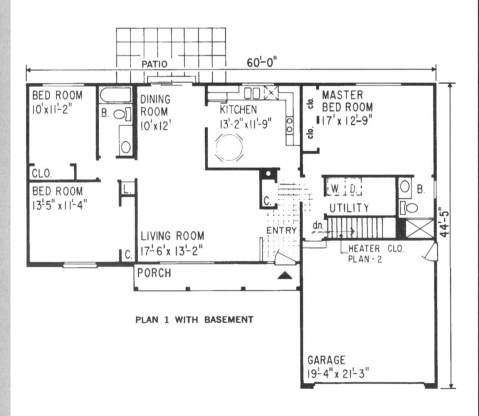

PLAN 1 WITH BASEMENT

PRICE CODE C

FUNCTIONAL FAMILY ROOM

No. 1064

■ This plan features:

— Four bedrooms

— Two full baths

■ Sheltered front porch leading into a tiled Foyer area and a formal Living Room with a bay window

■ Family Room featuring a heat-circulating fireplace flanked by bookshelves, a television shelf and a wood storage area

■ An efficient U-shaped Kitchen with a snack bar adjacent to the Utility Room/Garage and the Family Room

■ A Master Bedroom which offers two closets and a private bath

■ Three additional bedrooms share a full hall bath

MAIN FLOOR — 1,954 SQ . FT.
GARAGE — 431 SQ. FT.

**TOTAL LIVING AREA:
1,954 SQ. FT.**

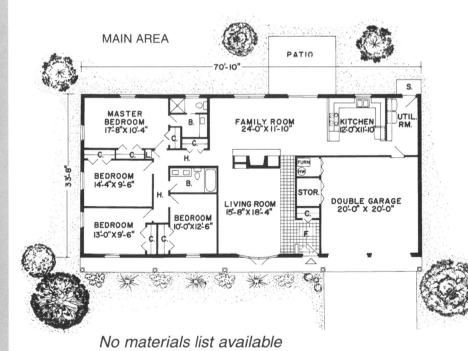

No materials list available

PRICE CODE E

SECLUDED BEDROOM

No. 10451

■ This plan features:

— Four bedrooms

— Three full and one half bath

■ A secluded Master Bedroom with a charming fireplace, individual dressing areas, and a sky-lit bathroom

■ A court yard effect created by the glassed-in living spaces overlooking the central covered patio

FIRST FLOOR — 2,864 SQ. FT.
GARAGE — 607 SQ. FT.

**TOTAL LIVING AREA:
2,864 SQ. FT.**

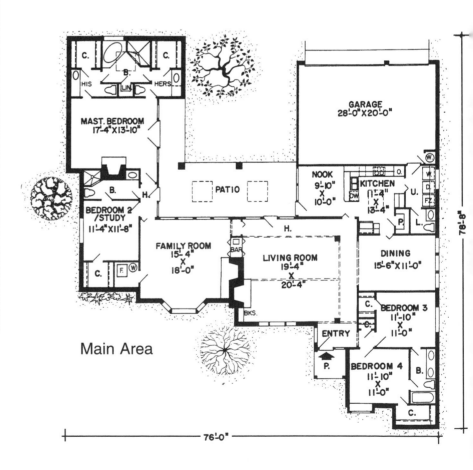

Main Area

PRICE CODE B

YOUR CLASSIC HIDEAWAY

No. 90423

■ This plan features:

— Three bedrooms

— Two full baths

■ A lovely fireplace in the Living Room, which is both cozy and a source of heat for the core area

■ An efficient country Kitchen connecting the large Dining and Living Rooms

■ A lavish Master Suite enhanced by a step-up sunken tub, more than ample closet space, and separate shower

■ A screened porch and patio area for outdoor living

■ An optional basement, slab or crawl space foundation — please specify when ordering

MAIN AREA — 1,773 SQ. FT.
SCREENED PORCH — 240 SQ. FT.

TOTAL LIVING AREA: 1,773 SQ. FT.

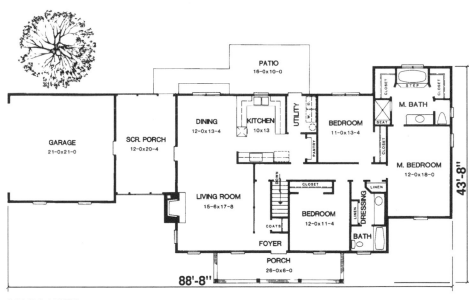

MAIN AREA

PRICE CODE A

COMPACT HOME IS SURPRISINGLY SPACIOUS

No. 90905

This plan features:

— Three bedrooms

— Two full baths

A spacious Living Room warmed by a fireplace

A Dining Room flowing off the Living Room, with sliding glass doors to the deck

An efficient, well-equipped Kitchen with a snack bar, double sink, and ample cabinet and counter space

A Master Suite with a walk-in closet and private full bath

Two additional, roomy bedrooms with ample closet space and protection from street noise from the two-car garage

MAIN AREA — 1,314 SQ. FT.
BASEMENT — 1,488 SQ. FT.
GARAGE — 484 SQ. FT.
WIDTH — 50'-0"
DEPTH — 54'-0"

TOTAL LIVING AREA:
1,314 SQ. FT.

An
EXCLUSIVE DESIGN
By Westhome Planners, Ltd.

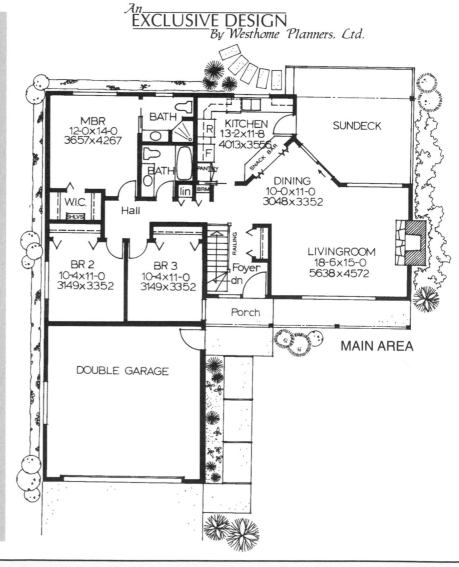

PRICE CODE A

SMALL SCALE, LOTS OF SPACE

No. 90390

■ This plan features:

— Two bedrooms with optional third bedroom/den

— Two full baths

■ Vaulted ceilings and corner windows

■ A Living Room enhanced by a cozy corner fireplace

■ A Master Suite featuring interesting angles and corner window treatments

MAIN AREA — 1,231 SQ. FT.

TOTAL LIVING AREA:
1,231 SQ. FT.

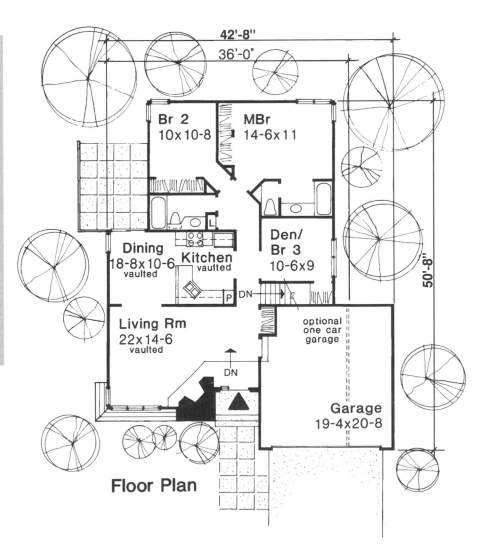

Floor Plan

PRICE CODE B

CAREFREE ONE-LEVEL CONVENIENCE

No. 10674

■ This plan features:

— Three bedrooms

— Two full baths

■ A galley Kitchen, centrally-located between the Dining, Breakfast and Living Room areas

■ A huge Family Room which exits onto the patio

■ The Master Suite with double closets and vanities

MAIN AREA — 1,600 SQ. FT.
GARAGE — 465 SQ. FT.

TOTAL LIVING AREA:
1,600 SQ. FT.

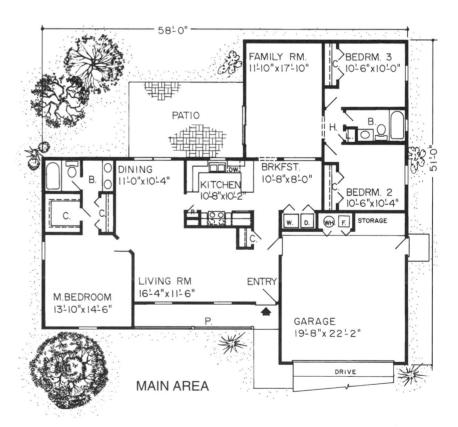

MAIN AREA

PRICE CODE A

AN OPEN CONCEPT HOME

No. 93021

■ This plan features:

— Three bedrooms

— Two full baths

■ An angled Entry creating the illusion of space

■ Two square columns that flank the bar and separate the Kitchen from the Living Room

■ A Dining Room that may service both formal and informal occasions

■ A Master Bedroom with a large walk-in closet

■ A large Master Bath with double vanities, linen closet and whirlpool tub/shower combination

■ Two additional bedrooms that share a full bath

FIRST FLOOR — 1,282 SQ. FT.
GARAGE — 501 SQ. FT.

TOTAL LIVING AREA:
1,282 SQ. FT.

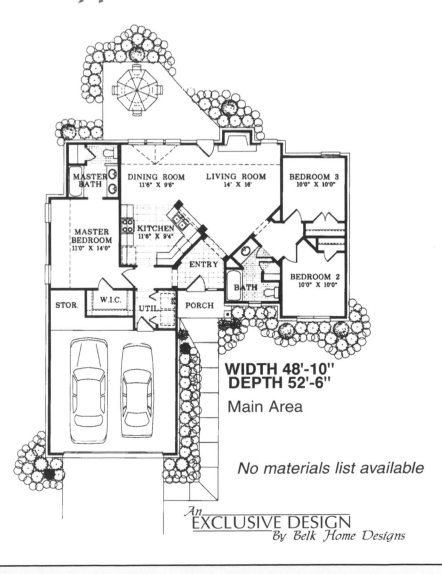

WIDTH 48'-10''
DEPTH 52'-6''

Main Area

No materials list available

An
EXCLUSIVE DESIGN
By Belk Home Designs

PRICE CODE B

CONVENIENT SINGLE LEVEL

No. 84056

■ This plan features:

— Three bedrooms

— Two full baths

■ A well-appointed U-shaped Kitchen that includes a view of the front yard and a built-in pantry

■ An expansive Great Room with direct access to the rear yard, expanding the living space

■ A Master Bedroom equipped with two closets—one is a walk-in— and a private bath

■ Two additional bedrooms that share a full hall bath

■ A step-saving, centrally located laundry center

FIRST FLOOR — 1,644 SQ. FT.
GARAGE — 576 SQ. FT.

**TOTAL LIVING AREA:
1,644 SQ. FT.**

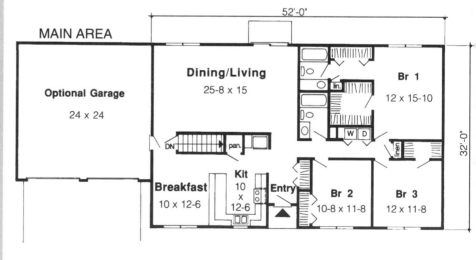

MAIN AREA

Optional Garage
24 x 24

Dining/Living
25-8 x 15

Br 1
12 x 15-10

DN   pan.

Breakfast
10 x 12-6

Kit
10 x 12-6

Entry

Br 2
10-8 x 11-8

Br 3
12 x 11-8

52'-0"

32'-0"

W D   linen   lin.

No materials list available

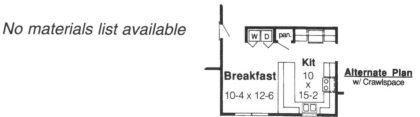

Breakfast
10-4 x 12-6

Kit
10 x 15-2

Alternate Plan
w/ Crawlspace

W D   pan.

PRICE CODE B

COMPACT PLAN ALLOWS FOR GRACIOUS LIVING

No. 90158

■ This plan features:

— Three bedrooms

— Two full baths

■ A Great Room, accessible from the Foyer, offering cathedral ceilings, exposed beams, and a brick fireplace

■ A Kitchen with a center island and cathedral ceiling, accented by a round-top window

■ A Master Bedroom with a full bath and a walk-in closet

■ An optional basement, slab or crawl space foundation — please specify when ordering

MAIN AREA — 1,540 SQ. FT.
BASEMENT — 1,540 SQ. FT.

TOTAL LIVING AREA:
1,540 SQ. FT.

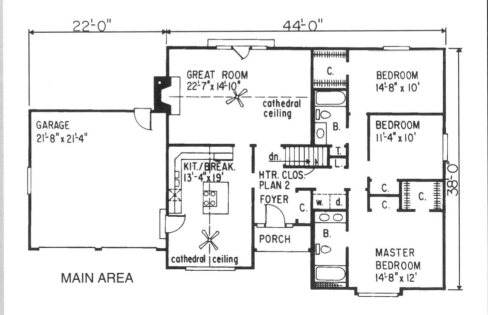

PRICE CODE B

VARIED ROOF HEIGHTS CREATE INTERESTING LINES

No. 90601

■ This plan features:

— Three bedrooms

— Two full baths

■ A spacious Family Room with a heat-circulating fireplace, which is visible from the Foyer

■ A large Kitchen with a cooktop island, opening into the dinette bay

■ A Master Suite with his-n-her closets and a private Master Bath

■ Two additional bedrooms which share a full hall bath

■ Formal Dining and Living Rooms, flowing into each other for easy entertaining

MAIN AREA — 1,613 SQ. FT.

**TOTAL LIVING AREA:
1,613 SQ. FT.**

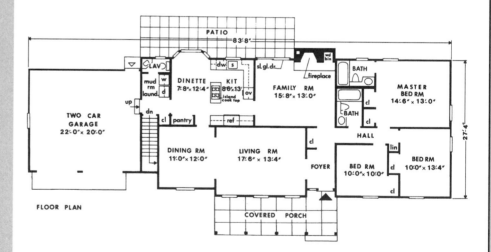

FLOOR PLAN

PRICE CODE A

HIGH IMPACT ANGLES

No. 90357

- This plan features:
  — Three bedrooms
  — Two full baths
- Soaring ceilings to give the house a spacious, contemporary feeling
- A fireplaced Great Room adjoining a convenient Kitchen, with a sunny Breakfast Nook
- Sliding glass doors opening onto an angular deck
- A Master Suite with vaulted ceilings and a private bath

MAIN AREA — 1,368 SQ. FT.

**TOTAL LIVING AREA:
1,368 SQ. FT.**

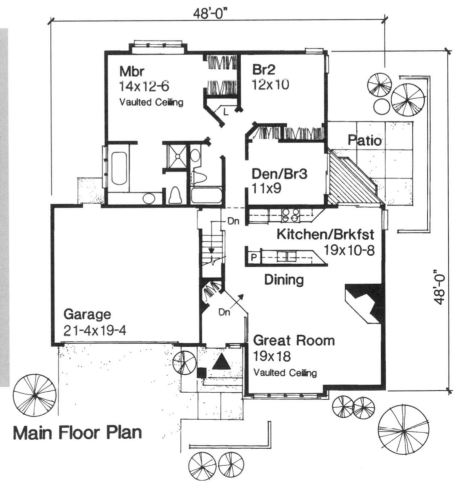

Main Floor Plan

PRICE CODE C

BEAMED CEILING ACCENTS FAMILY ROOM

No. 10465

■ This plan features:

— Four bedrooms

— Three full baths

■ A Family Room accentuated by a beamed ceiling, built-in bookcase, and a large fireplace

■ A Dining Room easily accessible from the efficient Kitchen

■ A Master Bedroom located along the opposite side of the home, with its own bath and spacious walk-in closets

FIRST FLOOR — 2,144 SQ. FT.
GARAGE — 483 SQ. FT.

TOTAL LIVING AREA:
2,144 SQ. FT.

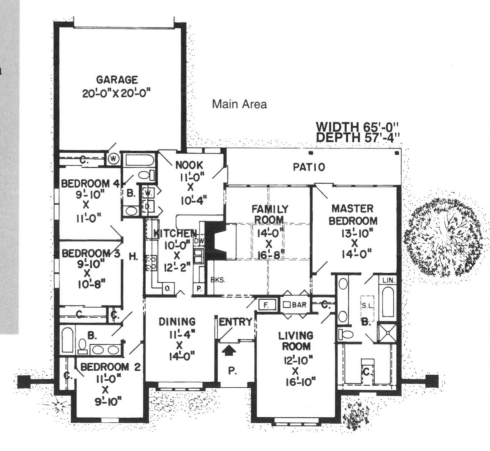

PRICE CODE B

TURRET DINING VIEWS

No. 93061

This plan features:

— Three bedrooms

— Two full baths

Front Porch and Entry lead into the Dining and Great Rooms

Expansive Great Room with a focal point fireplace and access to the rear yard

Angled counter with an eating bar and a built-in pantry in the Kitchen easily serves the Breakfast area, the Great Room and the outdoors

Comfortable Master Bedroom and Bath with a corner whirlpool tub, a double vanity and a huge walk-in closet

Two additional bedrooms with oversized closets, share a full bath

This plan is available with a Slab or Crawlspace foundation — please specify when ordering

MAIN FLOOR — 1,742 SQ. FT.
GARAGE — 566 SQ. FT.

TOTAL LIVING AREA:
1,742 SQ. FT.

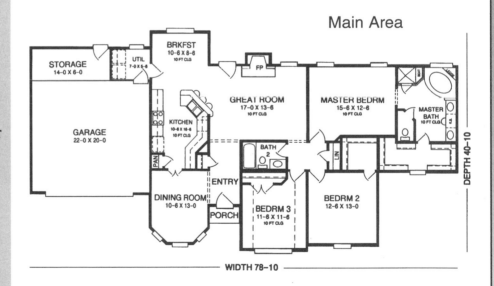

Main Area

An
EXCLUSIVE DESIGN
By Belk Home Designs

PRICE CODE C

RANCH OFFERS ATTRACTIVE WINDOW FACADE

An
EXCLUSIVE DESIGN
By Karl Kreeger

No. 10569

■ This plan features:

— Four bedrooms

— Three full baths

■ A Living Room with sloping, open-beamed ceilings and a fireplace with built-in bookshelves

■ A Dining Room with a vaulted ceiling, adding a feeling of spaciousness

■ A Master Bath with ample closet space and a private bath

■ A two-car garage

FIRST FLOOR — 1,840 SQ. FT.
BASEMENT — 1,803 SQ. FT.
GARAGE — 445 SQ. FT.

**TOTAL LIVING AREA:
1,840 SQ. FT.**

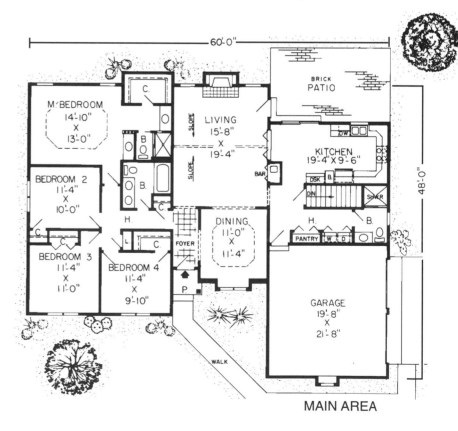

MAIN AREA

PRICE CODE B

SPANISH INSPIRATION

No. 90069

■ This plan features:

— Three bedrooms

— Two full baths

■ Spanish exterior with stucco walls, a heavy oak door, clay-top chimneys, arched garage doors and rugged wood beams

■ Central Foyer leads to the Living/Dining Room with a sliding glass door to the Patio, topped by a cathedral ceiling with exposed wood beams

■ Combination Family Room/Kitchen with a peninsula counter and a sliding glass door to the Patio

■ Secluded Master Bedroom with a walk-in closet and a private bath convenient to the laundry

■ Two additional bedroom share a full bath

■ This plan is available with a Basement or Slab foundation — please specify when ordering

MAIN FLOOR — 1,550 SQ. FT.
GARAGE — 440 SQ. FT.

TOTAL LIVING AREA:
1,550 SQ. FT.

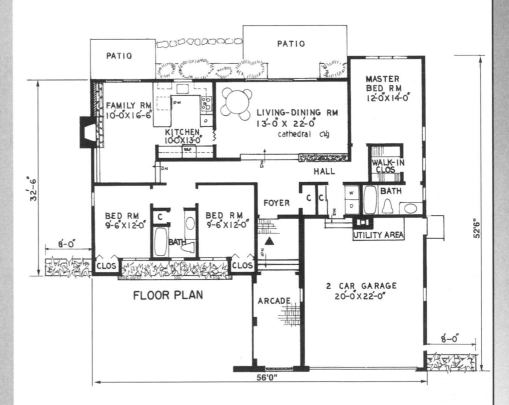

PATIO

PATIO

FAMILY RM
10'-0"X16'-6"

KITCHEN
10'-0"X13'-0"

LIVING-DINING RM
13'-0" X 22'-0"
cathedral clg

MASTER BED RM
12'-0"X14'-0"

WALK-IN CLOS

HALL

BATH

BED RM
9'-6"X12'-0"

BATH

BED RM
9'-6"X12'-0"

FOYER

C C

UTILITY AREA

CLOS

CLOS

32'-6"

8'-0"

FLOOR PLAN

ARCADE

2 CAR GARAGE
20'-0"X22'-0"

52'6"

8'-0"

56'0"

PRICE CODE A

SLOPED CEILINGS ENHANCE OPEN FLOOR PLAN

No. 90125

■ This plan features:

— Three bedrooms

— Two full baths

■ A step down into the tiled entrance area

■ An open Great Room and Living Room enhanced by sloping ceilings, cozy fireplace, and sliding doors to back patio

■ An L shaped Kitchen sharing snack bar with Dining Room

■ An optional basement or crawlspace foundation — please specify when ordering

MAIN AREA — 1,440 SQ. FT.

TOTAL LIVING AREA:
1,440 SQ. FT.

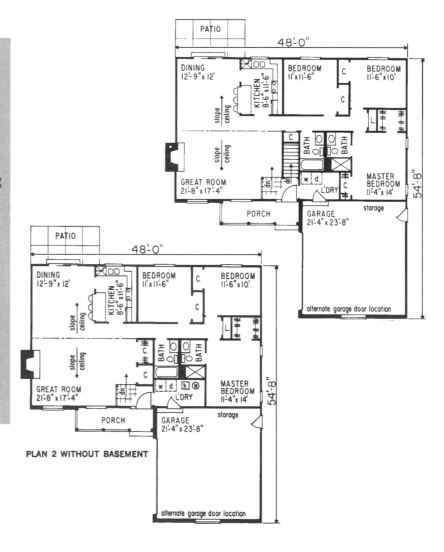

PRICE CODE A

EXTRA LARGE FAMILY KITCHEN IN COZY THREE BEDROOM

No. 90134

■ This plan features:

— Three bedrooms

— One full and one half baths

■ A sheltered porch providing a protected entrance

■ An extra large Kitchen, with a galley-style food preparation area, separated from the rest of the room by an eating bar

■ Three bedrooms clustered around the full bath

■ A large outdoor storage area built into the back of the carport

■ An optional basement, slab or crawl space foundation — please specify when ordering

MAIN AREA — 1,120 SQ. FT.

TOTAL LIVING AREA:
1,120 SQ. FT.

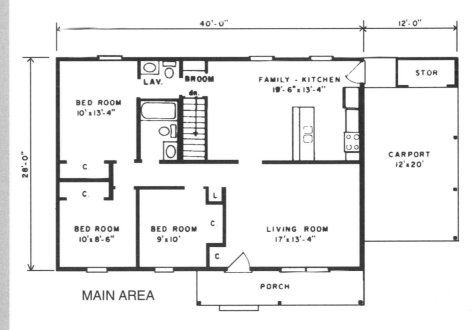

PRICE CODE A

DECORATIVE CEILINGS ADD DISTINCTION

No. 93134

This plan features:

— Three bedrooms

— Two full baths

Sheltered entrance and tiled Foyer lead into spacious Living Room with cathedral ceiling and hearth fireplace

Formal Dining Room opens to Living Room and accesses yard

Efficient, Eat-in Kitchen handy to Dining Room, Laundry, and Garage entrance

Master Bedroom suite accented by tray ceiling, walk-in closet and private bath

Two additional bedrooms with ample closets and window seats, share full bath

Central stairs to lower level offering many options

MAIN FLOOR — 1,387 SQ. FT.
BASEMENT — 1,387 SQ. FT.
GARAGE — 482 SQ. FT.
FOUNDATION — BASEMENT ONLY

**TOTAL LIVING AREA:
1,387 SQ. FT.**

No materials list available

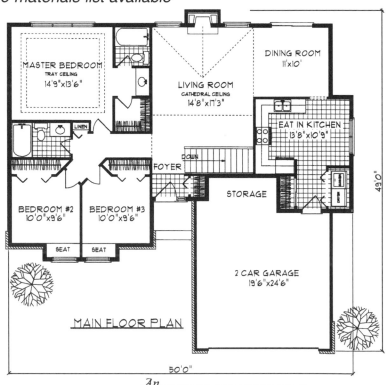

MAIN FLOOR PLAN

An
EXCLUSIVE DESIGN
By Ahmann Design Inc.

PRICE CODE C

OPEN, ONE-LEVEL FLOOR PLAN

No. 91084

■ This plan features:

— Three bedrooms

— Two full baths

■ A transom window and sidelights illuminating the entry

■ A multi-direction Foyer is complimented by a large, see-through fireplace

■ A formal Living Room and Dining Room makes home entertaining easy

■ A U-shaped Kitchen with a convenient bar sink and corner views

■ A Master Bedroom with a double door entry and a large bath suite, complete with separate shower and spa tub

■ A second bedroom with a built-in desk and window

MAIN LIVING AREA — 1,889 SQ. FT.

TOTAL LIVING AREA: 1,889 SQ. FT.

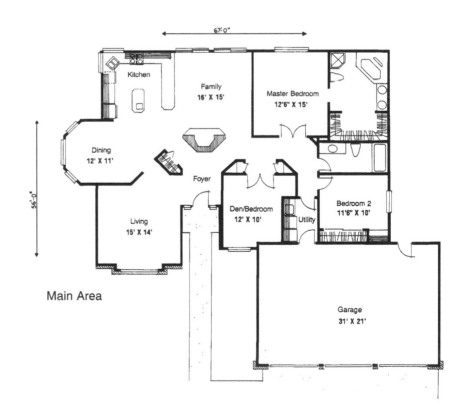

Main Area

PRICE CODE C

No. 93031

This plan features:

— Three bedrooms

— Two full baths

A traditional Southern elevation with an Entry flanked by large square columns and dominated by a gable finished with dentil molding

An angled Foyer which opens the home to a large Great Room with a fireplace

A Master Suite that is entered through double doors, and is privately located away from the other bedrooms

A Master Bath with an angled whirlpool tub, separate shower and double vanities

A Kitchen with a pantry and plenty of cabinet and counter space

A coffered ceiling treatment in the Breakfast Room which adds character

FIRST FLOOR — 1,955 SQ. FT.

**TOTAL LIVING AREA:
1,955 SQ. FT.**

ELEGANT COLUMNED ENTRY

Main Area

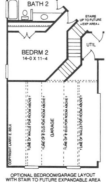

OPTIONAL BEDROOM/GARAGE LAYOUT
WITH STAIR TO FUTURE EXPANDABLE AREA

An
EXCLUSIVE DESIGN
By Belk Home Designs

No materials list available

PRICE CODE B

No. 90986

This plan features:

— Three bedrooms

— Two full baths

An Italian style, featuring columns and tile originally designed to sit on the edge of a golf course

■ An open design with panoramic vistas in every direction

■ Tile used from the Foyer, into the Kitchen and Nook, as well as in the Utility Room

■ A whirlpool tub in the elaborate and spacious Master Bedroom suite

■ A Great Room with a corner gas fireplace

■ A turreted Breakfast Nook and an efficient Kitchen with peninsula counter

■ Two family bedrooms that share a full hall bath

MAIN AREA — 1,731 SQ. FT.
GARAGE — 888 SQ. FT.
WIDTH — 74'-0"
DEPTH — 45'-0"

TOTAL LIVING AREA:
1,731 SQ. FT.

SURROUNDED WITH SUNSHINE

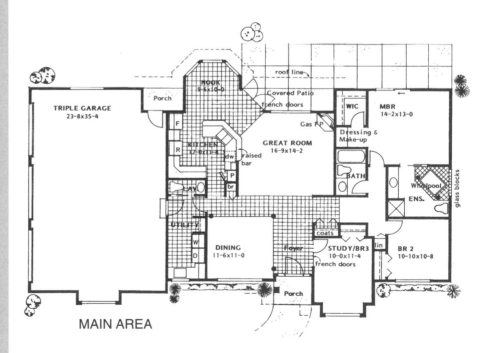

MAIN AREA

An
EXCLUSIVE DESIGN
By Westhome Planners, Ltd.

PRICE CODE B

CONTEMPORARY CONVENIENCE

No. 20008

■ This plan features:

— Three bedrooms

— Two full baths

■ A Living Room with vaulted ceilings and a fireplace

■ A Master Suite with vaulted ceilings, walk-in closet and the privacy of a Master Bath

■ An open Kitchen with a Breakfast Bay arrangement

FIRST FLOOR — 1,545 SQ. FT.
BASEMENT — 1,545 SQ. FT.
GARAGE — 396 SQ. FT.

TOTAL LIVING AREA:
1,545 SQ. FT.

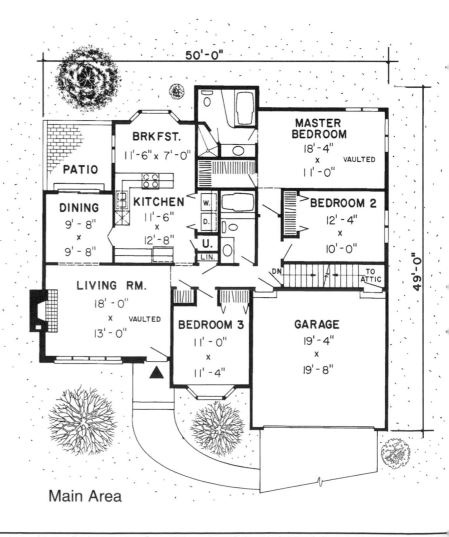

Main Area

PRICE CODE D

MASTER BEDROOM MERITS DECK

No. 10270

■ This plan features:

— Three bedrooms

— Two and one half baths

■ A large eat-in Kitchen with easy access to a step-saving Laundry Room

■ A Work Shop for the hobbyist

■ Two appealing rear decks and a basement terrace

FIRST FLOOR — 2,202 SQ. FT.
BASEMENT — 2,016 SQ. FT.
GARAGE & WORKSHOP — 677 SQ. FT.

TOTAL LIVING AREA:
2,202 SQ. FT.

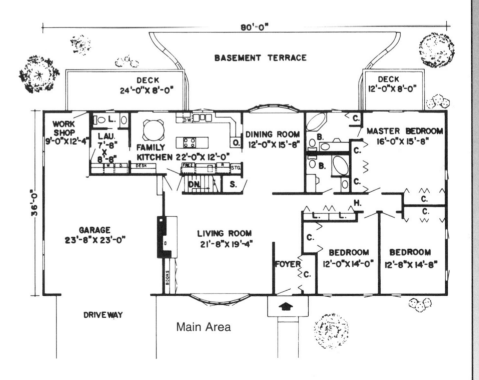

PRICE CODE A

FORMAL BALANCE

No. 90689

■ This plan features:

— Three bedrooms

— Two full baths

■ A cathedral ceiling in the Living Room with a heat-circulating fireplace as the focal point

■ A bow window in the Dining Room that adds elegance as well as natural light

■ A well-equipped Kitchen that serves both the Dinette and the formal Dining Room efficiently

■ A Master Bedroom with three closets and a private Master Bath with sliding glass doors to the Master Deck with a hot tub

FIRST FLOOR — 1,374 SQ. FT.
MUDROOM/LAUNDRY — 102 SQ. FT.
BASEMENT — 1,361 SQ. FT.
GARAGE — 548 SQ. FT.

TOTAL LIVING AREA:
1,476 SQ. FT.

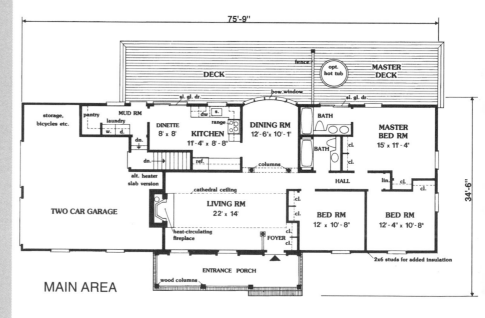

MAIN AREA

PRICE CODE F

A CELEBRATION OF TRADITIONAL ELEMENTS

No. 10749

■ This plan features:

— Four bedrooms

— Two full and two half baths

■ High ceilings with cooling fans and loads of built-in storage

■ Every bedroom adjoining a bath and the Master Suite enjoying access to the outdoor deck

■ A massive fireplace located the roomy Family Room

■ A Kitchen, Breakfast area, Sewing room, Dining Room and pantry all located within steps of each other for convenience

FIRST FLOOR — 3,438 SQ. FT.
GARAGE — 610 SQ. FT.

**TOTAL LIVING AREA:
3,438 SQ. FT.**

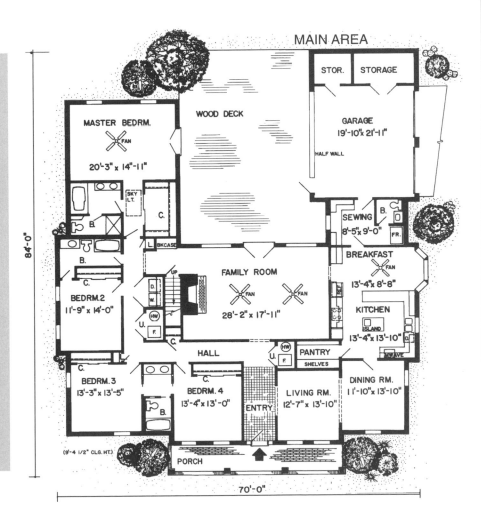

MAIN AREA

PRICE CODE E

SUPERIOR COMFORT AND PRIVACY

No. 9828

■ This plan features:

— Four bedrooms

— Three full baths

■ A natural stone exterior with slate floors in the Foyer and leading to the private patio off the Master Bedroom

■ A two-way fireplace between the Living Room and Family Room

■ A Breakfast Nook with a large bow window facing the terrace and pool

■ Four bedrooms grouped in one wing for privacy

FIRST FLOOR — 2,679 SQ. FT.
BASEMENT — 2,679 SQ. FT.
GARAGE — 541 SQ. FT.

TOTAL LIVING AREA: 2,679 SQ. FT.

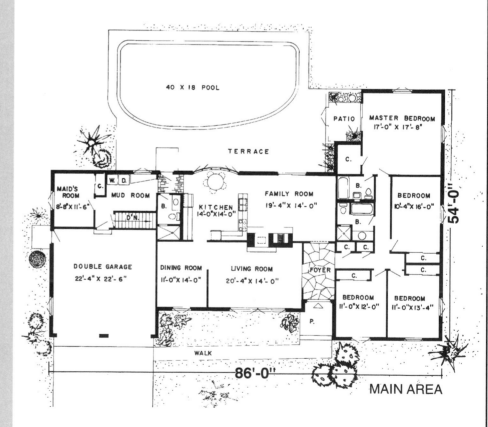

MAIN AREA

PRICE CODE B

INSPIRED BY COUNTRY PORCHES OF OLD

No. 20211

■ This plan features:

— Three bedrooms

— Two full baths

Decorative and sloped ceilings

A large country Kitchen with a central island, double sink, pantry, ample cabinet and counter space and access to deck

A Master Suite with a decorative ceiling, walk-in closet and a private Master Bath

A decorative Dining Room ceiling

A central fireplace in the sloped ceilinged Living Room, providing a focal point and adding warmth to the room

Two additional bedrooms that share use of a full hall bath

MAIN AREA — 1,609 SQ. FT.
GARAGE — 707 SQ. FT.
BASEMENT — 902 SQ. FT.

**TOTAL LIVING AREA:
1,609 SQ. FT.**

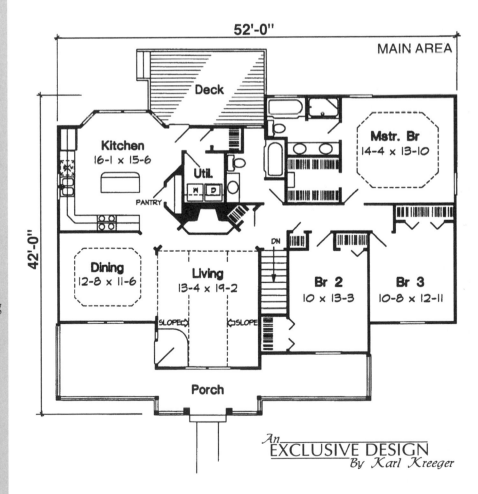

An
EXCLUSIVE DESIGN
By Karl Kreeger

PRICE CODE B

CAREFREE COMFORT

No. 91418

This plan features:

— Three bedrooms

— Two full baths

A dramatic vaulted Foyer

A range top island Kitchen with a sunny eating Nook surrounded by a built-in planter

A vaulted ceiling in the Great Room with a built-in bar and corner fireplace

A bayed Dining Room that combines with the Great Room for a spacious feeling

A Master Bedroom with a private reading nook, vaulted ceiling, walk-in closet, and a well-appointed private Bath

Two additional bedrooms sharing a full hall bath

MAIN AREA — 1,665 SQ. FT.
GARAGE — 2-CAR

**TOTAL LIVING AREA:
1,665 SQ. FT.**

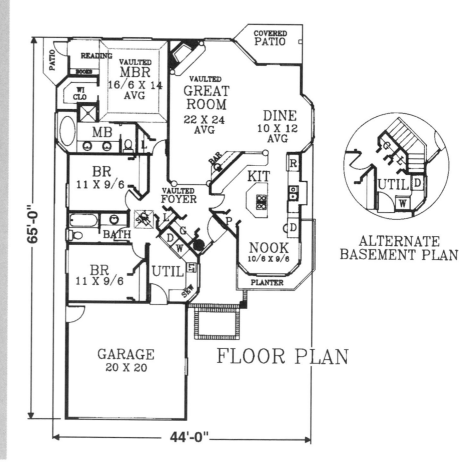

FLOOR PLAN

ALTERNATE
BASEMENT PLAN

PRICE CODE C

MASTER BEDROOM SUITE ACCENTUATES LUXURY

No. 9870

- ■ This plan features:
- — Three bedrooms
- — Two and one half baths
- ■ A French Provincial design adorned with pillars and a bow window
- ■ The Kitchen centered between a laundry room and Kitchen Nook for added convenience
- ■ A spacious Family Room which opens to the terrace
- ■ A Master Bedroom complete with a full bath and sitting room placed to allow full privacy

FIRST FLOOR — 2,015 SQ. FT.
BASEMENT — 2,015 SQ. FT.
GARAGE — 545 SQ. FT.

**TOTAL LIVING AREA:
2,015 SQ. FT.**

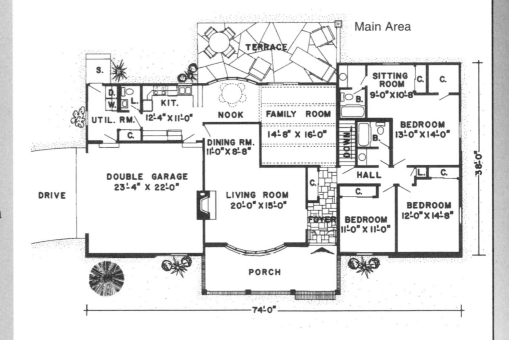

Main Area

TERRACE

S.

UTIL. RM.

KIT.
12'-4" X 11'-0"

NOOK

FAMILY ROOM
14'-8" X 16'-0"

SITTING ROOM
9'-0" X 10'-8"

BEDROOM
13'-0" X 14'-0"

DINING RM.
11'-0" X 8'-8"

DOUBLE GARAGE
23'-4" X 22'-0"

LIVING ROOM
20'-0" X 15'-0"

HALL

DRIVE

DOWN

BEDROOM
12'-0" X 14'-8"

FOYER

BEDROOM
11'-0" X 11'-0"

PORCH

38'-0"

74'-0"

PRICE CODE C

UNDERGROUND DELIGHT

No. 10376

■ This plan features:

— Three bedrooms

— Two full baths

■ A design that aids against the high cost of living, through many energy-saving features including the use of passive solar energy

■ Sliding glass doors leading to the front lawn from all three bedrooms

■ A large eat-in Kitchen open to the Family Room and near the Utility Room

■ Added features including a greenhouse, Sewing Room and Jacuzzi in the Master Bathroom

FIRST FLOOR — 2,086 SQ. FT.

TOTAL LIVING AREA: 2,086 SQ. FT

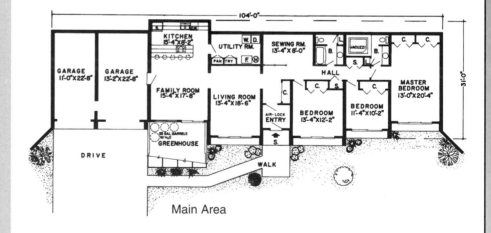

Main Area

PRICE CODE B

CAREFREE CONTEMPORARY

No. 90697

■ This plan features:

— Three bedrooms

— Two full baths

■ A corner fireplace adding intrigue to the sunny Living Room

■ Skylights in the high sloping ceiling of the Family Room, which also has a greenhouse bay window and a heat-circulating fireplace

■ An elegant formal Dining Room with a window alcove

■ A Master Bedroom with a private Master Bath and two closets

■ Two additional bedrooms which share a full hall bath

MAIN AREA — 1,597 SQ. FT.
BASEMENT — 1,512 SQ. FT.

TOTAL LIVING AREA:
1,597 SQ. FT.

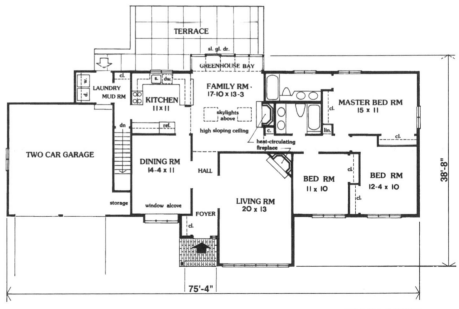

MAIN AREA

PRICE CODE B

STATELY ELEGANCE

No. 20506

■ This plan features:

— Three bedrooms

— Two full baths

■ Columned Foyer with a barrel vaulted ceiling

■ Showcase sunken Living Room with a fireplace and high stepped ceiling

■ Elegant columned Dining Room, with stepped ceiling open to the Foyer and the Living Room, and swinging doors to the Kitchen

■ Large L-shaped Kitchen, with stove top island, windowed double sink, ample counter and storage space, and access to Utility/Laundry Room

■ Secondary bedrooms with private door to compartmented full bath

■ Third Bedroom or Study with stepped ceiling

MAIN AREA — 1,778 SQ. FT.
GARAGE — 419 SQ. FT.

**TOTAL LIVING AREA:
1,778 SQ. FT.**

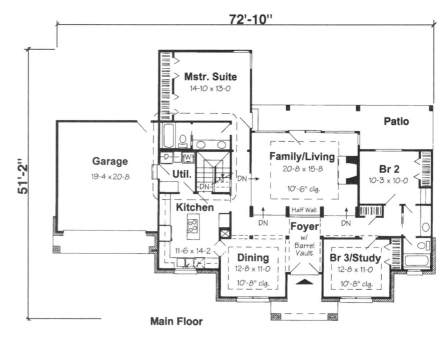

Main Floor

Alternate Crawl
Space/Slab Option

No materials list available

PRICE CODE A

Have it all

No. 20139

■ This plan features:

— Three bedrooms

— Two full baths

■ A classic brick and clapboard exterior adorned with an old-fashioned a window

■ An elegant Living Room with a fireplace flowing into a formal Dining Room with sliders to a rear deck

■ A compact Kitchen opening to the Dining Room for a spacious feel

■ A well-appointed Master Suite with ample closet space and a four-piece private bath

First floor — 1,488 sq. ft.
Basement — 1,488 sq. ft.
Garage — 484 sq. ft.

Total living area:
1,488 sq. ft.

Deck

Br 3
10 x 10

Dining
11 x 15

Kit
10 x 11-8

MBr 1
13 x 13-4

7-1/2" ceiling reveal

slope

plant shelf above

skylight

lin.

W
D

DN

Br 2
12-8 x 10-4

Living Rm
12-10 x 19-6

9'-0" ceiling height

Garage
21-4 x 22-2

42'-0"

First Floor

54'-0"

An
EXCLUSIVE DESIGN
By Karl Kreeger

PRICE CODE A

No. 20215

This plan features:

— Two bedrooms

— Two full baths

Front facade highlighted by a box window topped with a sunburst decoration

Covered entrance leads into the Living Room with a hearth fireplace and a double window overlooking the Deck

Dining Room offers a lovely bay window and access to the Deck

Efficient Kitchen with a built-in pantry and a peninsula counter/snackbar

Private Master Bedroom with a double window offers a large walk-in closet, a double vanity and a whirlpool tub

This plan is available with a basement, slab, or crawlspace foundation. Please specify when ordering.

MAIN FLOOR — 1,428 SQ. FT.
BASEMENT — 1,428 SQ. FT.
GARAGE — 528 SQ. FT.

TOTAL LIVING AREA:
1,428 SQ. FT.

QUIET DINING WITH A VIEW

No materials list available

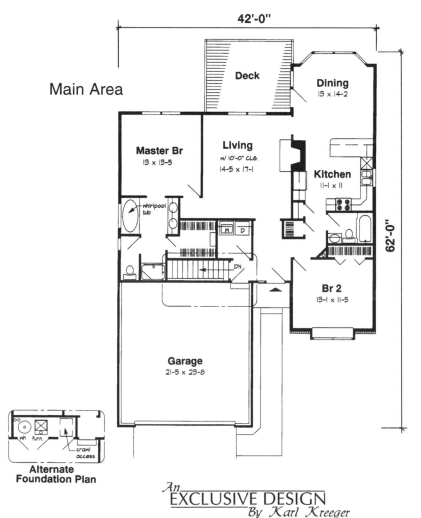

An EXCLUSIVE DESIGN *By Karl Kreeger*

PRICE CODE C

COZY TRADITIONAL

No. 93000

■ This plan features:

— Three bedrooms

— Two full baths

■ An angled eating bar separating the Kitchen, Breakfast Room and Great Room, while leaving these areas open for easy entertaining

■ An efficient, well-appointed Kitchen that is convenient to both the formal Dining Room and the sunny Breakfast Room

■ A spacious Master Suite with oval tub, step-in shower, double vanity and walk-in closet

■ Two additional bedrooms with ample closet space that share a full hall bath

FIRST FLOOR — 1,862 SQ. FT.
GARAGE — 520 SQ. FT.

TOTAL LIVING AREA:
1,862 SQ. FT.

No materials list available

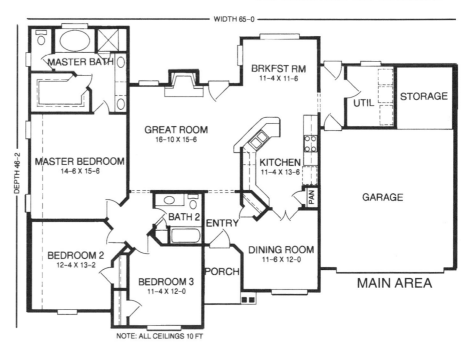

An EXCLUSIVE DESIGN
By Belk Home Designs

PRICE CODE B

FOR THE DISCRIMINATING BUYER

No. 92625

This plan features:

— Three bedrooms

— Two full baths

An attractive, classic brick design, with wood trim, multiple gables, and wing walls

A sheltered entrance into the Foyer

A sloped ceiling adding elegance to the formal Dining Room

A sloped ceiling and a corner fireplace enhancing the Great Room

A peninsula counter in the Kitchen and the Breakfast Room

A Master Suite equipped with a large walk-in closet and a private bath with an oval corner tub, separate shower and double vanity

Two additional bedrooms

MAIN AREA — 1,710 SQ. FT.
BASEMENT — 1,560 SQ. FT.
GARAGE — 455 SQ. FT.
WIDTH — 65'-10"
DEPTH — 56'-0"

TOTAL LIVING AREA:
1,710 SQ. FT.

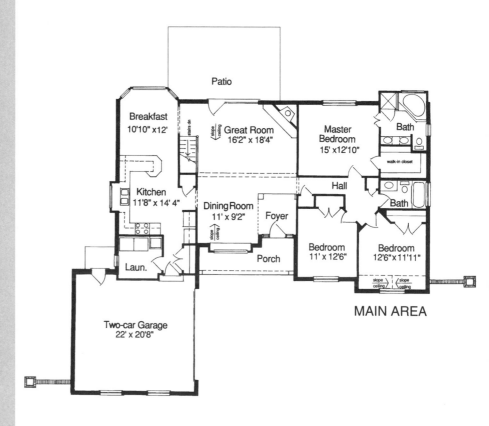

MAIN AREA

No materials list available

PRICE CODE C

PLUSH MASTER BEDROOM WING

No. 92705

■ This plan features:

— Three bedrooms

— Two full baths

■ A raised, tile Foyer with a decorative window leading into an expansive Living Room, accented by a tiled fireplace and framed by French doors

■ An efficient Kitchen with a walk-in pantry and serving bar adjoining the Breakfast and Utility areas

■ A private Master Bedroom, crowned by a stepped ceiling, offering an atrium door to outside, a huge, walk-in closet and a luxurious bath

MAIN FLOOR — 1,849 SQ. FT.
GARAGE — 437 SQ. FT.

**TOTAL LIVING AREA:
1,849 SQ. FT.**

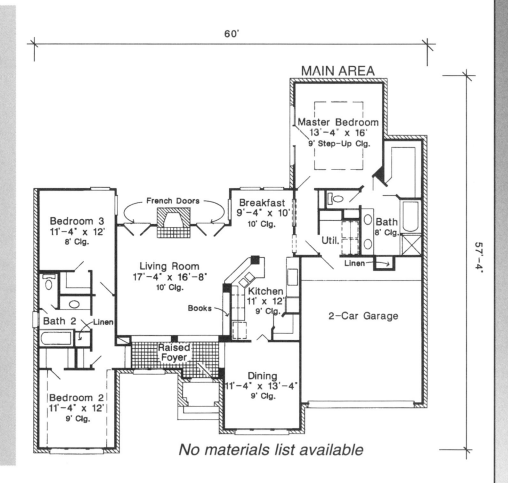

No materials list available

PRICE CODE C

CHARMING BRICK HOME

No. 93107

- This plan features:
— Three bedrooms
— Two full baths

- A covered entrance leading into a spacious Living Room with a fireplace and an airy Dining Room with access to the Patio

- An island Kitchen, open to the Dining Room, offering ample storage and easy access to theLaundry area and the Garage

- A Master Bedroom with a walk-in closet, access to the Patio and a plush bath offering a window tub, a step-in shower and a double vanity

- Two additional bedrooms, with decorative windows, sharing a full hall bath

MAIN FLOOR — 1,868 SQ. FT.
BASEMENT — 1,868 SQ. FT.

TOTAL LIVING AREA:
1,868 SQ. FT.

No materials list available

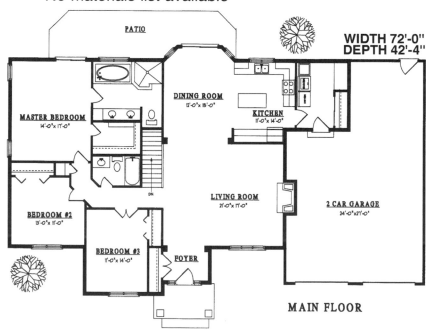

WIDTH 72'-0''
DEPTH 42'-4''

MAIN FLOOR

An EXCLUSIVE DESIGN
By Ahmann Design Inc.

PRICE CODE B

STYLISH SINGLE-LEVEL

No. 93100

■ This plan features:

— Three bedrooms

— Two full and one half baths

■ A well-appointed, U-shaped Kitchen separated from the Dining Room by a peninsula counter

■ A spacious Living Room, enhanced by a focal point fireplace

■ An elegant Dining Room with a bay window that opens to a screen porch, expanding living space

■ A Master Suite with a walk-in closet and private Master Bath

■ Two family bedrooms that share a full hall bath

MAIN AREA — 1,642 SQ. FT.
GARAGE — 591 SQ. FT.
BASEMENT — 1,642 SQ. FT.

TOTAL LIVING AREA:
1,642 SQ. FT.

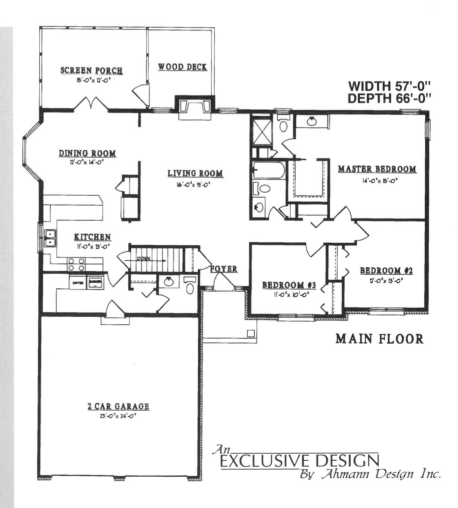

WIDTH 57'-0"
DEPTH 66'-0"

MAIN FLOOR

An
EXCLUSIVE DESIGN
By *Ahmann Design Inc.*

PRICE CODE G

No. 24244

This plan features (per unit):

— Three bedrooms

— Two full baths

Friendly front Porch that leads into the Dining area accented by arches

A Sloped ceiling above a decorative window and an atrium door to the Deck highlight the Living area

Compact, but open Kitchen easily serves the Dining and Living areas

Master Bedroom offers a walk-in closet and a double vanity bath

Two additional bedrooms with ample closets share a full bath

This plan is available with a Basement, Slab, or Crawlspace foundation. Please specify when ordering

MAIN FLOOR (PER UNIT) — 1,430 SQ. FT.
GARAGE (LEFT PER UNIT) — 338 SQ. FT.
GARAGE (RIGHT PER UNIT) — 310 SQ. FT.

TOTAL LIVING AREA: 1,430 SQ. FT.

DUPLEX FOR DOUBLE LIVING SPACE

Alternate Slab/ Crawl Space Option Left Unit

Alternate Slab/ Crawl Space Option Right Unit

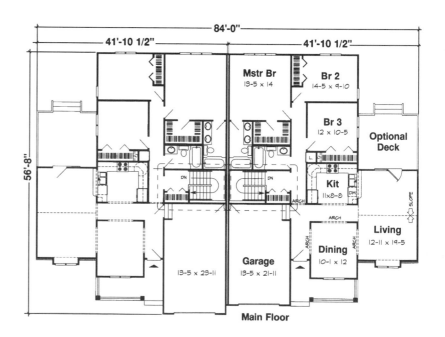

Main Floor

PRICE CODE A

Amenity packed with affordability

No. 92525

■ This plan features:

— Three bedrooms

— Two full baths

■ A sheltered entrance inviting your guests onward

■ A fireplace in the Den offering a focal point, while the decorative ceiling adds definition to the room

■ A well-equipped Kitchen flowing with ease into the Breakfast bay or Dining Room

■ A Master Bedroom, having two closets and a private Master Bath

MAIN AREA — 1,484 SQ. FT.

TOTAL LIVING AREA:
1,484 SQ. FT.

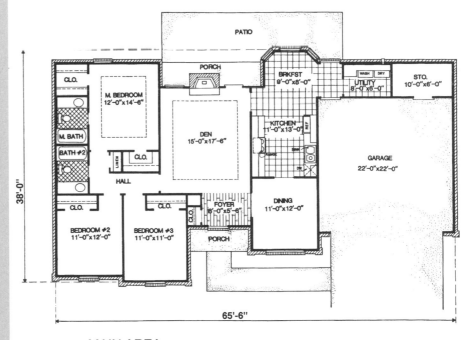

MAIN AREA

PRICE CODE C

No. 20504

■ This plan features:

— Two or three bedrooms

— Three full baths

■ Eye-catching octagon room with arched windows accents the sheltered front entrance

■ Open Living/Dining area with a cozy fireplace and built-in shelves below the decorative ceiling, and an atrium door to the Patio

■ Efficient Kitchen with a walk-in pantry, an island cooktop/snack bar, and a Nook

■ Private Master Bedroom with a vaulted ceiling, an atrium door to the Patio, a dressing area with two walk-in closets, and a raised whirlpool tub

■ Third bedroom with an oversized closet and a full bath

■ This plan is available with a slab or a crawlspace foundation. Please specify when ordering

MAIN FLOOR — 1,958 SQ. FT.
GARAGE — 405 SQ. FT.

**TOTAL LIVING AREA:
1,958 SQ. FT.**

DISTINCTIVE STYLE AND PRIVACY

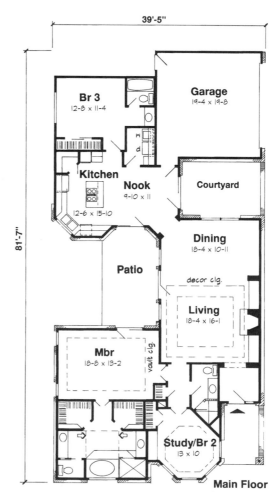

39'-5"

81'-7"

Br 3
12-8 x 11-4

Garage
19-4 x 19-8

Kitchen
12-6 x 15-10

Nook
9-10 x 11

Courtyard

Dining
18-4 x 10-11

Patio

decor clg.

Living
18-4 x 16-1

Mbr
18-8 x 13-2

vault clg

Study/Br 2
13 x 10

Main Floor

No materials list available

PRICE CODE C

CONVENIENT AND EFFICIENT RANCH

No. 93311

■ This plan features:

— Three bedrooms

— Two full and one half baths

■ A barrel vault ceiling in the Foyer

■ A stepped ceiling in both the Dinette and the formal Dining Room

■ An expansive Gathering Room with a large focal point fireplace and access to the wood deck

■ An efficient Kitchen that includes a work island and a built-in pantry

■ A luxurious Master Suite with a private bath that includes a separate tub and step-in shower

■ Two additional bedrooms that share a full hall bath

FIRST FLOOR — 1,810 SQ. FT.
GARAGE — 528 SQ. FT.

TOTAL LIVING AREA:
1,810 SQ. FT.

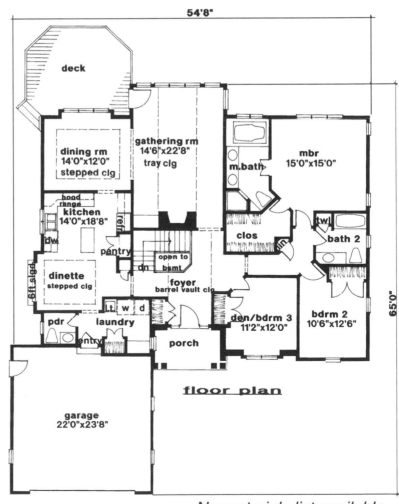

floor plan

An
EXCLUSIVE DESIGN
By Plan One Homes, Inc.

No materials list available

PRICE CODE C

No. 90421

This plan features:

— Three bedrooms

— Two full baths

A lovely French Provincial design

A large Family Room with a raised hearth fireplace and double doors to the patio

An L-shaped, island Kitchen with a Breakfast Bay and open counter to the Family Room

A Master Suite including one double closet and a compartmentalized bath with walk-in closet, step-up garden tub, double vanity and linen closet

Two front bedrooms sharing a full hall bath with a linen closet

An optional basement, slab or crawl space foundation — please specify when ordering

FIRST FLOOR — 1,940 SQ. FT.

TOTAL LIVING AREA:
1,940 SQ. FT.

IDEAL FOR FORMAL ENTERTAINING

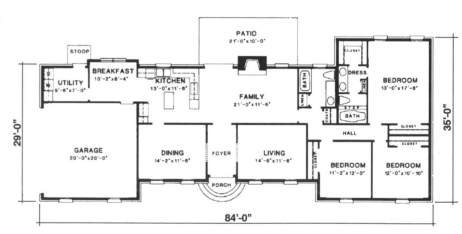

MAIN AREA

PRICE CODE B

CLASSIC FEATURES

No. 90691

■ This plan features:

— Three bedrooms

— Two full baths

■ A cathedral ceiling in the Living Room with a heat-circulating fireplace

■ A spectacular bow window and skylight in the Dining Room

■ A sliding glass door and skylight in the Kitchen

■ A Master Bedroom including a private Master Bath with a whirlpool tub

■ Two additional bedrooms that share a full, double-vanity hall bath

MAIN AREA — 1,530 SQ. FT.
BASEMENT — 1,434 SQ. FT.

**TOTAL LIVING AREA:
1,530 SQ. FT.**

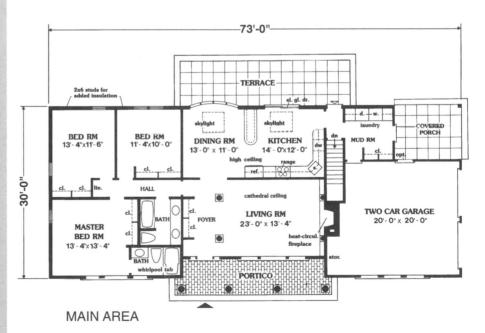

MAIN AREA

PRICE CODE A

COMPACT AND EFFICIENT

No. 91079

This plan features:

— Three bedrooms

— Two full baths

A covered porch entrance

A skylight over the Dining Room, that illuminates naturally

A vaulted ceiling and a cozy fireplace in the Living Room

An efficient and convenient Kitchen with an abundance of cabinets and counter space

A private Master Suite that includes a walk-in closet and a Master Bath

Two secondary bedrooms that share a full hall bath

FIRST FLOOR — 1,390 SQ. FT.
GARAGE — 440 SQ. FT.

TOTAL LIVING AREA:
1,390 SQ. FT.

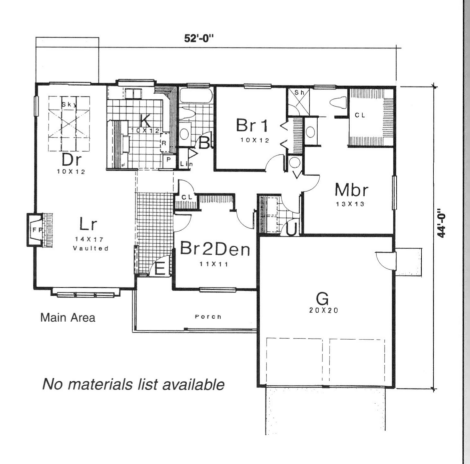

Main Area

No materials list available

PRICE CODE C

A LONG WRAP-AROUND PORCH

No. 99765

This plan features:

— Three bedrooms

— Two full and one half baths

A one story country-style Ranch with a contemporary floor plan

A corner fireplace adding warmth to the Living Room

A formal Dining Room with sliding glass doors to the deck

An eating bar and Nook area in the Kitchen

A vaulted ceiling with skylights in the Family Room

A Master Suite with private bath and a cedar closet as well as a walk-in closet

Two additional bedrooms that share a full bath

MAIN AREA — 1,998 SQ. FT.
BASEMENT — 1,998 SQ. FT.
GARAGE — 635 SQ. FT.
WIDTH — 87'-0"
DEPTH — 48'-0"

TOTAL LIVING AREA:
1,998 SQ. FT.

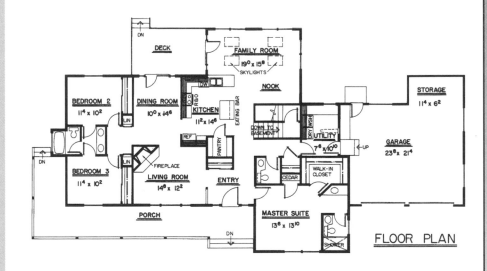

FLOOR PLAN

PRICE CODE A

No. 93222

- This plan features:
- — Three bedrooms
- — Two full baths
- A covered entrance sheltering and welcoming visitors
- An expansive Living Room enhanced by natural light streaming in from the large front window
- A bayed formal Dining Room with direct access to the Sun Deck and the Living Room for entertainment ease
- An efficient, galley Kitchen equipped with a double sink
- An informal Breakfast Room
- A large Master Suite equipped with a walk-in closet and a full private Bath
- Two additional bedrooms that share a full hall bath

MAIN AREA — 1,276 SQ. FT.
FINISHED STAIRCASE — 16 SQ. FT.
BASEMENT — 392 SQ. FT.
GARAGE — 728 SQ. FT.

TOTAL LIVING AREA:
1,292 SQ. FT.

FOR AN ESTABLISHED NEIGHBORHOOD

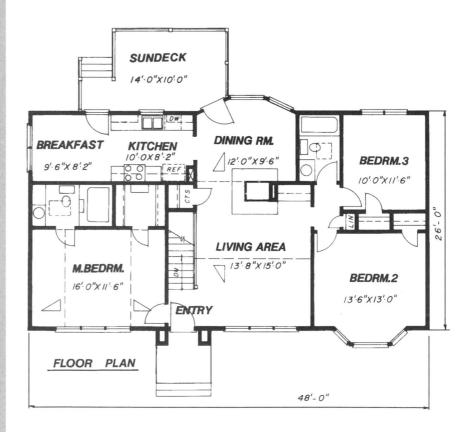

An EXCLUSIVE DESIGN
By Jannis Vann & Associates, Inc.

PRICE CODE A

FOR TODAY'S SOPHISTICATED HOMEOWNER

No. 93027

■ This plan features:

— Three bedrooms

— Two full baths

■ A formal Dining Room that opens off the foyer and has a classic bay window

■ A Kitchen notable for it's angled eating bar that opens to the Living Room

■ A cozy fireplace in the Living Room that can be seen from the Kitchen

■ A Master Suite that includes a whirlpool tub/shower combination and a walk-in closet

■ Ten foot ceilings in the major living areas, including the Master Bedroom

MAIN AREA — 1,500 SQ. FT.
GARAGE — 437 SQ. FT.

TOTAL LIVING AREA:
1,500 SQ. FT.

An
EXCLUSIVE DESIGN
By Belk Home Designs

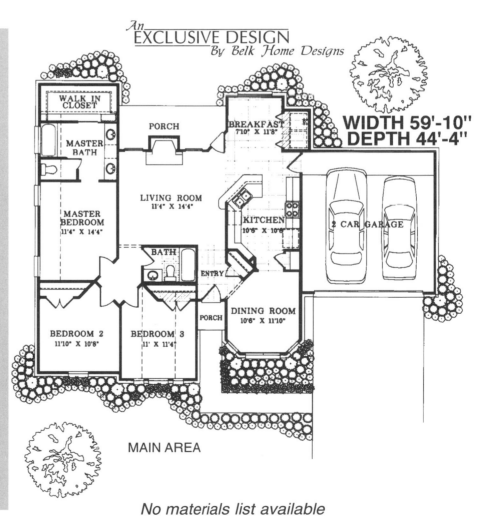

WIDTH 59'-10"
DEPTH 44'-4"

MAIN AREA

No materials list available

PRICE CODE C

DISTINCTIVE EUROPEAN DESIGN

No. 92516

■ This plan features:

— Three bedrooms

— Two full baths

■ A spacious Foyer leading into a grand Living Room, topped by a vaulted ceiling, a fireplace between built-in cabinets and a wall of glass leading to a covered Porch

■ A gourmet Kitchen with a peninsula counter/snackbar and a built-in pantry, that is central to the Dining Room, the bay window Breakfast area, the Utility Room and the Garage

■ A large Master Bedroom, crowned by a raised ceiling, with French doors leading to a covered Porch, a luxurious bath and a walk-in closet

MAIN FLOOR — 1,887 SQ. FT.
GARAGE & STORAGE — 524 SQ. FT.

TOTAL LIVING AREA:
1,887 SQ. FT.

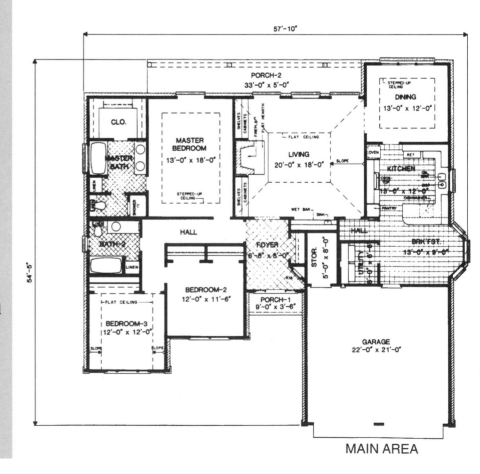

MAIN AREA

PRICE CODE D

AN OPEN CONCEPT FLOOR PLAN

No. 93050

■ This plan features:

— Four bedrooms

— Two full and one half baths

■ The Kitchen, Breakfast Room and the Family Room are adjacent to one another and open to one another, perfect for family gatherings

■ A stupendous fireplace on the center of the rear wall between the Family Room and the Breakfast Room

■ A private Master Suite with a large Master Bath

■ An oval tub, separate shower, compartmented toilet, double vanity and his-and-her walk-in closets in the Master bath

■ Two additional bedrooms with walk-in closets and a full hall bath in close proximity

MAIN FLOOR — 2,511 SQ. FT.

GARAGE — 469 SQ. FT.

TOTAL LIVING AREA:
2,511 SQ. FT.

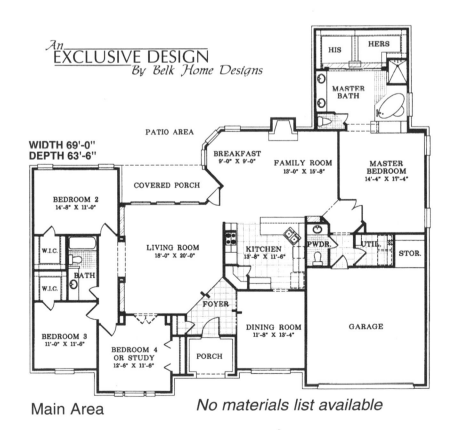

An
EXCLUSIVE DESIGN
By Belk Home Designs

WIDTH 69'-0"
DEPTH 63'-6"

Main Area

No materials list available

PRICE CODE B

Your ideal ranch

No. 93130

■ This plan features:

— Three bedrooms

— Two full baths

■ A spacious Living Room with a vaulted ceiling that catches your eye as you enter

■ An open floor plan, making the rooms seem more spacious

■ A private Master Suite with a walk-in closet and terrific Master Bath

■ Two additional bedrooms with ample closet space that share a full bath

■ Stairs off the Foyer that lead to a lower level, where there is plenty of room for future expansion

FIRST FLOOR — 1,508 SQ. FT.
BASEMENT — 1,508 SQ. FT.
GARAGE — 400 SQ. FT.

**TOTAL LIVING AREA:
1,508 SQ. FT.**

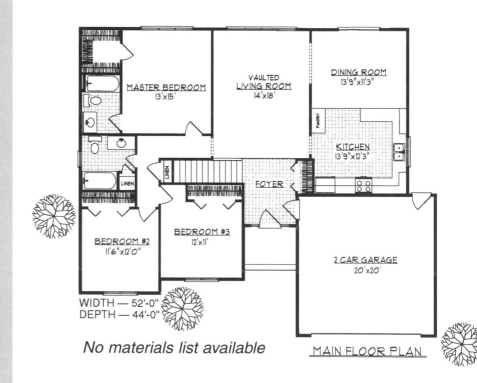

WIDTH — 52'-0"
DEPTH — 44'-0"

No materials list available

MAIN FLOOR PLAN

An
EXCLUSIVE DESIGN
By Ahmann Design Inc.

PRICE CODE B

ZONED FOR COMFORT

No. 90610

■ This plan features:

— Three bedrooms

— Two full baths

■ A spacious Kitchen with a built-in pantry, ample cabinet and counter space and a sunny Breakfast area

■ A large Family Room with a fireplace and sliding doors to a covered porch

■ A Master Suite with a walk-in closet and a private Bath

■ Two additional bedrooms with ample closet space and access to the full hall bath

■ A Dining and Living Room laid out for ease in entertaining

FIRST FLOOR — 1,771 SQ. FT.

TOTAL LIVING AREA: 1,771 SQ. FT.

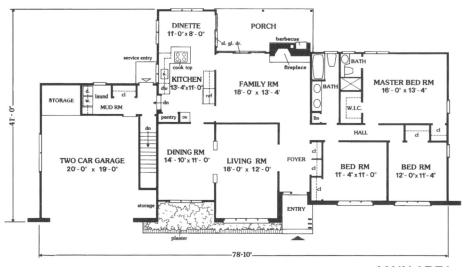

MAIN AREA

PRICE CODE D

DORMER WINDOWS ACCENT ELEVATION

No. 91415

■ This plan features:

— Four Bedrooms

— Two full baths

■ Portico double-door entrance leads into Living Room and Dining area with a Sunroom beyond

■ Living Room highlighted by cozy hearth fireplace between built-in shelves and French doors to Patio

■ Family Room with cozy wood stove, French doors to Patio

■ Open, hub Kitchen with island cooktop, built-in desk and angled serving counter/snack bar, and Family Room

■ Double decorative windows accent Master Bedroom with walk-in closet and private bath with double vanity and raised whirlpool tub

MAIN FLOOR — 2,546 SQ. FT.
GARAGE — 3 CAR
FOUNDATION — BASEMENT, SLAB OR CRAWL SPACE

TOTAL LIVING AREA:
2,546 SQ. FT.

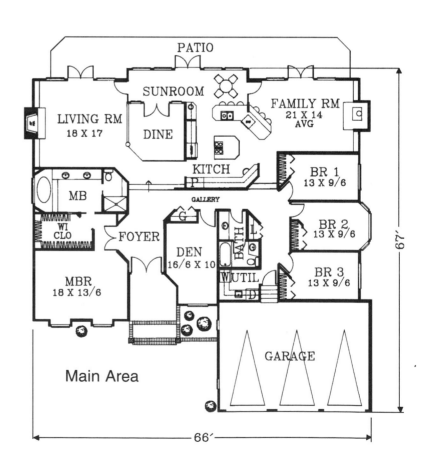

Main Area

PRICE CODE A

STATELY AND SPACIOUS CONTEMPORARY

No. 99710

This plan features:

— Three bedrooms

— Two full baths

Lofty brick columns flanking the high gabled entryway

A large corner fireplace in the Great Room which can be enjoyed from both the Dining Room and the Kitchen

An efficient wrap-around Kitchen with many built-ins, opening via an eating bar, to the Great Room and Dining Room

A privately situated Master Suite, complete with a full bath and a walk-in closet

Two additional bedrooms that share a full hall bath

Utility room, accessed from the garage, also serves as a Laundry Room

MAIN AREA — 1,459 SQ. FT.
GARAGE — 567 SQ. FT.
WIDTH — 56'-0"
DEPTH — 54'-0"

TOTAL LIVING AREA:
1,459 SQ. FT.

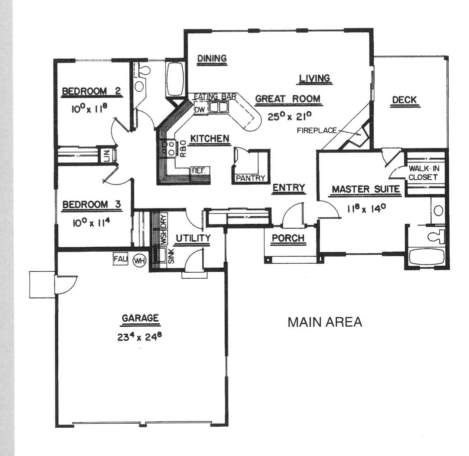

MAIN AREA

An
EXCLUSIVE DESIGN
By Landmark Designs, Inc.

PRICE CODE C

TRADITIONAL EMPHASIZES LIVING AREAS

No. 22014

- This plan features:
- — Three bedrooms
- — Two full and one half baths
- A twenty foot Family Room with a large fireplace and access to the patio
- A formal Dining Room and a Game Room, which can function as a formal Living Room if necessary
- Each of the three bedrooms adjoin a full bath
- A Master Bedroom with a luxurious his-and-her bath and walk-in closets

FIRST FLOOR — 2,118 SQ. FT.
GARAGE — 448 SQ. FT.

**TOTAL LIVING AREA:
2,118 SQ. FT.**

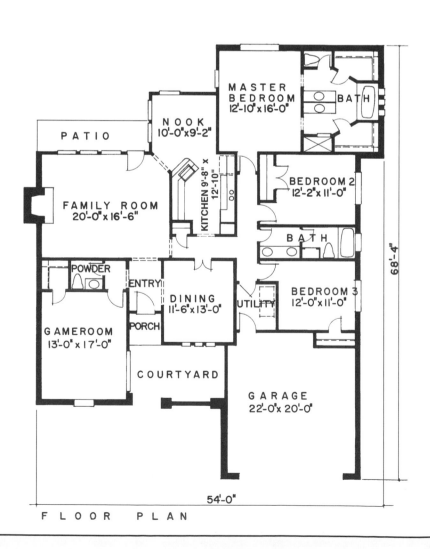

FLOOR PLAN

PRICE CODE D

ENTRY GRACED BY ARCHES

No. 93032

■ This plan features:

— Four bedrooms

— Two full baths

■ A combination of brick and wood siding finishes with a pair of graceful arches at the entry creating an all-time favorite curb elevation

■ An angled foyer design that provides views to the Great Room and the Dining Room

■ A see-through fireplace between the Great Room and the Dining Room as an elegant detail

■ A Kitchen that includes a cooktop work island and eating bar, plenty of cabinets and more than ample counter space

■ A Master Suite with a whirlpool tub, shower and double vanity with knee space, plus a walk-in closet

FIRST FLOOR — 2,250 SQ. FT.
GARAGE — 543 SQ. FT.

TOTAL LIVING AREA:
2,250 SQ. FT.

No materials list available

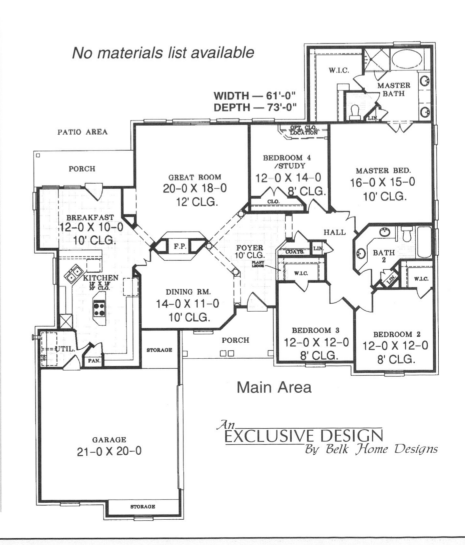

WIDTH — 61'-0"
DEPTH — 73'-0"

Main Area

An
EXCLUSIVE DESIGN
By Belk Home Designs

PRICE CODE A

ATTRACTIVE ROOF LINES

No. 90983

■ This plan features:

— Three bedrooms

— Two full baths

■ An open floor plan shared by the sunken Living Room, Dining and Kitchen areas

■ An unfinished daylight Basement which will provide future bedrooms, a bathroom and laundry facilities

■ A Master Suite with a big walk-in closet and a private bath featuring a double shower

FIRST FLOOR — 1,396 SQ. FT.
BASEMENT — 1,396 SQ. FT.
GARAGE — 389 SQ. FT.
WIDTH — 48'-0"
DEPTH — 54'-0"

TOTAL LIVING AREA:
1,396 SQ. FT.

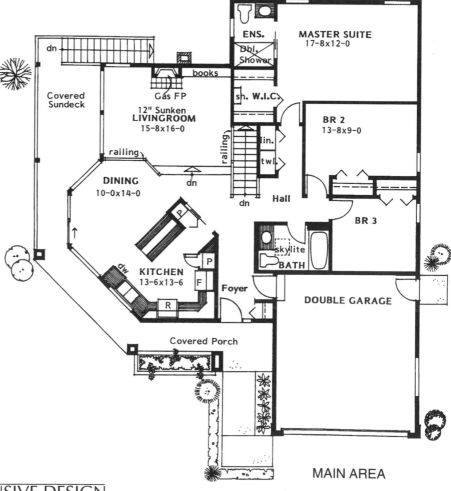

An
EXCLUSIVE DESIGN
By Westhome Planners, Ltd.

CHARMING SOUTHERN TRADITIONAL

No. 92503

■ This plan features:

— Three bedrooms

— Two full baths

■ A covered front porch with striking columns, brick quoins, and dental molding

■ A spacious Great Room with vaulted ceilings, a fireplace, and built-in cabinets

■ A Utility Room adjacent to the Kitchen, which leads to the two-car Garage and Storage Rooms

■ A Master Bedroom including a large walk-in closet and a compartmentalized bath

MAIN AREA — 1,271 SQ. FT.
GARAGE — 506 SQ. FT.

TOTAL LIVING AREA:
1,271 SQ. FT.

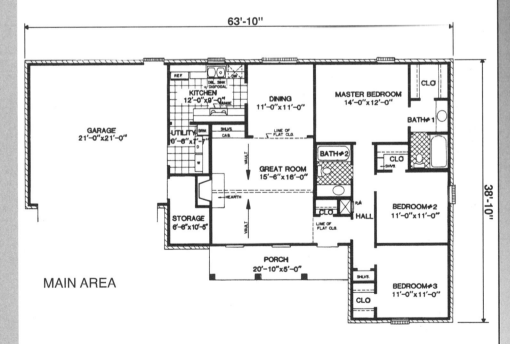

MAIN AREA

PRICE CODE C

FOUR BEDROOM CHARMER

No. 91346

This plan features:

— Four bedrooms

— Two full baths

A vaulted ceiling in the naturally lighted entry

A Living Room with a masonry fireplace, large windowed bay and vaulted ceiling

A coffered ceiling and built-in china cabinet in the Dining Room

A large Family Room with a wood stove alcove

An island cook top, built-in pantry and a telephone desk in the efficient Kitchen

A luxurious Master Bedroom with whirlpool garden tub, walk-in closet and double sink vanity

Two additional bedrooms sharing a full bath

A Study with a window seat and built-in bookshelves

FIRST FLOOR — 2,185 SQ. FT.

TOTAL LIVING AREA: 2,185 SQ. FT.

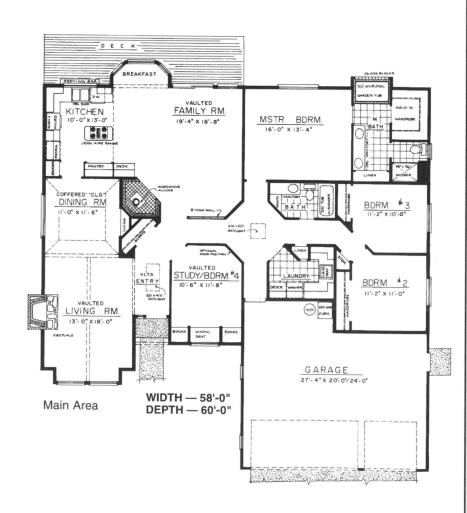

Main Area

WIDTH — 58'-0"
DEPTH — 60'-0"

PRICE CODE A

Low Maintenance, Southwestern Style

No. 10643

■ This plan features:

— Three bedrooms

— Two full baths

■ A stucco facade with an arched privacy wall, leading into a tiled entrance

■ An airy Living Room providing easy entertaining and access to other areas

■ A central Kitchen equipped with a cooktop island/breakfast bar, adjoining the Dining Room

■ A Master Suite offering a bay window area, a walk-in closet and a private bath with a skylight

■ Two additional bedrooms with oversized closets sharing a full hall bath

MAIN FLOOR — 1,285 SQ. FT.
GARAGE — 473 SQ. FT.

TOTAL LIVING AREA:
1,285 SQ. FT.

An

EXCLUSIVE DESIGN
By Karl Kreeger

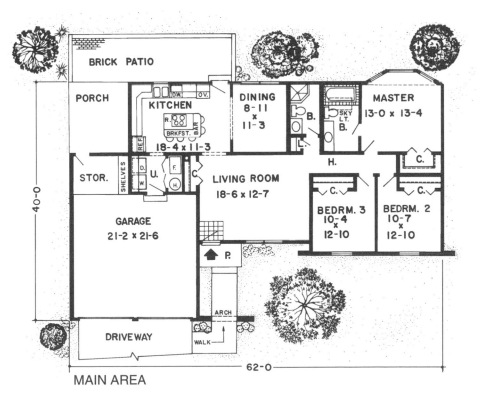

PRICE CODE C

DISTINGUISHED STYLING

No. 91548

■ This plan features:

— Three bedrooms

— Two full and one half baths

■ Impressive transom window entrance into the open layout of the Great Room, the Dining area and the Kitchen/Nook

■ Decorative ceiling in the Great Room crowns a corner fireplace and a double window overlooking the rear yard

■ Cooktop island/eating bar in the efficient Kitchen serves the Nook and Great Room and Dining areas

■ Master Suite with a decorative ceiling over an atrium door to the rear yard and a plush bath with a double vanity, a spa tub and a walk-in closet

■ This plan is available with a Crawlspace foundation only

MAIN FLOOR — 2,155 SQ. FT.
GARAGE — 430 SQ. FT.

TOTAL LIVING AREA:
2,155 SQ. FT.

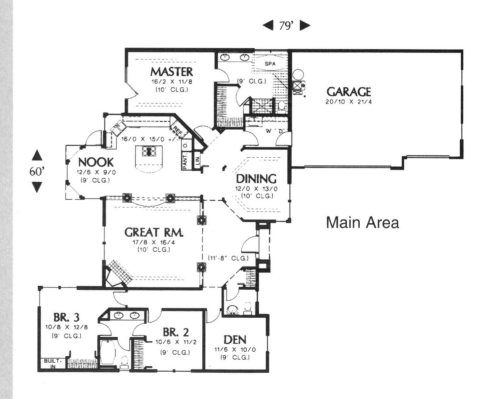

◄ 79' ►

60'

MASTER
16/2 X 11/8
(10' CLG.)

SPA
(9' CLG.)

GARAGE
20/10 X 21/4

16/0 X 15/0 +/-

NOOK
12/6 X 9/0
(9' CLG.)

DINING
12/0 X 13/0
(10' CLG.)

GREAT RM.
17/8 X 16/4
(10' CLG.)

(11'-8" CLG.)

BR. 3
10/8 X 12/8
(9' CLG.)

BR. 2
10/6 X 11/2
(9' CLG.)

DEN
11/6 X 10/0
(9' CLG.)

BUILT-IN

Main Area

PRICE CODE A

A LOVELY SMALL HOME

No. 93026

■ This plan features:

— Three bedrooms

— Two full baths

■ A large Living Room with a ten foot ceiling

■ A Dining Room with a distinctive bay window

■ A Breakfast Room located off the Kitchen

■ A Kitchen with an angled eating bar to open that opens the room to the Living Room

■ A Master Suite with ten foot ceiling and his-n-her vanities, a combination whirlpool tub and shower, plus a huge walk-in closet

■ Two additional bedrooms that share a full bath

MAIN AREA — 1,402 SQ. FT.
GARAGE — 437 SQ. FT.

**TOTAL LIVING AREA:
1,402 SQ. FT.**

An
EXCLUSIVE DESIGN
By Belk Home Designs

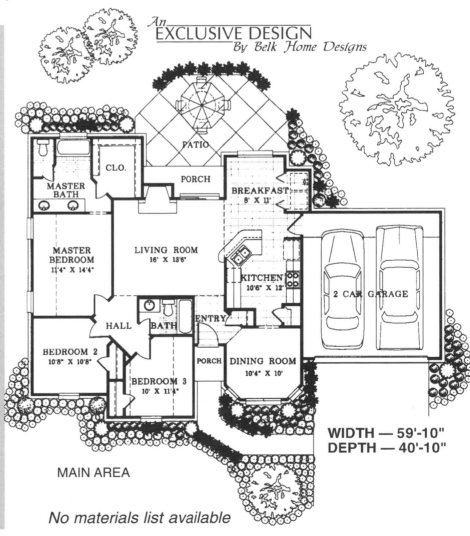

WIDTH — 59'-10"
DEPTH — 40'-10"

MAIN AREA

No materials list available

PRICE CODE B

CONVENIENT COUNTRY-STYLE LIVING

No. 24249

This plan features:

— Three bedrooms

— Two full baths

A Wrap-around Porch adds outdoor living space and provides a friendly entrance

A Large fieldstone fireplace below a sloped ceiling separates the Great Room from the Dining and Kitchen areas

Efficient Kitchen with an island breakfast bar serves the Dining area and the Deck beyond

Master Bedroom suite offers a large walk-in closet and a private bath with a double vanity

Two additional bedrooms, one with a walk-in closet, share a full bath

This plan is available with a Basement foundation only

MAIN FLOOR — 1,741 SQ. FT.
BASEMENT — 957 SQ. FT.

TOTAL LIVING AREA:
1,741 SQ. FT.

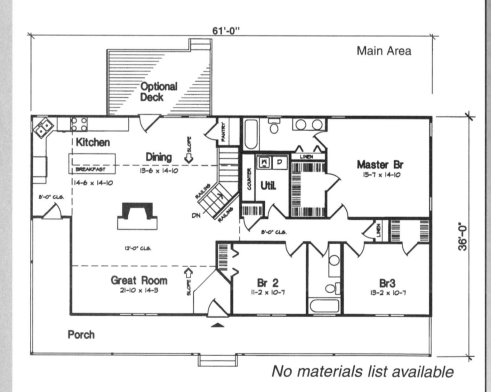

No materials list available

PRICE CODE B

GREEK REVIVAL

No. 99610

This plan features:

— Three bedrooms

— Two full baths

A large front porch with pediment and columns

A stunning, heat-circulating fireplace flanked by cabinetry and shelves in the Living Room

A formal Dining Room enhanced by a bay window

An efficient, U-shaped Kitchen with a peninsula counter and informal Dinette area

A Master Suite with a private Master Bath and direct access to the private terrace

Two additional bedrooms sharing a full hall bath

FIRST FLOOR — 1,460 SQ. FT.
LAUNDRY/MUDROOM — 68 SQ. FT.
BASEMENT — 1,367 SQ. FT.
GARAGE & STORAGE — 494 SQ. FT.

**TOTAL LIVING AREA:
1,528 SQ. FT.**

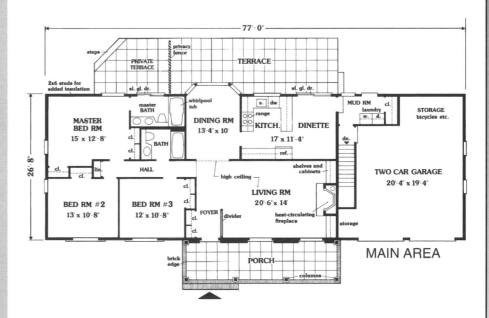

MAIN AREA

PRICE CODE B

WIDE OPEN LIVING AREAS

No. 91814

This plan features:

— Three bedrooms

— Two full baths

Adaptable for barrier-free living

An efficient Kitchen with double sink peninsula counter, that also serves as an eating bar

A covered Porch and a patio with decorative columns and half-round windows

A large Master Bedroom with a patio, double sinks, walk-in closet, spa tub, and a shower

Two additional bedrooms that share a full hall bath

An optional crawl space or slab foundation — please specify when ordering

MAIN AREA — 1,785 SQ. FT.
GARAGE — 672 SQ. FT.

**TOTAL LIVING AREA:
1,785 SQ. FT.**

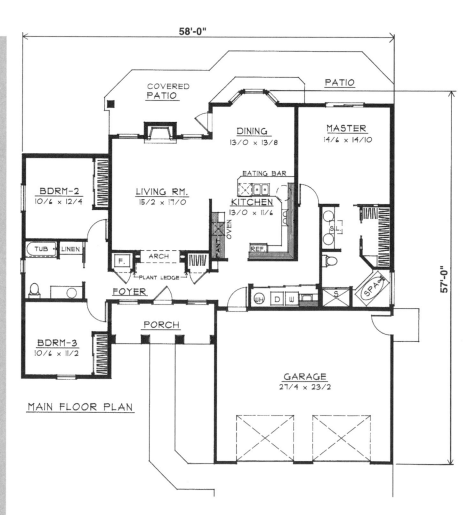

MAIN FLOOR PLAN

PRICE CODE C

BEAUTIFUL COMBINATION OF OLD AND NEW

No. 24256

■ This plan features:

— Three bedrooms

— Two full baths

■ Vaulted ceilings in the family living areas; Living Room, Dining Room, Family Room and Eating Nook

■ An open layout between the Kitchen, Nook, and Family Room, making the rooms appear even more spacious

■ A corner fireplace in the Family Room, which also has access to the patio

■ A peninsula counter in the island Kitchen that doubles as an eating bar

■ A lavish Master Suite that is equipped with a private bath and walk-in closet

■ Two family bedrooms that share a full hall bath

MAIN AREA — 2,108 SQ. FT.

TOTAL LIVING AREA:
2,108 SQ. FT.

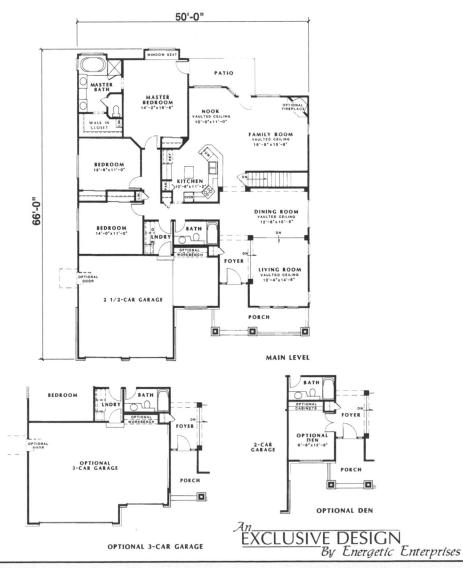

MAIN LEVEL

OPTIONAL 3-CAR GARAGE

OPTIONAL DEN

An *EXCLUSIVE DESIGN* By *Energetic Enterprises*

PRICE CODE B

PERFECT FOR A FIRST HOME

No. 92405

■ This plan features:

— Three bedrooms

— Two full baths

■ A spacious Master Suite including a separate Master Bath with a garden tub and shower

■ A Dining Room and Family Room highlighted by vaulted ceilings

■ An oversized patio accessible from the Master Suite, Family Room and Breakfast Room

■ A well planned Kitchen measuring 12′ x 11′

MAIN AREA — 1,564 SQ. FT.
GARAGE & STORAGE — 476 SQ. FT.

TOTAL LIVING AREA:
1,564 SQ. FT.

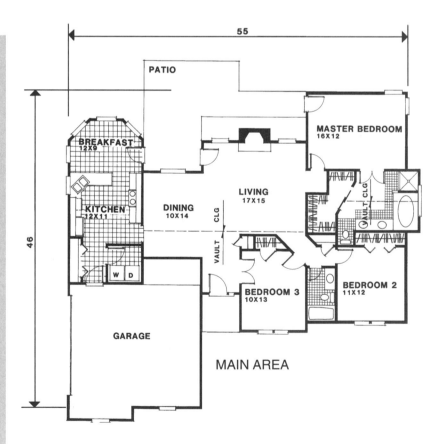

MAIN AREA

No materials list available

PRICE CODE B

SECLUDED MASTER SUITE

No. 92527

■ This plan features:

— Three bedrooms

— Two full baths

■ A convenient one-level design with an open floor plan between the Kitchen, Breakfast area and Great Room

■ A vaulted ceiling and a cozy fireplace in the spacious Great Room

■ A well-equipped Kitchen using a peninsula counter as an eating bar

■ A Master Suite with a luxurious Master Bath

■ Two additional bedrooms having use of a full hall bath

MAIN AREA — 1,680 SQ. FT.

**TOTAL LIVING AREA:
1,680 SQ. FT.**

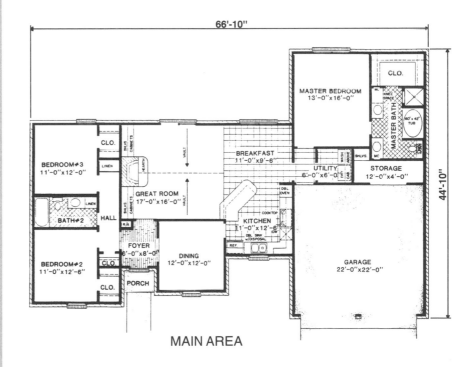

MAIN AREA

PRICE CODE C

ATTRACTIVE COMBINATION OF BRICK AND SIDING

No. 24259

- This plan features:
- — Three bedrooms
- — Two full baths
- A Great Room sunny bayed area, fireplace and built-in entertainment center
- A private Master Bedroom with luxurious Master Bath and walk-in closet
- Dining Room has a Butler Pantry
- Two additional Bedrooms have use of a full hall Bath

FIRST FLOOR — 2,010 SQ. FT.

TOTAL LIVING AREA:
2,010 SQ. FT.

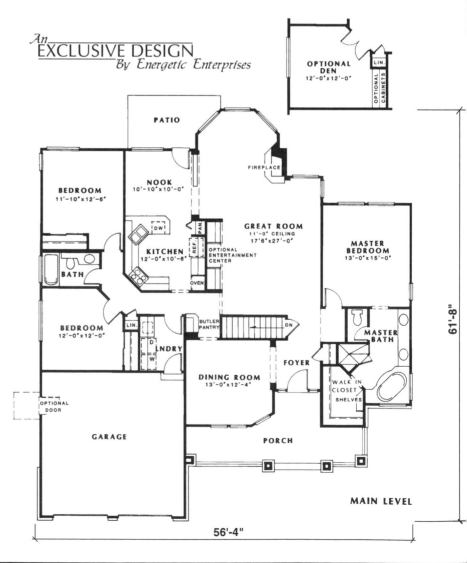

An EXCLUSIVE DESIGN
By Energetic Enterprises

PRICE CODE C

No. 24261

■ This plan features:

— Three bedrooms

— Two full baths

■ Inviting Porch leads into an open Foyer with theDining Room and the Great Room beyond

■ Great Room with a corner fireplace and a glass alcove overlooking the rear yard offers a built-in entertainment center

■ Central Kitchen with a built-in pantry and a pcninsula counter easily serves the Nook and Patio

■ Private Master Bedroom with a double window overlooking the rear yard, offers a plush bath with a double vanity, a whirlpool tub and a large walk-in closet

■ Two additional bedrooms with ample closets sharea full bath

■ This plan is available with a Basement, Slab or Crawlspace foundation. Please specify when ordering

MAIN FLOOR — 2,010 SQ. FT.
GARAGE — 482 SQ. FT.

TOTAL LIVING AREA:
2,010 SQ. FT.

MARVELOUS MASTER SUITE

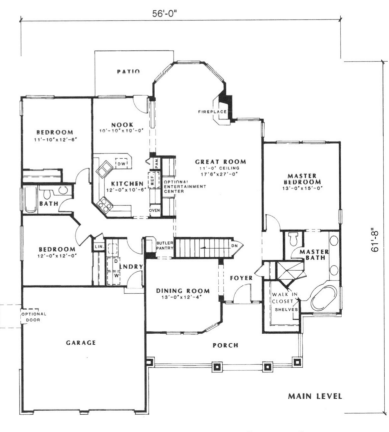

An EXCLUSIVE DESIGN
By Energetic Enterprises

PRICE CODE B

ENHANCED BY A COLUMNED PORCH

No. 92531

■ This plan features:

— Three bedrooms

— Two full baths

■ A Great Room with a fireplace and decorative ceiling

■ A large efficient Kitchen with Breakfast area

■ A Master Bedroom with a private Master Bath and walk-in closet

■ A formal Dining Room conveniently located near the Kitchen

■ Two additional bedrooms with walk-in closets and use of full hall bath

FIRST FLOOR — 1,754 SQ. FT.

TOTAL LIVING AREA: 1,754 SQ. FT.

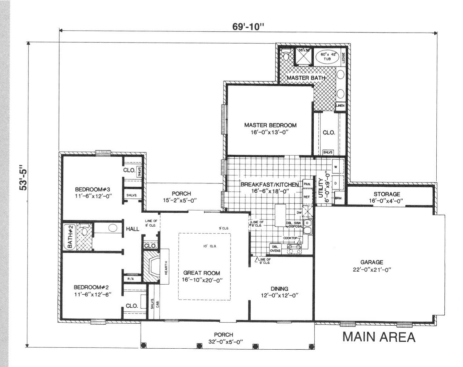

PRICE CODE B

SPECTACULAR RAMBLER

No. 91811

■ This plan features:

— Three bedrooms

— Two full baths

■ A twelve foot ceiling over the Foyer, Living Room, Kitchen and Dining Rooms

■ A sunken Living Room with custom-cut windows

■ A spacious Master Suite with a walk-in closet, and a private bath

■ A Family Room with a fireplace, separated from the Kitchen by an eating bar

■ An efficient Kitchen with a double sink, built-in pantry, and a peninsula counter

■ An optional basement, slab or crawl space foundation — please specify when ordering

MAIN AREA — 1,546 SQ. FT.
OPTIONAL BASEMENT — 1,588 SQ. FT.
GARAGE — 549 SQ. FT.

TOTAL LIVING AREA:
1,546 SQ. FT.

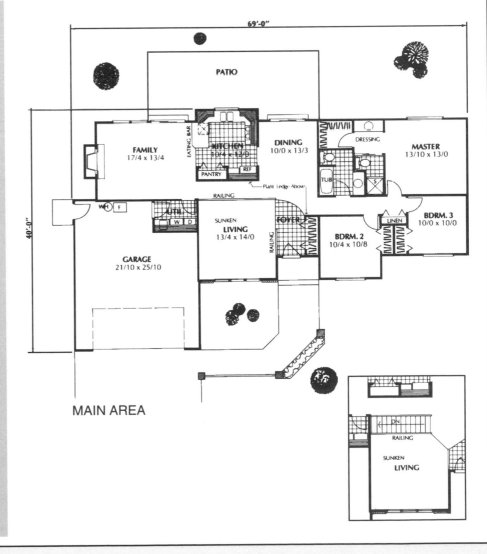

MAIN AREA

PRICE CODE B

SKYLIGHT WELCOME

No. 90695

This plan features:

— Three bedrooms

— Two full baths

A covered, double door entrance into the Foyer, with skylights, opening to the Living Room/Dining Room

A heat-circulating fireplace with an extended hearth in the Living Room, enhanced by a wall of glass and a sliding door to the Terrace in the Dining Room

A centrally-located Kitchen/Dinette with a skylight, a sliding glass door to the Sun Room

A Family Room with a built-in media center, more windows and a sliding glass door to the Terrace

A Master Bedroom suite with a walk-in closet, and a private bath with a whirlpool tub

Two additional bedrooms sharing a full hall bath

MAIN FLOOR — 1,726 SQ. FT.

TOTAL LIVING AREA:
1,726 SQ. FT.

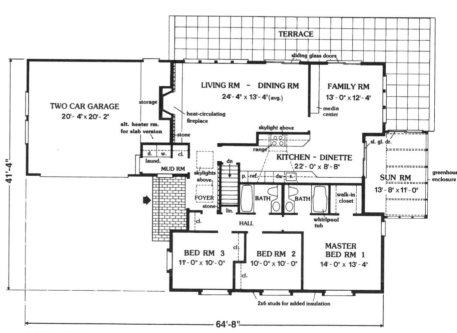

MAIN AREA

PRICE CODE A

SPECTACULAR TRADITIONAL

No. 92502

■ This plan features:

— Three bedrooms

— Two full baths

■ The use of gable roofs and the blend of stucco and brick to form a spectacular exterior

■ A high vaulted ceiling and a cozy fireplace, with built-in cabinets in the Den

■ An efficient, U-shaped Kitchen with an adjacent Dining Area

■ A Master Bedroom, with a raised ceiling, that includes a private bath and a walk-in closet

■ Two family bedrooms that share a full hall bath

MAIN AREA — 1,237 SQ. FT.
GARAGE — 436 SQ. FT.

TOTAL LIVING AREA:
1,237 SQ. FT.

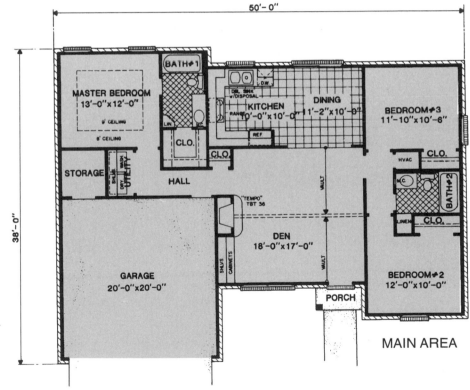

MAIN AREA

PRICE CODE A

SPANISH STYLING, AFFORDABLE DESIGN

No. 91340

■ This plan features:

— Two bedrooms

— Two full baths

■ A large Master Suite with vaulted ceilings and a handicap accessible private bath

■ Vaulted ceilings in the Great Room

■ An open Kitchen area with an eating bar

■ Accessibility Features:

— Level entry way

—Wide doorways (32″-36″ clear width)

—Chair height electrical controls/outlets

—Reinforced walls for installation of grab bars

MAIN AREA — 1,111 SQ. FT.

TOTAL LIVING AREA:
1,111 SQ. FT.

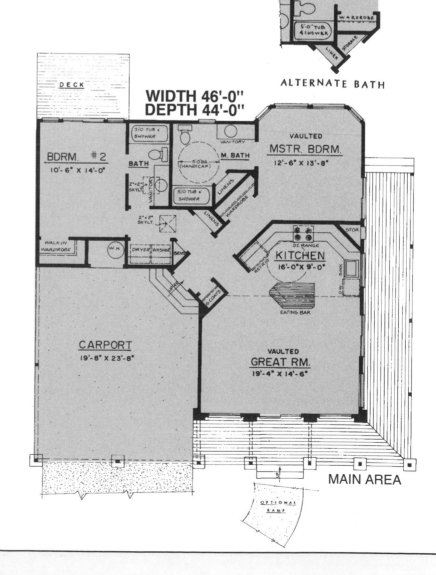

WIDTH 46'-0"
DEPTH 44'-0"

ALTERNATE BATH

PRICE CODE C

CAREFREE AND COZY

An
EXCLUSIVE DESIGN
By Mark Stewart

No. 91618

■ This plan features:

— Three bedrooms

— Two full and one half baths

■ A coved ceiling, fireplace and massive front window in the Living Room

■ A built-in, corner china cabinet in the elegant, formal Dining Room

■ A Kitchen with a large cook top island and snack counter

■ A secluded Master Suite with a bay window, coved ceiling, and a private bath with double vanities and garden spa tub

■ Accessibility Features:

— Level entry way

— Wide doorways (32"-36" clear width)

— Chair height electrical controls/outlets

— Reinforced walls for installation of grab bars

FIRST FLOOR — 2,087 SQ. FT.

**TOTAL LIVING AREA:
2,087 SQ. FT.**

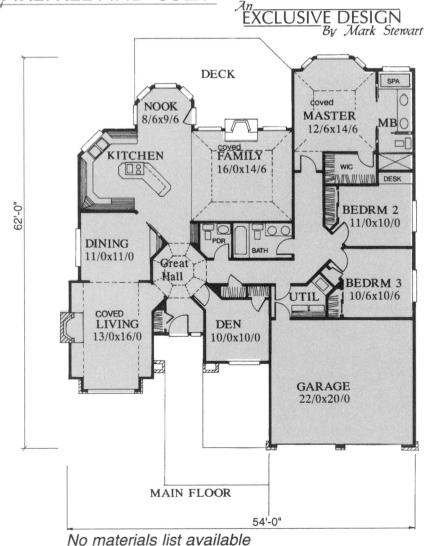

No materials list available

PRICE CODE A

ROOM FOR MORE

No. 24311

■ This plan features:

— Two bedrooms

— Two full baths

■ A Living Room with a fire-place and access to two decks, expanding the outdoor living space

■ An efficient Kitchen opening to the Dining area

■ A Master Bedroom, including a private bath with a corner spa/tub

MAIN AREA — 1,127 SQ. FT.

TOTAL LIVING AREA: 1,127 SQ. FT.

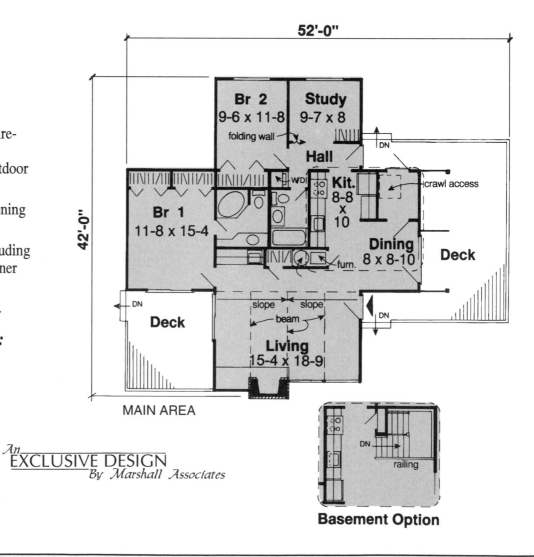

An EXCLUSIVE DESIGN
By Marshall Associates

PRICE CODE A

LOTS OF LIVING SPACE IN COMPACT DESIGN

No. 90368

■ This plan features:

— Two bedrooms with optional third bedroom/den

— Two full baths

■ Flowing living spaces and yard views

■ A Master Suite including a full bath and ample closet space

■ A Living and Dining Room combination, enhanced by a corner fireplace

MAIN AREA — 1,081 SQ. FT.

TOTAL LIVING AREA: 1,081 SQ. FT.

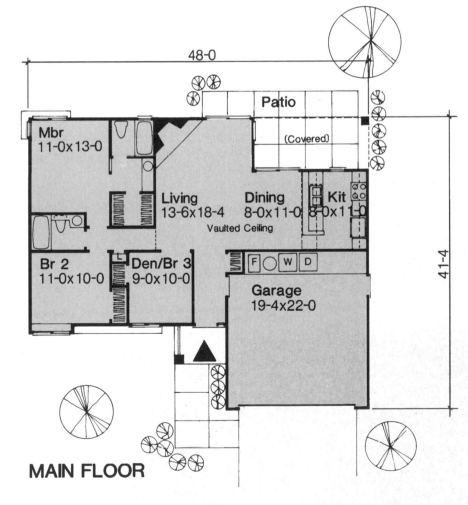

MAIN FLOOR

PRICE CODE B

ATTENTION TO DETAILS
DESIGN NO. 93262

An **EXCLUSIVE DESIGN**
By Jannis Vann & Associates, Inc.

■ This plan features:
— Three bedrooms
— Two full baths
■ Beautiful detailing around the windows and the doors, adding to its curb appeal
■ A large Living Room with a focal point fireplace in the center of the outside wall, and direct access to the rear yard
■ A Master Suite located at the opposite end of the house from the secondary bedrooms, insuring privacy
■ A decorative ceiling in the Master Bedroom and a private Master Bath and walk-in closet
■ An informal Breakfast Room and formal Dining Room both located next to the efficient Kitchen
■ A Laundry Room and a double Garage

FIRST FLOOR — 1,708 SQ. FT.
GARAGE — 400 SQ. FT.

TOTAL LIVING AREA:
1,708 SQ. FT.

No materials list available

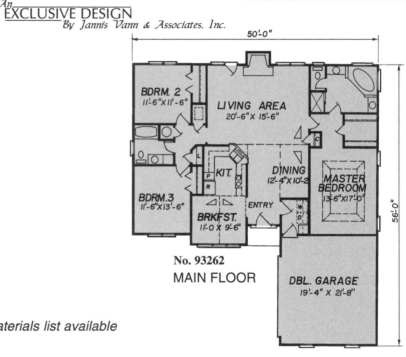

No. 93262
MAIN FLOOR

OPEN SPACES
DESIGN NO. 93279

■ This plan features:
— Three bedrooms
— Two full baths
■ A Family Room, Kitchen and Breakfast Area that all connects to form a great space
■ A central, double fireplace adding warmth and atmosphere to the Family Room, Kitchen and the Breakfast area
■ An efficient Kitchen that is highlighted by a peninsula counter and doubles as a snack bar
■ A Master Suite that includes a walk-in closet, a double vanity, separate shower and a tub bath
■ Two additional bedrooms sharing a full hall bath

MAIN FLOOR — 1,388 SQ. FT.
GARAGE — 400 SQ. FT.

TOTAL LIVING AREA:
1,388 SQ. FT.

An **EXCLUSIVE DESIGN**
By Jannis Vann & Associates, Inc.

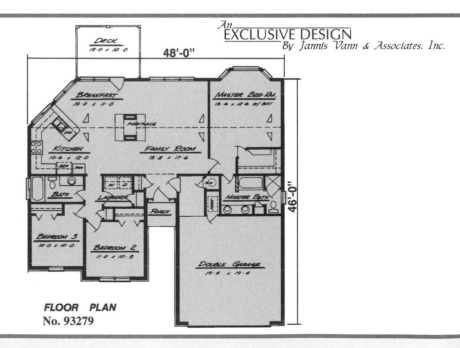

FLOOR PLAN
No. 93279

PRICE CODE B

NOSTALGIC EXTERIOR

DESIGN NO. 99771

- This plan features:
— Three bedrooms
— Two full baths
- Cedar shakes, gables and a brick facade
- A huge Great Room complete with skylights, a bay window, a wide hearth in front of the fireplace and a wood box
- A large work island in the center of the Kitchen that has a built-in range and oven
- A triangular step-in pantry and a long eating bar that enhance the Kitchen's conveniences
- A Master Suite equipped with a private bath and walk-in closet
- Two additional bedrooms that share a full hall bath

FIRST FLOOR — 1,578 SQ. FT.
GARAGE — 685 SQ. FT.
ATTIC — 724 SQ. FT.

TOTAL LIVING AREA:
1,578 SQ. FT.

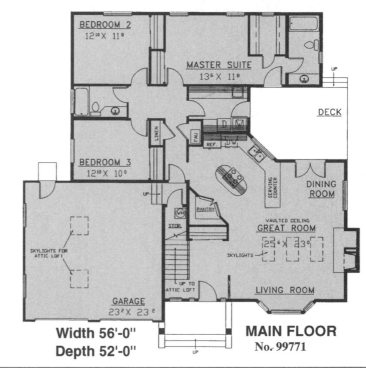

Width 56'-0"
Depth 52'-0"

MAIN FLOOR
No. 99771

PRICE CODE A

WELCOMING FRONT PORTCH ACCENTED BY COLUMNS
DESIGN NO. 92542

■ This plan features:
— Three bedrooms
— Two full baths

■ Open Foyer leads into the Dining Room defined by columns and a spacious Den

■ Cozy fireplace in the Den with built-in shelves and sliding glass doors to the rear Porch below a decorative ceiling

■ Efficient, U-shaped Kitchen with a peninsula snackbar and a glass Breakfast area

■ Secluded Master Suite with a decorative ceiling, a huge walk-in closet and a private bath

■ Two additional bedrooms with ample closets, share the double vanity bath

■ This plan is available with a Slab or Crawlspace foundation. Please specify when ordering

MAIN FLOOR — 1,866 SQ. FT.
GARAGE/STORAGE — 538 SQ. FT.

TOTAL LIVING AREA:
1,866 SQ. FT.

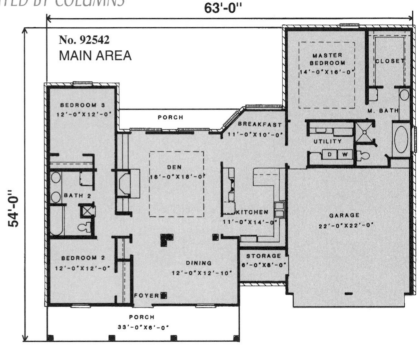

No. 92542
MAIN AREA

63'-0"
54'-0"

MASTER BEDROOM 14'-0"X16'-0"
CLOSET
M. BATH
BEDROOM 3 12'-0"X12'-0"
PORCH
BREAKFAST 11'-0"X10'-0"
UTILITY
D W
DEN 18'-0"X18'-0"
BATH 2
KITCHEN 11'-0"X14'-0"
GARAGE 22'-0"X22'-0"
BEDROOM 2 12'-0"X12'-0"
DINING 12'-0"X12'-10"
STORAGE 6'-0"X6'-0"
FOYER
PORCH 33'-0"X6'-0"

BRICK DETAIL WITH ARCHES
DESIGN NO. 92544

■ This plan features:
— Four bedrooms
— Two full and one half baths

■ Front and back porches expand the living space and provide inviting access to the open layout

■ Spacious Den with a fireplace flanked by built-in shelves and double access to the rear Porch

■ Formal Dining Room with an arched window and direct access to the Kitchen

■ Efficient, U-shaped Kitchen with a snackbar counter, a bright Breakfast area and an adjoining laundry and Garage

■ Secluded Master Bedroom suite with a walk-in closet and a double vanity bath

■ Three additional bedrooms with walk-in closets, share one and half baths

■ This plan is available with a Slab or Crawlspace foundation. Please specify when ordering

MAIN FLOOR — 1,987 SQ. FT.
GARAGE/STORAGE — 515 SQ. FT.

MAIN AREA
No. 92544

TOTAL LIVING AREA:
1,987 SQ. FT.

BEDROOM 4 11'-0"X12'-6"
LIN.
PORCH 6'-0"X29'-8"
MASTER BEDROOM 14'-0"X15'-0"
BEDROOM 3 11'-0"X12'-0"
BREAKFAST 8'-0"X12'-0"
W D
STO.
DEN 18'-0"X18'-0"
KITCHEN 10'-0"X12'-0"
GARAGE 21'-6"X22'-0"
FOYER
PORCH 6'-0"X16'-0"
DINING 12'-0"X12'-0"
BEDROOM 2 11'-0"X12'-0"

67'-0" Width
49'-0" Depth

CHARMING RANGE STYLE

DESIGN NO. 92630

■ This plan features:
— Three bedrooms
— Two full baths

■ A Great Room and Dining Room accented by a sloped ceiling

■ An outstanding Breakfast Area with a sloped ceiling and French doors, which lead to a spacious Screened Porch

■ A convenient and efficient Kitchen with a peninsula counter/eating bar and a built-in pantry

■ A tray ceiling crowning the Master Bedroom

■ An ultra Master Bath with whirlpool tub, a double-vanity and a large walk-in closet

■ Two additional bedrooms that share a full hall bath

MAIN FLOOR — 1,782 SQ. FT.
BASEMENT — 1,735 SQ. FT.
GARAGE — 407 SQ. FT.

TOTAL LIVING AREA:
1,782 SQ. FT.

MATERIALS LIST NOT AVAILABLE

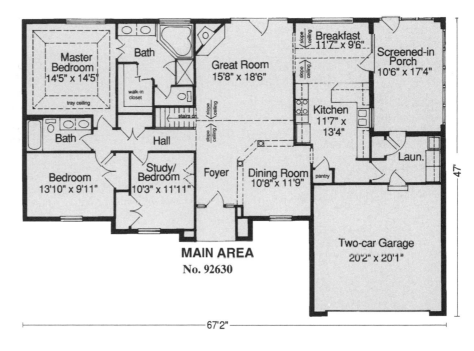

MAIN AREA
No. 92630

Master Bedroom 14'5" x 14'5"
Bath
Great Room 15'8" x 18'6"
Breakfast 11'7" x 9'6"
Screened-in Porch 10'6" x 17'4"
walk-in closet
tray ceiling
Kitchen 11'7" x 13'4"
Bath
Hall
Laun.
Bedroom 13'10" x 9'11"
Study/ Bedroom 10'3" x 11'11"
Foyer
Dining Room 10'8" x 11'9"
pantry
Two-car Garage 20'2" x 20'1"

47'
67'2"

SLIGHT WESTERN TOUCH
DESIGN NO. 92521

■ This plan features:
— Three bedrooms
— Two full baths
■ A vaulted ceiling in the Den to add to the spacious feeling
■ A U-shaped Kitchen with ample storage and counter space flowing into the Eating area with a built-in pantry
■ A Master Bedroom enhanced by a decorative ceiling and private bath
■ Two additional bedrooms having use of a full hall bath

FIRST FLOOR — 1,203 SQ. FT.

TOTAL LIVING AREA:
1,203 SQ. FT.

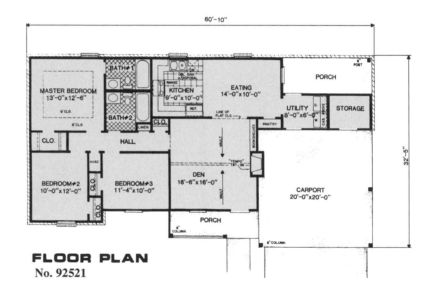

FLOOR PLAN
No. 92521

SYMMETRICAL AND STATELY
DESIGN NO. 92546

■ This plan features:
— Four bedrooms
— Two full and one half baths
■ Double column Porch leads into the open Foyer.
■ Decorative ceiling crowns the Den with a hearth fireplace, built-in shelves and window access to the rear Porch
■ Large, efficient Kitchen with a peninsula serving counter, a Breakfast area, adjoining the Utility and the Garage
■ Master Bedroom suite with a decorative ceiling, two vanities and a large walk-in closet
■ Three additional bedrooms with double closets.
■ This plan is available with a Slab or Crawlspace foundation. Please specify when ordering

MAIN FLOOR — 2,387 SQ. FT.
GARAGE — 462 SQ. FT.

No. 92546
TOTAL LIVING AREA:
2,387 SQ. FT.

MAIN FLOOR

ELEGANT AND EFFICIENT

DESIGN NO. 92515

- This plan features:
  — Three bedrooms
  — Two full baths
- Covered entrance into the Foyer leads to a spacious Den with a decorative ceiling above a hearth fireplace and French doors to the patio area
- Decorative window and ceiling highlight the formal Dining Room
- Large, country Kitchen with double ovens, a cooktop and a peninsula snackbar serving the bright Breakfast area
- Large Master Bedroom suite with a decorative ceiling, a walk-in closet and a plush bath with a double vanity and a whirlpool tub
- Two additional bedrooms with walk-in closets share a full bath
- This plan is available with a Slab or Crawlspace foundation. Please specify when ordering

MAIN FLOOR — 1,959 SQ. FT.
GARAGE — 484 SQ. FT.

TOTAL LIVING AREA:
1,959 SQ. FT.

No. 92515
MAIN FLOOR

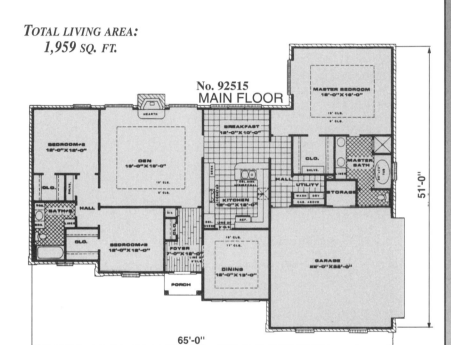

PRICE CODE D

ARCHED WINDOWS ACCENT SOPHISTICATED DESIGN

DESIGN NO. 92509

■ This plan features:

— Four bedrooms

— Two full and one half baths

■ Graceful columns and full-length windows highlight front t Porch leading into central Foyer flanked by formal Living and Dining rooms

■ Spacious Great Room with decorative ceiling over hearth fireplace between built-in cabinets and sliding glass door to covered back Porch

■ Efficient Kitchen with peninsula counter, Breakfast alcove and adjoining Dining Room, Utility room and Garage

■ Secluded Master Bedroom suite offers access to back Porch, decorative ceiling and plush bath with walk-in closet, double vanity and spa tub

■ Three additional bedrooms with loads of closets space share double vanity bath

MAIN FLOOR — 2,551 SQ. FT.

GARAGE — 484 SQ. FT.

FOUNDATION — SLAB OR CRAWL SPACE

TOTAL LIVING AREA: 2,551 SQ. FT.

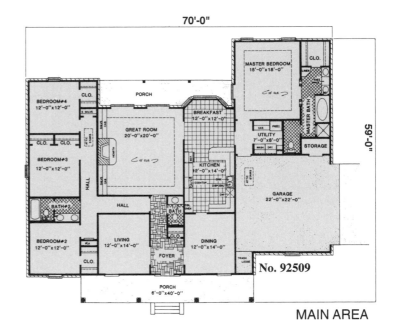

No. 92509

MAIN AREA

BAY WINDOWS AND A TERRIFIC FRONT PORCH

DESIGN NO. 93261

■ This plan features:

— Three bedrooms

— Two full baths

■ A country front porch

■ An expansive Living Area that includes a fireplace

■ A Master Suite with a private Master Bath and a walk-in closet, as well as a bay window view of the front yard

■ An efficient Kitchen that serves the sunny Breakfast Area and the Dining Room with equal ease

■ A built-in pantry and a desk add to the conveniences in the Breakfast Area

■ Two additional bedrooms that share the full hall bath

■ A convenient main floor Laundry Room

MAIN AREA — 1,778 SQ. FT.

BASEMENT — 1,008 SQ. FT.

GARAGE — 728 SQ. FT.

TOTAL LIVING AREA: 1,778 SQ. FT.

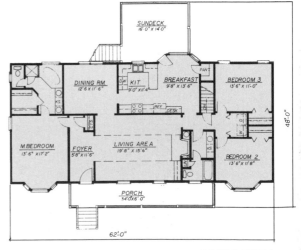

MAIN AREA

No. 93261

An EXCLUSIVE DESIGN
By Jannis Vann & Associates, Inc.

244

SOUTHERN COUNTRY FLAIR

DESIGN NO. 94619

- This plan features:
  - —Four bedrooms
  - —Two full baths
- Great wrap-around front Porch leads into the central Foyer and a formal Dining room
- Spacious Family Room with a tray ceiling topping the corner fireplace and access to the Covered Porch
- Efficient, country Kitchen with a peninsula counter/eating bar, a glass Breakfast area and a nearby Utility room
- Master Bedroom suite with a decorative ceiling and a lavish Master Bath with two vanities and walk-in closets and an atrium tub
- Three additional bedrooms share a double vanity bath
- This plan is available with a Slab or Crawl space foundation. Please specify when ordering

MAIN FLOOR — 2,355 SQ. FT.

GARAGE — 553 SQ. FT.

TOTAL LIVING AREA:
2,355 SQ. FT.

MAIN AREA

Width 58'-10"
Depth 81'-0"

Garage
24'-2" X 19'-8"

Cov. Porch
31'-1" X 7'-0"

Ma. Bedrm.
14'-0" X 17'-10"

Ma. Bath

Brkfst.
11'-10" X 11'-0"

Family
18'-6" X 20'-6"

Bn 2

Bedrm. 2
11'-9" X 11'-8"

Kit.
11'-10" X 14'-0"

Hall

Bedrm. 3
11'-10" X 12'-2"

Util.

Dining
12'-0" X 14'-6"

Foyer

Bedrm. 4
12'-0" X 12'-0"

Porch
43'-6" X 6'-0"

No. 94619
MAIN AREA

TRIANGULAR ENTRANCE EXTENDS INTO FOYER

DESIGN NO. 99614

■ This plan features:

— Three bedrooms

— Two full and one half baths

■ A triangular ceiling in the entrance porch that extends into the foyer

■ A large glazed bay window that extends the full width of the Living Room

■ A heat-circulating fireplace flanked by shelves and cabinets in the Living Room

■ A Dinette with a six-sided shape, four sides being windows

■ A Family Room with a sloped ceiling, sliding glass doors to the terrace and easy access to an angled Kitchen counter acting as a snack bar

■ A Master Suite with walk-in closet, private terrace, private Master Bath with whirlpool tub, a separate shower and a double vanity

■ Two additional bedrooms that share a full hall bath

FIRST FLOOR — 2,282 SQ. FT.

LAUNDRY/MUDROOM — 114 SQ. FT.

BASEMENT — 2,136 SQ. FT.

GARAGE — 509 SQ. FT.

TOTAL LIVING AREA:
2,396 SQ. FT.

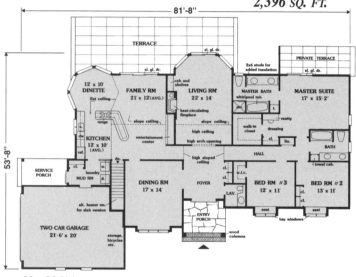

No. 99614
MAIN AREA

TAILORED FOR A VIEW TO THE SIDE

DESIGN NO. 93708

■ This plan features:

— Three/Four bedrooms

— Three full and one half baths

■ A designed for a homesite with a view to the side, perfect for entertaining and everyday living

■ A sheltered entrance with windows over the door and a side light

■ A large entry Foyer highlighted by a ceiling dome and French doors leading to the private study or guest bedroom with a vaulted ceiling

■ An elegant formal Dining Room with a high ceiling and a columned and arched entrance

■ A sunken Great Room with a high tray ceiling and arched and columned openings and a fireplace further enhancing the room

■ A Breakfast Room, with an optional planning desk, opens to the Kitchen via the eating bar

■ An island and walk-in pantry adding to the Kitchen's efficiency

■ A tray ceiling and lavish bath pamper the owner in the Master Suite

■ Two additional bedrooms that share a split vanity bath

MAIN FLOOR — 2,579 SQ. FT.

GARAGE — 536 SQ. FT.

TOTAL LIVING AREA:
2,579 SQ. FT.

Materials list not available

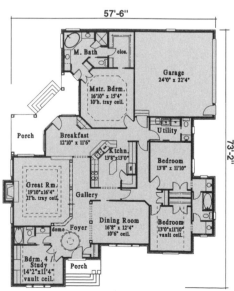

MAIN AREA
No. 93708

Main Level Floor Plan

PRICE CODE B

TRANSOM WINDOWS EXTEND VIEW AND LIGHT

DESIGN NO. 98317

- This plan features:
- — Three bedrooms
- — Two full baths
- Impressive one and half-story gable entrance leads into the Living Room and the formal Dining area with a triple window and pillars
- Living Room with a transom window below a vaulted ceiling opens into the Family Room and Deck beyond
- Open Kitchen with a glass Breakfast alcove, a built-in desk and a pantry
- Master Suite with a vaulted ceiling above a double window, two closets and a private bath
- Two additional bedrooms with ample closets, share a full bath
- This plan is available with a Basement foundation only

MAIN FLOOR — 1,700 SQ. FT.
BASEMENT — 1,700 SQ. FT.
GARAGE — 393 SQ. FT.

TOTAL LIVING AREA:
1,700 SQ. FT.

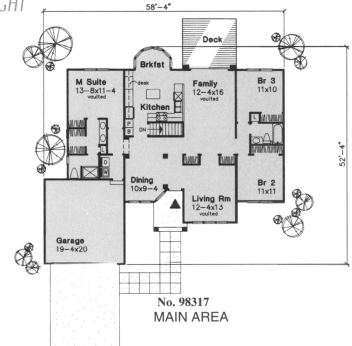

No. 98317
MAIN AREA

PRICE CODE D

GARAGE PLANS

Save money by Doing-It-Yourself using our Easy-To-Follow plans. Whether you intend to build your own garage or contract it out to a building professional, the Garlinghouse garage plans provide you with everything you need to price out your project and get started. Put our 85 years of experience to work for you.
Order now!!

ITEM NO. 06016C — $86.00
Apartment Garage With One Bedroom

ITEM NO. 06015C — $86.00
Apartment Garage With Two Bedrooms

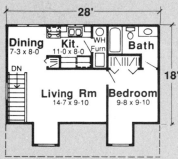

- 24' x 28' Overall Dimensions
- 544 Square Foot Apartment
- 12/12 Gable Roof with Dormers
- Slab or Stem Wall Foundation Options

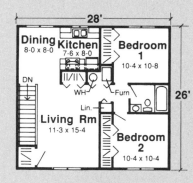

- 26' x 28' Overall Dimensions
- 728 Square Foot Apartment
- 4/12 Pitch Gable Roof
- Slab or Stem Wall Foundation Options

ITEM NO. 06012C — $54.00
30' Deep Gable &/or Eave Jumbo Garages

- 4/12 Pitch Gable Roof
- Available Options for Extra Tall Walls, Garage & Personnel Doors, Foundation, Window, & Sidings
- Package contains 4 Different Sizes
  - 30' x 28'   • 30' x 32'   • 30' x 36'   • 30' x 40'

ITEM NO. 06013C — $68.00
Two-Car Garage With Mudroom/Breezeway

- Attaches to Any House
- 24' x 24' Eave Entry
- Available Options for Utility Room with Bath, Mudroom, Screened-In Breezeway, Roof, Foundation, Garage & Personnel Doors, Window, & Sidings

ITEM NO. 06001C — $48.00
12', 14', & 16' Wide-Gable 1-Car Garages

- Available Options for Roof, Foundation, Window, Door, & Sidings
- Package contains 8 Different Sizes
- 12' x 20' Mini-Garage ● 14' x 22' ● 16' x 20' ● 16' x 24'
- 14' x 20'   ● 14' x 24' ● 16' x 22' ● 16' x 26'

ITEM NO. 06003C — $48.00
24' Wide-Gable 2-Car Garages

- Available Options for Side Shed, Roof, Foundation, Garage & Personnel Doors, Window, & Sidings
- Package contains 5 Different Sizes
- 24' x 22'   ● 24' x 24'   ● 24' x 26'
- 24' x 28'   ● 24' x 32'

ITEM NO. 06007C — $60.00
Gable 2-Car Gambrel Roof Garages

- Interior Rear Stairs to Loft Workshop
- Front Loft Cargo Door With Pulley Lift
- Available Options for Foundation, Garage & Personnel Doors, Window, & Sidings
- Package contains 5 Different Sizes
- 22' x 26' ● 22' x 28' ● 24' x 28' ● 24' x 30' ● 24' x 32'

ITEM NO. 06006C — $48.00
22' & 24' Deep Eave 2 & 3-Car Garages

- Can Be Built Stand-Alone or Attached to House
- Available Options for Roof, Foundation, Garage & Personnel Doors, Window, & Sidings
- Package contains 6 Different Sizes
- 22' x 28'   ● 22' x 32'   ● 24' x 32'
- 22' x 30'   ● 24' x 30'   ● 24' x 36'

ITEM NO. 06002C — $48.00
20' & 22' Wide-Gable 2-Car Garages

- Available Options for Roof, Foundation, Garage & Personnel Doors, Window, & Sidings
- Package contains 7 Different Sizes
- 20' x 20'   ● 20' x 24'   ● 22' x 22'   ● 22' x 28'
- 20' x 22'   ● 20' x 28'   ● 22' x 24'

ITEM NO. 06008C — $60.00
Eave 2 & 3-Car Clerestory Roof Garages

- Interior Side Stairs to Loft Workshop
- Available Options for Engine Lift, Foundation, Garage & Personnel Doors, Window, & Sidings
- Package contains 4 Different Sizes
- 24' x 26'   ● 24' x 28'   ● 24' x 32'   ● 24' x 36'

Here's What You Get

- Three complete sets of drawings for each plan ordered.
- Detailed step-by-step instructions with easy-to-follow diagrams on how to build your garage (not available with apartment/garages).
- For each garage style, a variety of size and garage door configuration options.
- Variety of roof styles and/or pitch options for most garages.

- Complete materials list.
- Choice between three foundation options: Monolithic Slab, Concrete Stem Wall or Concrete Block Stem Wall.
- Full framing plans, elevations and cross-sectionals for each garage size and configuration.
- And Much More!!

Order Information For Garage Plans:

All garage plan orders contain three complete sets of drawings with instructions and are priced as listed next to the illustration. Additional sets of plans may be obtained for $10.00 each with your original order. UPS shipping is used unless otherwise requested. Please include the proper amount for shipping.

GARLINGHOUSE

Build-It-Yourself PROJECT PLAN

Garage Order Form

Order Code No. G96L5

Please send me 3 complete sets of the following GARAGE PLAN:

Item no. & description	Price
_____	$ _____
Additional Sets	
_____ (@ $10.00 each)	$ _____
Shipping Charges: UPS-$3.75, First Class- $4.50	$ _____
Subtotal:	$ _____
Resident sales tax: KS-6.15%, CT-6% (*Not Required For Other States*)	$ _____
Total Enclosed:	$ _____

My Billing Address is:

Name _____

Address _____

City _____

State _____ Zip _____

Daytime Phone No. _____

My Shipping Address is:

Name _____

Address _____
(UPS will not ship to P.O. Boxes)

City _____

State _____ Zip _____

Send your order to:
(With check or money order payable in U.S. funds only)
The Garlinghouse Company

P.O. Box 1717
Middletown, CT 06457

For Faster Service...Charge It!
U.S. & Canada Call
1(800)235-5700
All foreign residents call 1(860)343-5977
❏ Mastercard ❏ Visa

Card # | | | | | | | | | | | | | | | | |

Signature _____ Exp. ___ / ___

If paying by credit card, to avoid delays:
billing address must be as it appears on credit card statement
or FAX us at (860) 343-5984

No C.O.D. orders accepted; U.S. funds only. UPS will not ship to Post Office boxes, FPO boxes, APO boxes, Alaska or Hawaii. Canadian orders must be shipped First Class.

Prices subject to change without notice.

Ignoring Copyright Laws Can Be A $1,000,000 Mistake

Recent changes in the US copyright laws allow for statutory penalties of up to **$100,000** per incident for copyright infringement involving any of the copyrighted plans found in this publication. The law can be confusing. So, for your own protection, take the time to understand what you can and cannot do when it comes to home plans.

——— What You Cannot Do ———

You Cannot Duplicate Home Plans

Purchasing a set of blueprints and making additional sets by reproducing the original is *illegal*. If you need multiple sets of a particular home plan, then you must purchase them.

You Cannot Copy Any Part of a Home Plan to Create Another

Creating your own plan by copying even part of a home design found in this publication is called "creating a derivative work" and is *illegal* unless you have permission to do so.

You Cannot Build a Home Without a License

You must have specific permission or license to build a home from a copyrighted design, even if the finished home has been changed from the original plan. It is *illegal* to build one of the homes found in this publication without a license.

What Garlinghouse Offers

Home Plan Blueprint Package

By purchasing a single or multiple set package of blueprints from Garlinghouse, you not only receive the physical blueprint documents necessary for construction, but you are also granted a license to build one, and only one, home. You can also make any changes to our design that you wish, as long as these changes are made directly on the blueprints purchased from Garlinghouse and no additional copies are made.

Home Plan Vellums

By purchasing vellums for one of our home plans, you receive the same construction drawings found in the blueprints, but printed on vellum paper. Vellums can be erased and are perfect for making design changes. They are also semi-transparent making them easy to duplicate. But most importantly, the purchase of home plan vellums comes with a broader license that allows you to make changes to the design (ie, create a hand drawn or CAD derivative work), to make an unlimited number of copies of the plan, and to build up to three homes from the plan.

License To Build Additional Homes

With the purchase of a blueprint package or vellums you automatically receive a license to build one home or three homes, respectively. If you want to build more homes than you are licensed to build through your purchase of a plan, then additional licenses may be purchased at reasonable costs from Garlinghouse. Inquire for more information.

Everything You Need to M
You pay only a fraction of the original cost

You've Picked Your Dream Home!

You can already see it standing on your lot... you can see yourselves in your new home... enjoying family, entertaining guests, celebrating holidays. All that remains ahead are the details. That's where we can help. Whether you plan to build-it-yourself, be your own contractor, or hand your plans over to an outside contractor, your Garlinghouse blueprints provide the perfect beginning for putting yourself in your dream home right away.

We even make it simple for you to make professional design modifications. We can also provide a materials list for greater economy.

My grandfather, L.F. Garlinghouse, started a tradition of quality when he founded this company in 1907. For over 85 years, homeowners and builders have relied on us for accurate, complete, professional blueprints. Our plans help you get results fast... and save money, too! These pages will give you all the information you need to order. So get started now... I know you'll love your new Garlinghouse home!

Sincerely,

TYPICAL WALL SECTIONS

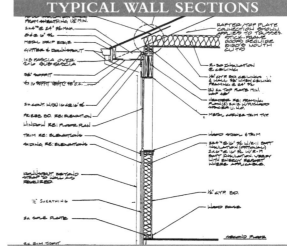

Detailed views of your exterior walls, as though sliced from top to bottom. These drawings clarify exterior wall construction insulation, flooring, and roofing details. Depending on your specific geography and climate, your home will be built with either 2x4 or 2x6 exterior walls. Most professional contractors can easily adapt plans for either requirement.

KITCHEN & BATH CABINET DETAILS

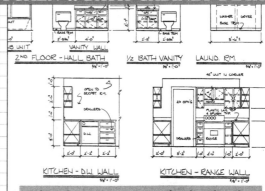

These plans or, in some cases, elevations show the specific details and placement of the cabinets in your kitchen and bathrooms as applicable. Customizing these areas is simpler beginning with these details. Kitchen and bath cabinet details are available for most plans featured in our collection.

EXTERIOR ELEVATIONS

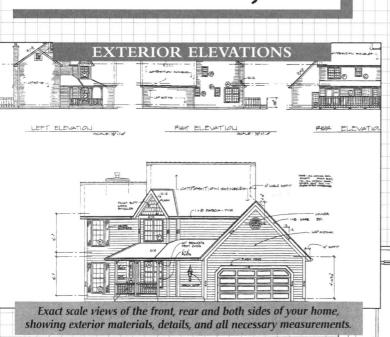

Exact scale views of the front, rear and both sides of your home, showing exterior materials, details, and all necessary measurements.

DETAILED FLOOR PLANS

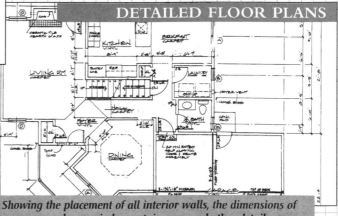

Showing the placement of all interior walls, the dimensions of rooms, doors, windows, stairways, and other details.

ake Your Dream Come True!

for home designs by respected professionals.

FIREPLACE DETAILS

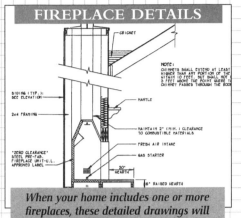

When your home includes one or more fireplaces, these detailed drawings will help your mason with their construction and appearance. It is easy to review details with professionals when you have the plans for reference.

TYPICAL CROSS SECTION

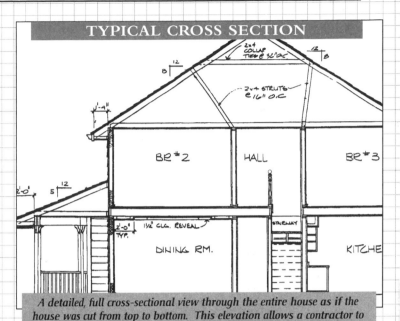

A detailed, full cross-sectional view through the entire house as if the house was cut from top to bottom. This elevation allows a contractor to better understand the interconnections of the construction components.

FOUNDATION PLAN

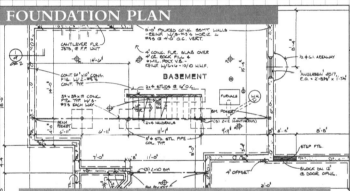

With footings and all load-bearing points applicable to your home, including all necessary notation and dimensions. The type of foundation supplied varies from home to home. Local conditions and practices will determine whether a basement, crawlspace or a slab is best for you. Your professional contractor can easily make the necessary adaption.

SCHEMATIC ELECTRICAL LAYOUTS

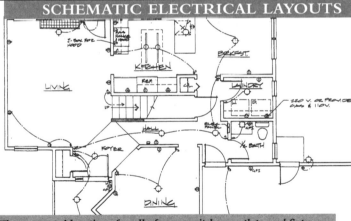

The suggested locations for all of your switches, outlets and fixtures are indicated on these drawings. They are practical as they are, but they are also a solid taking-off point for any personal adaptions.

ROOF PLAN

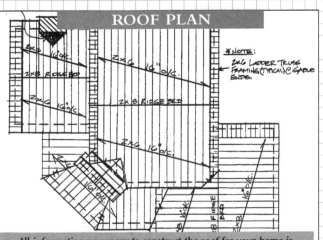

All information necessary to construct the roof for your home is included. Many blueprints contain framing plans showing all of the roof elements, so you'll know how these details look and fit together.

STAIR DETAILS

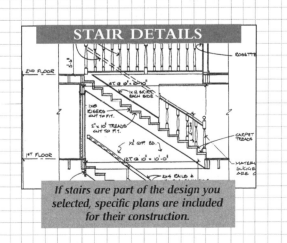

If stairs are part of the design you selected, specific plans are included for their construction.

GARLINGHOUSE OPTIONS & EXTRAS
MAKE THE DREAM TRULY YOURS.

Reversed Plans Can Make Your Dream Home Just Right!

"That's our dream home... if only the garage were on the other side!"

You could have exactly the home you want by flipping it end-for-end. Check it out by holding your dream home page of this book up to a mirror. Then simply order your plans "reversed". We'll send you one full set of mirror-image plans (with the writing backwards) as a master guide for you and your builder.

The remaining sets of your order will come as shown in this book so the dimensions and specifications are easily read on the job site... but they will be specially stamped "REVERSED" so there is no construction confusion.

We can only send reversed plans with multiple-set orders. But, there is no extra charge for this service.

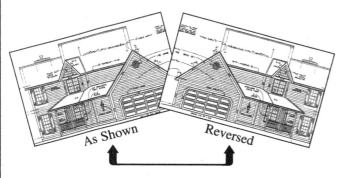

As Shown   Reversed

Modifying Your Garlinghouse Home Plan

Easy modifications to your dream home such as minor non-structural changes and simple material substitutions, can be made between you and your builder and marked directly on your blueprints. However, if you are considering making major changes to your design, we strongly recommend that you purchase our reproducible vellums and use the services of a professional designer or architect. For additional information call us at 1-860-343-5977.

Our Reproducible Vellums Make Modifications Easier

With a vellum copy of our plans, a design professional can alter the drawings just the way you want, then you can print as many copies of the modified plans as you need. And, since you have already started with our complete detailed plans, the cost of those expensive professional services will be significantly less. Refer to the price schedule for vellum costs. Call for vellum availability for plan numbers 90,000 and above.

Reproducible vellum copies of our home plans are only sold under the terms of a license agreement that you will receive with your order. Should you not agree to the terms, then the vellums may be returned unopened for a full refund.

Yours FREE With Your Order
FREE
SPECIFICATIONS AND CONTRACT FORM

provides the perfect way for you and your builder to agree on the exact materials to use in building and finishing your home before you start construction. A must for homeowner's peace of mind.

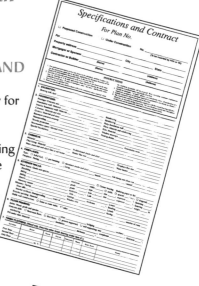

Remember To Order Your Materials List

It'll help you save money. Available at a modest additional charge, the Materials List gives the quantity, dimensions, and specifications for the major materials needed to build your home. You will get faster, more accurate bids from your contractors and building suppliers — and avoid paying for unused materials and waste. Materials Lists are available for all home plans except as otherwise indicated, but can only be ordered with a set of home plans. Due to differences in regional requirements and homeowner or builder preferences... electrical, plumbing and heating/air conditioning equipment specifications are not designed specifically for each plan. However, non plan specific detailed typical prints of residential electrical, plumbing and construction guidelines can be provided. Please see next page for additional information.

Questions?

Call our customer service number at 1-860-343-5977.